The Polliticke Courtier
Spenser's *The Faerie Queene* as a Rhetoric of Justice

Michael Dixon applies rhetorical theory to *The Faerie Queene*, highlighting the importance of rhetoric and locating the *inventio*, or organizing principle, of Spenser's epic narrative in the conception of justice. He demonstrates how Spenser adapts classical rhetoric to the poetics of romance-epic and illustrates the usefulness of rhetorical analysis as a complement to allegorical studies and the New Critical and new historicist approaches that currently dichotomize Spenserian scholarship.

Although pervasive in Spenser's art, the role of rhetoric has not been adequately addressed by critics. This disregard of the importance of rhetoric in *The Faerie Queene*, Dixon argues, obscures Spenser's larger rhetorical method and the structural dynamic it generates. Dixon identifies Britomart's evolution in Books III-V as the poem's centre and elucidates the rhetorical strategies that invest Spenser's "argument" for justice. Building on Kenneth Burke's conception of courtship in rhetoric as "the use of suasive devices for the transcending of social estrangement," Dixon interprets *The Faerie Queene* as a narrative of courtship in purpose as well as content, arguing that its tales of questing knights compose an artifact of suasive devices whereby Spenser courts a meeting of minds with his audience on the subject of justice.

MICHAEL F.N. DIXON is associate professor of English, University of Toronto.

The Polliticke Courtier

Spenser's The Faerie Queene *as a Rhetoric of Justice*

MICHAEL F.N. DIXON

McGill-Queen's University Press
Montreal & Kingston • London • Buffalo

© McGill-Queen's University Press 1996
ISBN 0-7735-1425-2

Legal deposit fourth quarter 1996
Bibliothèque nationale du Québec

Printed in Canada on acid-free paper

This book has been published with the help of grants
from the Humanities and Social Science Federation of
Canada, using funds provided by the Social Sciences
and Humanities Research Council of Canada, and
New College, University of Toronto.

Canadian Cataloguing in Publication Data

Dixon, Michael F.N.
   The polliticke courtier : Spenser's The Faerie Queene as
   a rhetoric of justice
   Includes bibliographical references and index.
   ISBN 0-7735-1425-2
   1. Spenser, Edmund, 1552?–1599. Faerie queene.
   2. Persuasion (Rhetoric). 3. Justice in literature. I. Title.
   PR2358.D59 1996   821'.3   C96-900334-X

Typeset in Palatino 10/12
by Caractéra inc., Quebec City

To Dulcie

Contents

Acknowledgments

Much trial and more error attended development of protocols for this study. Any case for kinship between the dry formalism of rhetorical theory and the rich dynamics of Spenserian epic is neither self-evident nor established by recent custom, and I am indebted to more students and colleagues in English and other disciplines at the University of Toronto than I can acknowledge individually. Their good will made the trials possible and the errors palpable. They not only tolerated politely but often engaged critically my abstruse preoccupations with rhetoric, its unstable terminology, and its problematic history.

Particularly helpful in identifying theoretical problems were weekly sessions of the "Old Peculiars" reading group at New College which included regularly F.J. Asals, Peter Dyson, Guy Hamel, Linda Hutcheon, and Patricia Merivale. Also at New College, Hugh Mason founded the Humanism Program with me and through patient dialogue helped to develop its rhetorical components from classical roots.

Problems of practice in adapting rhetoric to Spenser's art for this study were greatly clarified by the contribution of anonymous readers for the Aid to Scholarly Publications Programme and McGill-Queen's University Press. They proved an ideal audience: informed, articulate about their puzzlements, and perceptively constructive in their suggestions for improvement.

Like many Spenserians I am especially indebted to the uncommon generosity, as well as the editorial skill and critical acuity, of A.C.

Hamilton, who read an earlier version of this essay and whose searching, detailed commentary identified crucial issues of presentation, technical vocabulary, and analytical focus.

My most tolerant, patient, and encouraging critic throughout the development of this book is the subject of its dedication.

Eftsoones the time and place appointed were,
  Where all, both heauenly Powers, and earthly wights,
  Before great Natures presence should appeare,
  For triall of their Titles and best Rights:
  That was, to weet, vpon the highest hights
  Of Arlo-hill (Who knowes not Arlo-hill?).
  That is the highest head (in all mens sights)
  Of my old father Mole, whom Shepheards quill
Renowmed hath with hymnes fit for a rural skill.   (VII.vi.36)

Introduction:
Rhetorical Structure and
Critical Re-construction

Impetus for this study derives in significant part from the efforts of A.C. Hamilton and his fellow editors more than a decade ago to organize appropriate representation of rhetorical topics for *The Spenser Encyclopedia*. Their task proved difficult, and Hamilton identified the source of strain by quoting James Murphy: "few Spenserians know rhetoric well, while no rhetoricians know Spenser at all."[1] Although hyperbole is often the fruit of gnomic economy, Murphy's bleak judgment might well serve as an epigram for this essay insofar as it encapsulates adequately both an imbalance in Spenserian commentary which I seek to ameliorate and the problematical nature of the dual audience of Spenserians and students of rhetorical history I seek to address. Explication and analytical detail that seem excessive to one may strike the other as inadequate, and I hope my inevitable lapses from this austere negotiation between plethora and dearth will not exceed the range of tolerance allowed by either audience.

Rhetorical analysis of Spenser's poetry, while perhaps more varied and voluminous than Murphy implies, has tended to adopt a narrow focus, concentrating primarily on identification and elucidation of tropes and schemes which comprise the oratorical "office" of *elocutio* (style and ornamentation).[2] This limited approach reflects the authority of venerable precedent. Renaissance theorists, themselves biased by tradition to stress the rhetoric of lawcourts, pulpits, and political assemblies, cited poets in their textbooks mainly as examples of style,

and Spenser's first commentator, the enigmatic E.K., in his gloss to
The Shepheardes Calender limits his rhetorical observations to a random
selection of often obscure figures of ornament. Spenser's poetry is
not alone: Renaissance writers in general suffer from a constricted
rhetorical focus on their work that is limited to ornament and pathos.[3]
Practice, however, could hardly remain circumscribed within such
narrow theoretical boundaries. Poets strove to emulate in vernacular
literature the achievements of admired classical models, and in the
process necessarily adapted the rhetorical principles and practices of
those models to their needs. Such adaptations, perforce, involved
more than the devices of elocutio. Indeed, Aristotle himself refined
the standard definition of rhetoric to stress that "the art of persuasion" is primarily one of *inventio* – of discovery, selection, and organization – rather than ornamentation. He admonishes his orator first
to discover for each case the existing means of persuasion and then
to select the best means from those available and appropriate (*Rhetoric*: I.1.14). Suasion is thus a function of appropriateness, or *decorum*,
and I will elaborate on this pivotal concept in chapter 1. Exactly what
selections from available resources will satisfy decorum becomes a
function in turn of occasion, audience, subject, genre, and many
related contingencies,

Such factors govern patterns of selection which breed the suasive
dynamic of Spenser's poetry. He subordinates ornamental and sty-
listic devices not only to elements of inventio (especially topoi of
genre and subject, methods of proof, and enthymemes with their
demonstrative exempla) but also to strategies of narrative adapted
from the oratorical office of *dispositio* (the arrangement of an oration
to form a suasive presentation). Insofar as they accord with criteria
of decorum, his selections create a contingent relationship between
conception and execution that makes systematic analysis possible.
For the audience Spenser could anticipate, a circle of readers schooled
like himself in the disciplines of classical rhetoric (or a Tudor distillate
from such disciplines), the offices of the rhetor afforded a schematic
system of interpretation directly complementary to those of composition.[4] To discern Spenser's purpose, his audience could expect to
abstract principles of decorum from the detail of dispositio as well
as elocutio, and to move inferentially from this base to the conception
comprehended in his inventio. The contours of one such trace, seeking to apprehend the conceptual resonance of "justice" in Spenser's
inventio for *The Faerie Queene*, constitute the substance of this study.

Of course, despite its schematic simplicity in theory, such analytical
inference in practice proves complex and demanding. This complexity has two sources: Spenser's particular application of rhetorical

theory and factors inherent in that theory itself. The particular rhetorical structure Spenser disposes in his best work supports not one discrete network of decorous relationships but a dense matrix of fronding patterns expressing the poet's copia and reflecting his allegorical temper. Theorists traditionally classified *allegoria* as a trope, a figure of elocutio functioning as a somewhat extended *metaphora*, but in Spenser's practice it has evolved into a *genre* and hence into an element of inventio.[5] In this generic mode allegoria functions as both a method of exegesis for prophecies, divinations, myths, or signs and a species of *apologia*, or extended narrative, in which one sequence of events invites multiple interpretations by alluding to other sequences. Once a poet opts to use allegoria, he is committed by the demands of decorum to the conventions (*topoi*) of the genre. These include primarily formal and functional characteristics abstracted from admired models of allusive narrative or exegetical exposition, and Spenser's debt to topoi available in this tradition is well documented. Furthermore, decorum as a principle dictates that poets not simply adhere slavishly to their sources but select and where necessary adapt or concoct topoi appropriate to their particular vision, enriching the rhetorical tradition they inherit. Common to both the configuration of one narrative sequence evocative of others and the notion of exegetical exposition is the implicit concept of a unity underlying apparent diversity, a concept central to the Platonic strain in Spenser's Humanism and fundamental to his inventio of justice in *The Faerie Queene*.[6] Indeed, it occupies what is arguably (and I will so argue) the culminating focus of the epic in Dame Nature's juridical decision at the court on Arlo Hill concerning Mutabilitie's "appeale" against Jove's denial of her case for universal sovereignty (VII.vii.58). By merging topoi of allegoria with those of other rhetorical genre (*elegia*, *epithalamion*, *fabula*, *heroica* [epic], *lyrica*, *pastoralia*, and *sonnet*) he subsumes all as species of allegoria, producing matrices that, as the history of Spenserian commentary abundantly attests, engender multiple and diverse interpretations.

My purpose in essaying an explication of Spenser's rhetorical structure is not pandemic refutation of such allegorical interpretations: allegoria is, of course, a valid genre of critical discourse as well as epic structure, and in any case rhetorical analysis provides no meta-narrative to resolve us of all ambiguities. Rather I hope to provide a context in which this multiplicity and diversity of interpretation may find a measure of common provenance and at least partial accommodation. Commentators occupied primarily with other problems of analysis and interpretation understandably tend to deal only incidentally and selectively with *The Faerie Queene* as a rhetorical artifact.[7] Historical and political occasions, religious motives, strategies of encomium and structures of allegoria, elocutional topoi of pastoral and romance gain varying degrees of attention, sometimes substantial, while other elements of Spenser's rhetorical method suffer neglect. This selective, often indirect treatment of rhetorical issues isolates such elements from their context, obscuring their functional interplay within the structure Spenser's method generates. Through systematic rather than incidental analysis, and by focusing on Spenser's inventio and dispositio rather than his elocutio, my aim is to reintegrate rhetorical elements within their structure of decorum and elucidate its dynamics.

This is precisely the point where I suspect the "fewness" of Murphy's "few Spenserians" has its source. Such an aim as mine is hardly difficult to formulate, and its theoretical validity is surely now beyond dispute: G.A. Kennedy, Murphy, Michael Murrin, Walter Ong, Thomas Sloan, and, pre-eminently, Brian Vickers have made classical rhetoric accessible and have advocated repeatedly, with persuasive authority, the case for rhetorical analysis as requisite to a fully informed reading of Renaissance texts.[8] Nothing remains, it would appear, but to practice the theory on Spenser's text. Unfortunately the theory contains no ready protocols for its application to epic poetry; indeed, the inherent principle of decorum itself precludes any protocol of application to any rhetorical artifact that is not contingent on the artifact. Analysts, like the poets they analyse, must adapt rhetorical theory to their practices. In chapter 1 I will engage directly issues specific to this study provoked by such requirements for adaptation, but I should like as prologue and context to address briefly some more general manifestations of these adaptive issues current within Spenserian commentary.

2   CRITICAL "RECONSTRUCTION"

Such adaptive issues find a focus in the term "structure," which is itself currently a virtual allegoria of conflicted topoi within the lively theoretical *controversia* engaging advocates variously labelled "Structuralist," "Post-structuralist" and "Deconstructionist." Given this context, it might seem prudent to choose a less volatile substantive for "rhetorical" to modify, or at the very least to display it in some less prominent venue than the title of an introduction. However, my imprudence, or perhaps impudence, is calculated; indeed, my subject makes it scarcely avoidable. Incompatibilities focused in the term "structure" provide an occasion to confront the incipient drift of implication in Spenserian studies that commentators necessarily function within a closed, dichotomous field of theoretical polarity, an implication quite incompatible with the concept of "rhetorical structure" adumbrated in my prefatory title. That concept encompasses, or stands logically prior to, the principles organizing any interpretive discourse: every interpretation is, among other things, a rhetorical act. Every "school" of criticism has its own theoretical topoi and principles of decorum; every discourse devolved from those topoi and principles necessarily demonstrates them in a rhetorical construct, including those "structuralisms" labelled with ironically insistent privatives ("de-," "pre-" and "post-"). Such labels are always rhetorically problematical: they enhance *controversia* but hinder *perspicuitas*.

In Spenserian commentary, "deconstructive" methods have general currency among those theorists who influence a group of scholars labelled "New Historicist." Despite the significant theoretical and procedural differences among them that this univocal classification obscures,[9] their common insistence that Spenser's discourse must be situated among other discourses, especially synchronous political and economic discourses, creates a locus of commentary polarized adversarily against the position occupied by those who stress the integrity and autonomy of an author's text and tend to be lumped, with similar obfuscation of significant difference, under the designators "New Critical" or sometimes "Formalist," or even "Textual." Whatever the label, and regardless of the theoretical halter it tries to fit on the literary pony, any species of critical commentary, even "deconstructive" commentary, is "reconstructive" in rhetorical function; in Hamilton's memorable phrasing, it "juggles words out of context."[10] The poet's *dispositio* invariably becomes a selective reservoir of elements for the commentator's own discourse, which informs a new *dispositio* expressing an *inventio* with principles of decorum and topoi, including cultural topoi, necessarily different, often radically different, from those of the poet. The rhetorical imperatives dictating that all critical narrative will be reconstructive narrative seem to be what David Lee Miller eloquently laments as a deterministic decorum, a "deeper structure" underlying all critical discourse regardless of the ideology it seeks to invest. "We may construct a counter-canonical criticism, but for richer or poorer this revisionism will repeat the deeper structure of the literary canon whose authority it seeks to volatilize."[11] Critical commentary itself, in this technical but important sense, thus demonstrates the rhetorical genre of *allegoria*: it constitutes one discourse alluding to another, or possibly several others.

That both New Historicist and Formalist criticism are "reconstructive" does not, of course, minimize their differences. Topoi available to Spenser certainly include those of synchronous culture, and if New Criticists tend to evoke criteria of decorum that undervalue the exemplary ethos, and hence the persuasiveness, of synchronous discourses, New Historicists evoke criteria of decorum which undervalue the exemplary ethos of the author's text. Their techniques of argument diverge accordingly: like jazz musicians, New Historicists play improvisational riffs on a score which New Criticists try to render in accord with the composer's notation. Such differences are surely complementary as well as competitive: they provide insufficient polarity to require that commentators on Spenser, certainly those who are rhetorical analysts, declare exclusive adherence to one and rejection of the other. Indeed, the notion that we can accept one as a source of enlightenment only by rejecting the other as benighted creates the type of uneasiness Gilbert Ryle finds symptomatic of dilemmas that arise when we treat answers to different questions as if they were competing answers to the same question.[12] Although both New Historicist and New Critical positions imply an epistemology and a hermaneutic, the principles of decorum governing proof in literary criticism are not those of philosophy: neither position develops its notions with sufficient rigour to establish that their respective answers to questions about "what" or "how" Spenser's poem "means" are logically contradictory, hence mutually exclusive, predicates of the same subject. We can justifiably avoid Ryle's sort of dilemma, therefore, not by impaling ourselves on one of its horns but by situating the issue within rhetorical contingencies rather than logical absolutes, defining the question each asks by the procedures it follows. The question "What inventio does the textual evidence of the poem in isolation from other discourses demonstrate?" is quite different from one interrogating the inventio evidenced by some synchronic, diachronic (or even deliberately anachronic[13]) discourses that include the poem. Each of their differing procedures determines a range of possible answers; those ranges may overlap locally but do not cancel one another globally.[14]

Nor (to extend the territorial metaphor one more step) do they circumscribe between themselves the entire field of possible answers: procedures of rhetorical analysis generate their own range of interrogations from outside the frontiers of both New Historicists and New Criticists and intersect with both. As commentators we will always deal selectively and fragmentarily with a poet of Spenser's copia, focusing on one "level" of allegory at a time; stressing historical occasions while ignoring philosophical or religious motives; dwelling on one set of commonplaces or topics in preference to others; promoting pretextual or intertextual over intratextual decorum, and the principles of one aesthetic over another. Our journals in consequence will no doubt always comprehend a rhetoric of interpretations by providing a locus of confrontation between text and footnote, between what is being said and what has been said. Surely, however, it is not the survivor of a battle of interpretations, especially a circumscribed dichotomy of interpretations, that will prove adequate to the complexity of Spenser's vision and poetic, but the dialectical product of all the interpretations in concert, an inclusive "grammar" rather than a reductive rhetoric. I would think it as indecorous, therefore, to exclude either New Historicist or New Critical discourse from accommodation within the multiplicity and diversity of commentary on Spenser as to allow the preoccupations of their *controversia* to circumscribe that accommodation; or, symptomatically, to allow appropriation of the umbrella-term "structure" for the exclusive use of one of their advocates.

3 "COURTSHIP"

Indeed, the issue of "structure" illustrates how readily terminology becomes a major locus of disaccommodation. "Unfortunately," laments David Lodge in an academic postmodernist's *apologia pro vita sua*, "this discourse is so opaque and technical in its language that the first glance – baffled, angry, or derisive – is likely to be the last one. An unhappy consequence of recent developments has certainly been the loss of a common language of critical discourse which used to be shared between academic critics, practising writers, literary journalists and the educated common reader."[15] Lodge refers here to the source of critical idiom for New Historicism, the structuralist discourse developed in response to Ferdinand de Saussure's *Course in General Linguistics* primarily in the work of Roland Barthes, Jacques Derrida, Michel Foucault, and Jacques Lacan. Yet Jonathan Goldberg, one of its influential practitioners in Spenserian commentary, finds himself "not comfortable with the critical vocabulary"[16] of Judith Anderson, whose idiom surely represents that "common language of critical discourse" Lodge regrets as lost. Elocutio demonstrates inventio, and such mutual discomfort with critical idiom evokes Edward Pechter's definition of critical "jargon" as "the kind of language used by people who believe differently from us."[17]

Rhetorical terms, while not immune to the forces of jargonization, have been, most of them, so long out of common currency as to gain a kind of affective neutrality. This advantage is qualified rather severely, however, by the distraction, even intimidation, of the unfamiliar in language, and I have attempted to minimize both the number of rhetorical terms in this study and their degree of obscurity. Indeed, since I hope an understanding of rhetorical structure will further in some measure an accommodation among Pechter's "readers who believe differently," I should like to withdraw initially from the welter of terminology, detail, and specialism that critical enquiry, of every "school," so often necessarily entails, and orient our perspective first to some general features of topography mapping Spenser's adaptations of rhetoric to poetic in *The Faerie Queene*.

One highly versatile resource for such orientation lies in the distance, both temporal and ideological, available through a range of Modernist and Postmodernist efforts to adapt classical rhetoric to new theoretical constructs. Sources so various as Walter Benjamin, Roland Barthes, Jacques Derrida, T.S. Eliot, Marshall McLuhan, W.K. Wimsatt, and Paul de Man have, to varying degrees, re-envisioned and reconstituted the preoccupations of rhetorical theory, and all have influenced (both in emulation and defiance) my approach to rhetorical analysis. None, however, presents a theoretical analogue as appropriate to Spenser's adaptive practice as Kenneth Burke. Several different modes of correlation compose this analogy and justify using Burke as an adaptive strategy of my own to pursue this study. I shall explore these facets of congruence in some detail as this essay develops, but here my purpose is simply to introduce Burke's resonant concept of "courtship." The structures produced by Spenser's merging of rhetorical genre, with their resultant capability to generate such a diversity of readings, can be represented schematically in configurations which express abstractly this generalized and relatively jargon-free concept.

Burke, citing rhetorical motives in Castiglione's *The Book of the Courtier*, adduces a useful definition: "By the 'principle of courtship' in rhetoric we mean the use of suasive devices for the transcending of social estrangement."[18] For Spenser, as for Castiglione and many other Renaissance artists, the concept has broad ramifications. Three principal motives for courtship correspond to three fundamental sources of perceived estrangement between subject and object, between the "I" here and the "other" out there: those between sexes, those between social classes, and those between different orders of Being (Humanity, Nature, and God). Estrangement creates a mystery that motivates desire and defines the asymmetric conditions of power; patently, we find these estrangements intolerable and seek to overcome them. Each accordingly generates its own dynamic of courtship (erotic, social, and transcendent respectively), creating three analogous rhetorical structures all conforming schematically to the hierarchical pyramid we associate particularly with models of social privilege: broad at the base where the masses dwell in the lowest stratum of power, narrowing to a small elite of nobility (Castiglione's literal "courtiers"), and converging to an apex, the seat of sovereignty. As Burke's definition specifies, this social model patterns erotic and transcendent structures. In each, highly formalized strategies exist to overcome estrangement, to "ascend" the hierarchy and approach identification with its triadic apex, or "ultimate term." The erotic courtier seeking physical union with his beloved, or the Christian courting spiritual unity with God, like the poet courting his Muse, stand in relation to their respective objects of courtship as inferior to superior in the social model, traditionally adopting a stance of humility, supplication, and servitude. Spenser's invocation to his sovereign Elizabeth in the Proem to *The Faerie Queene* merges idioms decorous with all three mysteries, projecting onto an object of social courtship the tonalities of erotic, poetic, and transcendent courtship while himself assuming the bardic posture of courtier to that multivalent object:[19]

> ... O Goddesse heauenly bright,
> Mirrour of grace and Maiestie diuine,
> Great Lady of the greatest Isle, whose light
> Like Phoebus lampe throughout the world doth shine
> Shed thy faire beames into my feeble eyne,
> And raise my thoughts too humble and too vile,
> To thinke of that true glorious type of thine,
> The argument of mine afflicted stile:
> The which to heare, vouchsafe, O dearest dred a-while.   (I.Pr.4)[20]

Because erotic, social, and transcendent courtship structures are thus both formally and functionally analogous, any one of them may ·stand surrogate for the others, thereby providing Spenser with a source of considerable allegorical flexibility.

This model of courtship also conforms by analogy with the conceptual structure derived from Platonic idealism that not only distinguishes hierarchically between ideal and material poles of opposition but also provides an ordered progression between them through the strategies of Socratic dialectic. Like all processes of Platonic abstraction, and its pandemic post-Platonic or "neo-Platonic" derivatives, the dialectic may be "frozen" into a static scheme composing a triad in two dimensions or a pyramidal cone in three dimensions.[21] Both triad and cone configure a wide base consisting of undifferentiated alternative answers to a specific question as data (What is Good? What is Love? What is Beauty? What is Virtue? What is Justice?), narrowing inductively through a series of ordered abstractions to a single principle of principles at the apex (Good, Beauty, Justice, or any other absolute, abstract "Idea") from which, in turn, all objects partaking of such an abstraction could be deduced. None of the original answers is adequate but no answer is eliminated from the structure: rather all are positioned in an ordered series, a "grammar" of alternatives, each situated according to criteria of order determined by the principle of principles that necessarily transcends any individual answer. By extension, if we transposed this "frozen" triad to a dynamic structure, the same ultimate term would be a generative source or "motive" of all such deducible particulars. Thus the Platonic Idea of "justice" or "beauty" as an ultimate term is both the "motif" common to and abstractable from all just or beautiful artifacts and the "motive" generating them.

Rhetorically, the "motive" of a work is the inventio generating its dispositio; the inventio represents in rhetorical structure a locus corresponding schematically and functionally to both the ultimate term in a structure of courtship and, as noted above, the "end" of induction in a dialectical structure. Thus Plato's "idea" of good, beauty, or justice is the inventio of his dialogue; its dispositio is a dramatic narrative of Socrates and his interlocutors, simultaneously demonstrating the topoi which compose that inventio and depicting their courtship of it.[22]

Epic is not discursive dialogue: their generic topoi and principles of decorum differ significantly, and Spenser's inventio announced in the letter to Raleigh is multivalent, a complex of abstractions:

I labour to pourtraict in Arthure, before he was king, the image of a braue knight, perfected in the twelue priuate morall vertues, as Aristotle hath deuised, the which is the purpose of these first twelue bookes: which if I finde to be well accepted, I may be perhaps encoraged, to frame the other part of polliticke vertues in his person, after that hee came to be king.[23]

Knightly quest provides a narrative sequence and a vehicle for interwoven progressions of erotic, social, and transcendent courtship that allow Spenser to exploit the rhetorical potential in their analogous configurations. His dispositio, however, conforms only marginally with the inventio both stated and implied in the letter to Raleigh. Three discrepancies command particular attention: the dispositio shows only the most vestigial realization of the announced twelve-part anthology of separate demonstrations in separate books of twelve distinct "priuate morall vertues"; Arthur's erotic quest for Gloriana is far less significant to the actual dispositio of The Faerie

Queene than Britomart's for Artegall; and the intended sequestering of "priuate morall" from public or "polliticke" virtues does not survive Book III, and could hardly do so decorously given the political resonance of its subject – "chastitie" – in Elizabethan England.[24] Such discrepancies make it obvious that the letter offers no shortcut to comprehending Spenser's inventio, but these particular discrepancies offer one path of inference, however lengthy and ill-defined, from and through the glorious copia of Spenser's dispositio to his actual, and (by decorum) equally copious inventio. Even cursory analysis of this dispositio against the letter demonstrates an inventio composing not a catalogue of mutually independent virtues but an iterative series of interdependent virtues; indeed, a "grammar of virtues," insofar as the meaning of each depends upon its position in a sequence relative to other virtues and to some principle of order which, perforce, transcends any single component in the sequence.

My choice of "justice" to label that supervalent motive[25] derives entirely from what was intended initially to be simply a seriatim analysis of Spenser's dispositio. As the evidence of rhetorical structure mounted, however, it became increasingly apparent that by the time he began work on Book IV, possibly already in Book III, Spenser's shift from a catalogue to a grammar of virtues was in place, and that "justice," the subject of Book V, informed topoi determining both the direction of shift and a syntax of interdependency among the virtues preceding and succeeding it in the narrative sequence. As one would expect from its authority in humanist ideology, the Platonic inventio of justice resonates in Spenser's topoi, and this shift at the juncture of Books III and IV, among its other characteristics, collapses Spenser's original partition of "priuate morall" from "polliticke" virtues, arguing that for the poet, as for Plato, the virtues of the polis and the virtues of the individual soul are metonymic components in justice.[26] The specific direction of shift in rhetorical motive thus argues a clarification of Spenser's "end," announced in the letter to Raleigh, from demonstrating two-dozen discrete virtues that "fashion" an individual "gentleman or noble person in vertuous and gentle discipline" to demonstrating the coalescence of virtues that "fashions" a polity where private virtues find realization in a "polliticke" order.

Book I and Book II precede this shift and are less central than succeeding books to the demonstration of justice as a focal source of structural decorum. To comprehend Spenser's inventio through his rhetorical structure, however, with as little "re-construction" as cautiously mimetic procedure can promote, I consider the dispositio of *The Faerie Queene* in the order that Spenser chose as the decorous expression of his inventio, preserving especially the serial order of his major sequential division into "Books." In doing so I make no implicit case for "privileging" authorial intentions; rather I privilege execution, particularly the sequence of execution, because in rhetorical proof, for reasons I will outline shortly, sequence has consequence. My procedure equally implies no argument against privileging authorial intention. If we have some way of knowing or assuming with a fair degree of probability what Spenser's intentions were, it seems decorous to give him precedence over any other source of intention, and at least to acknowledge, even if we exceed them, the limits on connotation an author determines by context. Practicality as much as principle would justify Miller's statement of purpose, "neither to ignore the poet's intentions nor to violate them capriciously, but to read those intentions within a critical frame of reference that does not coincide with them, and that will allow their strategic exclusions to become manifest."[27] This effect on "strategic exclusions" is of course reciprocal: Spenser's text transgresses and so exposes the limits of his critics' frames of reference. The notion of authorial irrelevance as an absolute, however, is surely a sublimated symptom of industrial capitalism at its apotheosis, alienating the author entirely from the product of his labour; or perhaps the ultimate mirage of "late-capitalist" consumerism, making epics one with food at the supermarket or "Sesame Street" in the Sony: goods produced by spontaneous generation out of a cultural ether at the point of delivery.

Book I is the structural model for Book II and provides a paradigm of Spenser's rhetorical method throughout the epic, and I use it in chapters 1 and 2 as a serviceable resource for exempla to introduce Spenser's adaptation of rhetoric to poetic. Book II, although closely tracking Book I in structure, provides significant variations of dispositional proof in the episodes of Mammon and Acrasia, and I shall deal briefly with those also in chapter 2 before turning in the following chapters to the rhetorical texture of Books III through VII and the inventio of justice that texture opens to inference.

PART ONE

Inventio Heroicae

1 Decorum, Sequence, and Proof: The Problematics of Analogy

1 NARRATIVE AS "COURTSHIP"; SPENSER AS RHETOR

Aristotle's primal definition of rhetoric, "the art of persuasion," implies a motivation to implicate an "other" in our point of view. "Persuasion" both acknowledges Burke's "estrangement" (we are not "of the same mind") and seeks to overcome the estrangement. In the course of this chapter I will propose two improvisations on Aristotle's formula ("the art of contingent closure" and "the arts of analogy"), but this Burkean elaboration of rhetoric in the classical definition opens an avenue of tentative first approach (more accessible, I think, than any available alternative) to Spenser in his unfamiliar, even alienating, posture as "rhetorician." Here "persuasion" involves the reader in a kinetic tension, and the suasive act becomes a narrative of resolution. Rhetor becomes Burke's "courtier"; *The Faerie Queene* becomes a "narrative of courtship" in purpose as well as content, its tales of questing knights from Gloriana's court compose an artifact of suasive devices composed *to court* a meeting of minds between the poet and his estranged audience.

In Book I the subject is "Holinesse" and the "legende of the Knight of the Red Crosse" is Spenser's instrument of persuasion, constructed to forge an identification of perspectives between his vision and that of his reader. Because it is probably the best-known segment of the epic and certainly displays its most transparent rhetorical structure, I will use the "legende" of Redcrosse in this chapter and the next to adduce protocols of analysis and basic principles implicated in the theory of rhetoric as courtship, especially the concepts which I find to be most problematic: "decorum," "proof," and "sequence."

Treatments of Spenser's text as suasive artifact and instrument of courtship have tended, implicitly or explicitly, to limit its audience to Elizabeth Tudor and its purpose to courtly preferment. Any broader interpretive resonance latent within the analogical elision of rhetoric with courtship remains undeveloped. Indeed, the very aptness of the elision to Spenser's literal, historical position as a social courtier seems ironically to compel a limited and selective focus: in this posture as rhetor, Spenser shares with his poetry a tradition of unsystematic, highly selective rhetorical analysis. Some recent postmodernist versions illustrate the tradition and repay analysis.

Stephen Greenblatt gives perhaps the most unqualified statement of a common enthymeme: "*The Faerie Queene* is ... wholly wedded to the autocratic ruler of the English state,"[1] and Miller provides the most concise catalogue of topoi defining social posture: "As Englishman, poet, bureaucrat, colonist, and political subject, Spenser was himself *constituted* by Elizabeth's 'imperiall powre' and was economically dependent on her 'bountie.'"[2] Miller thus argues that the poet who "frames his ideal portrait of Elizabeth within complex allegorical images of the social hierarchy seeks at the same time and in the same gesture – by reflex as it were – to be himself constituted in the image of sovereignty" (31). Cultural topoi representing what Cain terms "the humanist promotion of Orpheus as civilizer"[3] prepare the ground for Spenser's defining within and through his texts a hierarchical position of "Laureate" for himself, a place possessed of ethos much higher than his birth or "bureaucratic" function would provide. Montrose summarizes the strategy of this courtship succinctly: "Spenser's authorial self-fashioning proceeds by the constitution of the writer as a subject of and in his own discourse; and also by the insertion of his text into the economy of courtly service and reward – that is, by its constitution as a book, a tangible commodity that functions as a vehicle of the writer's social and material advancement."[4]

My citation of this composite argument is not a prelude to refutation. The contention is plausible and, within its limits, persuasive. Those limits, however, are significant to central concerns of this study. In making their case, its advocates create an epideictic dispositio of "Spenser" through selective biographical exempla that isolate him in the posture of social courtier fractured from any erotic, aesthetic, or transcendent analogues. Burke's theory, precisely because it insists on these analogies and resists such "fracturing," provides a theoretical model for application to Spenser's purposes and practice which minimizes the distortions of fragmented selection. The postmodernist case for social motivation epitomizes the problem of selective rhetorical analysis that Burke's theory addresses, and does so in a form immediately available to the nonspecialist because "plausibility" in this argument fails to conceal, even from a rhetorical neophyte, that its persuasive range is severely restricted. Readers may be convinced that Spenser deployed his art to foster ambitions for a sinecure at Elizabeth's court but few will find this attribute sufficient to accommodate their experience of *The Faerie Queene*, which like Machiavelli's *The Prince*, quickly overflows the provisions of an advocatory niche labelled "employment application." Yet these same readers would surely concede that the case attributing social instrumentation to Spenser's poem does, in some way, affect their experience of it, and such affects seem immune to admonitions from New Criticism about autobiographical and intentional "fallacies." Good rhetoric is often fallacious logic, for reasons I will address shortly, but if postmodern historicism would privilege Elizabeth as Spenser's addressed audience to the point of exclusivity, New Criticism would make her a ghost. Spenser addresses Elizabeth Tudor certainly, but he does so in the presence of a larger audience, each audience aware of the other and of "Spenser" as constituted in an occasion of social courtship. We function corporately with Spenser's sovereign and her court as the addressed witness not only to that courtship but also to its multivalent analogues, which are driven by estrangements between rhetor and audience of which the "social" is simply one embedded component.

Of course to concede that extra-textual attributions affect "in some way" our response to the text leaves "the way" unmapped, and efforts to mark a clearer trail will encounter resistance. Recipes of explanation tend to falter when the logical binaries they assume fail to hold. A case of recognized limitations is nevertheless suasive – "extraneous" yet "influential," both inadequate and significant to our response. The process whereby an argument achieves such affects is much less transparent than its limitations and, without specialized discourse, less readily articulated.

Rhetorical theory constitutes such a discourse: its long history is founded precisely on the recognition that what we know or think we know about speakers, and about their purpose in speaking, always "makes a difference" to our experience of their oration, as in turn do the speakers' perceptions and anticipations of their audience and the sense both share, or fail to share, of specific demands on oratory made by specific occasions. My concern here is not to adjudicate the validity of either the postmodernist argument and its ambiguous affect on readers or any modernist rebuttal but to identify the interactive process they illustrate as a bedrock phenomenon of rhetoric. At issue is the most fundamental, and most problematic, of all rhetorical concepts, traditionally labelled "decorum."

Arcane, awkward, and virtually obsolete, decorum gives place in current usage to a generous selection of alternatives: applicability, appropriateness, aptness, fitness, computability, pertinence, propriety, relevance, and suitability are most common, although I suspect every specialty and demographic sub-group has its dialect version. In this study I revert persistently, if not exclusively, to decorum. Neither fastidiousness nor nostalgia prompts this reversion, and I hope readers will resist the understandable temptation to ease any resulting discomfort by silently emending decorum with putative synonyms. Its very awkwardness and murky obsolescence allow *decorum* to signal a problematic indeterminacy in the concept it labels that more familiar, comfortable terms camouflage. The problematics of decorum underlie those of rhetorical proof, and both germinate from a deep structure of indeterminacy rooted in the concept and processes of analogy. Rhetorical theory attempts to systematize the inchoate potential of analogy, driven by an ironic imperative that it be analogous with logic and depend primarily on a methodology of proof. Spenser's legend of Redcrosse illustrates with particular richness and variety the applied arts of analogy.

2   "PROOF" BY ANALOGY

Book I of *The Faerie Queene*, in effect, asserts a concept of holiness and sets out to prove it. Traditionally, such assertions were designated "enthymemes," and the old term, like "decorum," is worth preserving if only to focus a distinction between rhetorical assertions and the "premises" of logic. Plato disingenuously uses rhetorical strategies to denigrate rhetoric as counterfeit philosophy, but Aristotle, while fastidiously chastising rhetoric's propensity for fraud, concedes it the status of *antistrophos* to dialectic, its necessary partner in the dance of reason. Reason needs rhetoric to complement logic because it must deal with open systems: ones not amenable to the certainties of dialectic. Closed systems, like those of mathematics or metaphysics, have logical premises which can be systemically proved to be true or false within fixed procedures that deliver a conclusion whose certainty is that of *a priori* definition. "The square on the hypotenuse of a right-angled triangle is equal to the sum of squares on the other two sides" states a Pythagorean axiom of given truth-value within the closed system of Euclidean geometry, and permits deductions that, if the rules of that system are followed without error, are certain. No reference to anything outside the system is required for its proofs to be valid. Indeed, when David Hume, in *A Treatise of Human Nature* (I.iii), linked causality to probability, arguing that causal relationships are psychological fictions generated from experience and amenable only to such external, *a posteriori*, evidence for proof, he shifted causality from the realm of logic into its antistrophic complement, rhetoric, awakening Kant from his dogmatic slumber and dislocating central paradigms of Western thought. Currently, there are many logical systems using mathematical axioms that seem to preclude the possibility of any external referent in observable or imaginable nature, adducing proof only from other theories, but their deductions are demonstrably valid within the closed system that defines them.

Rhetorical proofs, in contradistinction, are complicated by the uncertainties of open systems and a consequent radical dependency on external reference. The axiomatically certain premise as a point of departure gives place to the problematic, and at best probable, enthymeme: "The free market system has failed us"; "The free market system will save us"; "Violence is as American as apple pie"; "All interpretation is misinterpretation"; "If any strength we have, it is to ill"; "Man is the measure of all things." We cannot prove such assertions by teasing out through systematic syllogism the predicates tangled in their subjects. Extramural contiguity, not intramural consistency, demonstrates validity, and this contiguity is manufactured from discontiguous elements. Aristotle's orator discovers the existing means of persuasion and selects the best from those available and appropriate. Exactly which selections from available resources are appropriate becomes a function of occasion, audience, subject, genre, and many related contingencies. The "art of persuasion" might more usefully be defined as the art of contingent closure; suasion is a function of decorum and the principles of decorum can mimic the inherent consistency of logical systems, allowing open systems to be artificially, and arbitrarily, closed.

Such mimicry participates in the species of rhetorical proof labelled *logos*, a procedure, as its tag implies, with greater pretensions to the desiderata of logic than Aristotle's two alternatives, *pathos* and *ethos*. Proof by pathos (pathetic proof) seeks to create community by suasion on purely emotional grounds; proof by ethos (ethical proof) seeks consent to an enthymeme on grounds of authority either conceded to its source or won by the performance of its advocate. In both pathetic and ethical proofs, while closure of estrangement ostensibly occurs around a proposition, the proposition itself bears no necessary relationship to the engendered sense of conviction, that dangerous *doppelgänger* of logical certainty which occurs when an audience fuses into community at the common places of shared emotions or communal norms of authority evoked by the rhetor. We may indeed always get the government we deserve, but we seldom get the one we voted for.

Logos, however, is comparatively ideocentric and proceeds by selection and ordering of exempla. Its suasiveness depends upon a shared perception that the exempla chosen are decorous with both the enthymeme they purport to prove and the available reservoir of exempla they purport to represent synecdochally. Exempla themselves also carry varying degrees of emotional and ethical appeal. For Spenser and the audience he could anticipate, scriptural exempla were more authoritative than historical or literary (fabulous) exempla, and among fabulous exempla citations from classical authors outranked later sources.

Whatever the source and authority of exempla, proof by logos demands their selection according to rules of decorum. But what is decorum other than a synonym for "accepted" or at least "acceptable analogy"? In an open system the best or most persuasive choice from among a given field of commonplaces is determined by a perception of which commonplaces are most analogous to the enthymeme under scrutiny. No choice is possible unless some factor enables us to limit the infinity of possible choices implicit in an open system. Through logos we impose such limits by a selection process that depends upon perceived analogies between discrete possibilities or, more exactly, upon analogies whose acceptability is either given or conceded under suasion. Nothing logical limits the cultural, geographical, and historical variety of acceptable analogies, since all connections among entities that are not predicates of the same subject are arbitrary and alogical. Thus nothing logical distinguishes one school of theory about the polis or its artifacts from another; distinctions reside in diverse principles of decorum, in the analogies and commonplace sources each will accept and/or preclude. Bereft of logic, all proof, the very possibility of ordering experience in an open system, depends for such ground as it has on analogy. Even choices based on ethos and pathos involve a perceived analogy between the figure of authority or object of emotional commitment and the issue demanding choice of an audience.

3   THE ARTIFICE OF DECORUM

Spenser's choosing to treat holiness as a rhetorical issue declares the subject open to controversy and commits him to these alogical, analogical methods of proof. His choices immediately narrow, constrained by a species of decorum we might label "decorum of precedent," the same species that allows allusions to occasions and social purpose prior to or from outside Spenser's art to affect our experience of that art. Book I of *The Faerie Queene* is a secular fable on holiness, not a treatise or sermon, and decorum forbids Spenser's directly citing the kinds of exempla suitable to formal argument: "Fierce warres and faithfull loues" must "moralize" his song (I.Pr.1.9). Appeals to biblical, historical, or literary authority "prior to" or "from outside" his dispositio are indirect, or allusive, achieved through a suggestive phrase or detail of description; that is, through techniques of elocutio not elements of inventio. Spenser's inventio consists, in fact, of mixed topoi which include those of rhetorical genre suitable to "fierce warres and faithfull loues," particularly heroica (epic), fabula (fairy tale, myth, romance), and pastoralia, all merged with allegoria. It also includes topoi of subject, represented in Book I by the aspects of "holinesse" comprising Spenser's vision. Each of these aspects is either praiseworthy (*eulogistic*) or blameworthy (*dyslogistic*) and they generate enthymemes which, stated simplistically, conform to either the pattern "x is holy" or "x is unholy."

"Proof" of such enthymemes requires Spenser to conform to precedents for allegoria and heroica; of particular interest here is their constituent requirement for "characters." "Character" implies a measure of predictability, demanding consistency through space and time as a necessary condition; "characters" are always the product of decorum by precedent. Spenser incorporates each aspect of his subject in heroes and villains, fictional loci of actions, words, and descriptions, who represent analogically the particular topoi of holiness each embodies, be they eulogistic (e.g., Una, Arthur, Caelia, Fidelia, and her sisters, Mercie and Contemplation) or dyslogistic (e.g., Errour, Archimago, Duessa, Lucifera, Orgoglio, and Despaire). Characters, in short, are Spenser's true exempla, some of whose characteristics may evoke scriptural, historical, or literary authority.[5]

Spenser favours three schemes of elocutio to adduce such authority: *prosopographia* (the description of a person by his form, stature, manners, studies, activities, and affections), *topothesia* (the description of an imaginary place), and *icon* (a specialized form of description by use of multiple comparisons to other persons or things). Some uses of prosopographia are extremely simple, involving little more than a suggestive name attached to an exemplum (e.g., Fidelia, Zele, Reverence, Repentance), or a detail of appearance, as in the initial description of Redcrosse (I.i.2) with its allusion to the "whole armour of God" in Ephesians vi. Similar economy marks the topothesia of "Morpheus house" (I.i.39,40) with its echo of passages from *Aeneid*, *Odyssey*, and *Metamorphoses*. Other schemes are highly elaborate. A lengthy, complex icon (vii.16–18) characterizes Duessa through a series of comparative identifications with the woman riding the seven-headed beast of Revelation. Sometimes both topothesia and prosopographia interweave to present place and person as analogues. The treacherous master of illusion, Archimago, for instance, is characterized by his monkish disguise (I.i.29) and precious habitat (I.i.34), both conveying the exaggerated perfection a stage-manager might create to reinforce highly conventional audience expectations of a hermit and his hermitage, and eliding with apparent seamlessness to the hyperbolized cliche of Archimago's verbal elocutio: "He told of Saintes and Popes, and euermore / He strowd an Aue-Mary after and before" (i.35). By contrast, the appearance of Despaire and his cave afford no disguise (ix.33–6); person and place seem transparently consistent with each other and continuous with the nihilistic "greedie graue" they figure iconically. Equally transparent is Spenser's use of icon to depict Lucifera's counsellors, the Deadly Sins. Their names evoke religious dyslogy, and every detail of description stands in appositional, sometimes synonymic, relationship to every other detail and to the abstract name. Thus Idlenesse bears such epithets as "sluggish," "lawlesse," "lustlesse," and "euill"; he rides a "slouthfull Asse"; his actions consist of avoiding devotions and "manly exercise" while "drownd in sleepe" of "lawlesse riotise" and, like all Lucifera's counsellors, he incorporates a disease appropriate to his name: "For in his lustlesse limbs through euill guise / A shaking feuer raignd continually" (iv.20).

Explications of decorum occur, of course, after the fact, and these citations are typical in representing "decorousness" as if it were a given quality of exempla, like a genetic code that sorts them into groups. Explication of decorum invariably drifts towards a deterministic idiom, but this drift should not go unexamined, even if it cannot be avoided. Indeed, so "transparent" and "apparent" are continuities and correspondences in examples such as these from Spenser that their origins in artifice easily become occluded; like Roland Barthes' "bourgeois norms" they develop a tendency to be "experienced as the evident laws of a natural order.[6] When perceived as "natural," analogical orders blur functionally into their logical complement. In his deconstruction of a notorious example, Edward Said argues that "so far as it existed in the West's awareness, the Orient was a word which later accrued to it a wide field of meanings, associations, and connotations, and ... these did not necessarily refer to the real Orient but to the field surrounding the word."[7] By "accruing" such a "field of meanings" the linguistic label "Semitic" became not an enthymeme asserting analogies but the subject premis of a logical system, "a transtemporal, transindividual category, purporting to predict every discrete act of 'Semitic' behavior on the basis of some pre-existing 'Semitic' essence, and aiming as well to interpret all aspects of human life and activity in terms of some common 'Semitic' element."[8] The confusion of natural and artificial origins that occasions this inversion of logical and rhetorical proofs is symptomatic of deeper confusions, or fusions, among patterns of "priority" that I shall address shortly because they engage issues of rhetorical proof raised by narrative sequence. Here I wish to stress how dependent is such proof on these confusions: the rhetor's suasiveness increases the more his artificial analogies "are experienced as evident laws of a natural order," and "decorum" labels the necessary condition of such experience.

Logic requires that natural and artificial orders remain distinct; rhetoric requires that they be analogous, that is, ambiguously both distinct and identical. Thus analogy, as a concept, epitomizes within its ambiguity the conditions of rhetoric as courtship: estrangement is the condition necessarily prior to the assertion of community. "Ambiguity" is the static disposition of which "courtship" is the dynamic. All the most fundamental strategies of rhetorical organization (metaphor, metonymy, and synecdoche) embody the same alogical ambiguity inherent in the very concept of analogy.

Decorum naturalizes artifice and "logicizes" analogy, and we need an elaborated understanding of Aristotle's "appropriateness" to accommodate complexities of the kind pandemic in Spenser and centralized in the critiques of radical indecorum undertaken by Barthes and Said. Decorum does not signify a stable attribute adhering or failing to adhere to discrete elements but a dynamic field of contingency both defining and defined by the relationship among elements. When Aristotle's orator selects something "most appropriate" from a field of available "means of persuasion" he conditions all further selections. The "available field" of choice "organizes around" (as it were) that first selection. But even that first selection is conditioned by a "principle of organization" which must be in place necessarily "before" (logically, temporally, and causally) all selection. Decorum records the coordinates of that Archimedean point of organization; or to use a less classical and more destabilizing analogy, it functions, I suggest, like the "attractor" postulated in the mathematics of Chaos theory to explain the patterns which coalesce, accumulate, and reiterate around a locus of organization from a totally random field. "Orient" and "Semitic" with their accrued "field of meanings" function as such "attractors" for Said, as do "bourgeois norms" in their pervasive hegemony for Barthes. All three generate structures of such self-referential, self-sustaining coherence out of the field they organize that their reconstruction demands that Barthes, and especially Said, employ immense resources of critical ingenuity and energy to persuade us that the structures are flawed at the source; that their rules of organization define an attractor whose inadequate selection distorts the field it claims to comprehend. To discredit those rules is to prove indecorum.

4   PATTERN RECOGNITION AND "ATTRACTORS"

With Spenser's structures of decorum our purpose is exploration not refutation, but the notion of attractor, although perhaps a disconcerting intrusion upon the technical vocabulary of rhetoric, tenders helpful service in establishing procedures for rhetorical analysis. It flags the obscured disposition of two components under a singular label, making a functional distinction within decorum between a process of organization and its generating rules. These components are reciprocal and mutually defining, but the rules become accessible only by inference from their consequences. The analyst's first operational concern is to recognize the presence of an attractor and diagnose its field of organization.

In using such displaced terms unconventionally, I hope to shift the ground under conventional misconceptions of rhetorical analysis as a set of fixed protocols applying univocal definitions from time-tested handbooks to discriminate among finely sutured parts of a dispositio and to generate a running marginal gloss on its figures of elocutio. We can apply handbook formulae to a text only by yet another act of analogy. The problematics adduced for decorum thus illustrate a general case: definitions in rhetorical textbooks and treatises are suggestive, not prescriptive – enthymemes, not premises – and provide no computer template for automatic processing. Protocols for their application are not given: they must be developed in context, and such school-exercises as figure-identification have analytical significance only if the isolated figure instances an organizational pattern. Patterns become discernable only through repetition.

Spenser's icon depicting Lucifera's counsellors, for instance, signals the presence of such a pattern with unusual clarity: each abstract character-name operates obtrusively as an attractor, organizing around itself diverse elements selected from copious fields of available epithets, actions, animals, and diseases. Even this unusually lucid attractor, however, owes the clarity and obtrusiveness of its presence to an atypically focused and contained configuration of repetition. Spenser repeats the constitution of his icon for each counsellor with ritualistic consistency, then groups the icons in a procession: isolated, uninterrupted, sequential. Sheer contiguity and formal consistency seem to resolve any issues of analogy before they arise. More typically, patterns of repetition reiterate diffusely across episodes, cantos and books, even the entire epic, and the analyst usually must discern analogies of function among different figures rather than consistency of form in repetitions of the same figure.

Lucifera's episode will serve to illustrate in brief synecdoche this decorum of functional interplay between such dominant schemes as icon, prosopographia and topothesia, and other, ancillary, elements of elocutio. The topothesia of Lucifera's house carries intrinsic rhetorical signs that depict, without ambiguity, the ethos of the place. The most obvious and fundamental of these is *antithesis*. Her "Pallace" is "stately" but mortarless, its walls "high" but "nothing strong, nor thicke," and its "faire mould" set on "weake" foundations (iv.4–5). These antitheses serve as attractors associating the notion of duality with the conjunction of falseness and disguise. The seductive, brilliant appearance of the palace disguises "cunningly" an ugly scene of corruption and decay, and Redcrosse's guide to Lucifera's court, Duessa, functions as exemplum of the same association. She is "duality" personified, "that false Lady faire, / The fowle Duessa" (iv.13, 37), deceitful by nature, and disguised as the attractive Fidessa until revealed by Arthur as a "loathly, wrinckled hag" (viii.46–9).

Antithesis, as a vehicle of duality, functions in concert with two related figures, *hyperbole* and *ironia*, to infuse duality with moral significance. Hyperbole occurs repeatedly as a descriptive element characterizing not only the palace but also its mistress, through her throne, dress, and person, as an object of social courtship (iv.4.3–5; 7.5–7; 8.6–9). The figure repeatedly denotes excessive brightness, and Spenser amplifies this hyperbolic stress on the brilliance of Lucifera and her habitation with *conduplicatio*, "too exceeding shone, / Exceeding shone," a *similtudo* linking Lucifera to Phaeton (iv.9.1–5), and a *gradatio* on "high-higher-highest" anticipating the ambitious tropes of Mutabilitie:

Yet did she thinke her pearelesse worth to pas
That parentage, with pride so did she swell,
And thundering *Ioue*, that high in heauen doth dwell,
And wield the world, she claymed for her syre,
Or if that any else did Ioue excell:
For to the highest she did still aspyre,
Or if ought higher were then that, did it desyre.   (iv.11.3–9)

Each of these figures conveys excess: it is the quality of decorum that attracts them into a common organization. In concert they cluster functionally to demonstrate both cause and effect of pride in material possessions, worldly power, and physical beauty or prowess. Excessive material brilliance not only "confound[s]" the "frayle amazed sense" of those who follow the "broad high way" to become courtiers at Lucifera's court, but also dazzles the "feeble eyen" of Lucifera herself (iv.9.6). Precedents of vision and reason as analogues stretch into antiquity and Lucifera, in believing herself "higher" than the "highest," clearly demonstrates self-induced unreason.

Furthermore, courtiers and courted at Lucifera's throne serve as loci for identical attributes and in so doing epitomize with dramatic clarity a structural principle of some importance to this study. Identity is the antithesis of estrangement; it is, therefore, the desired end of courtship. We are what we court. Lucifera is what her courtiers "would be" in the sequence of time and "are" in motivation. The prideful, including Redcrosse, demonstrate by dramatic action Lucifera's topos of failed intellect, the "blindness" whereby they deceive themselves into accepting the false appearance of "goods" instead of goodness itself. Antithesis and hyperbole thereby become elocutional analogues of the knight's blindness and its ironic consequences: the antithesis describes Lucifera and her court as they are while the hyperbole and related figures of hyperbolical effect describe the same things as Redcrosse and the others apprehend them through "frayle amazed senses."

Privileged by Spenser's narrator, we do not share Redcrosse's bedazzlement because our structure of analogies differs from his. We "perceive" from the outset that behind the brilliant appearance of Lucifera and her palace lie hidden an usurping tyrant and a rotting foundation. Every hyperbolical description of material seductivenes in this episode implies disapprobation rather than praise: eulogism argues dyslogism; an elocutio of excess asserts privation; physical beauty implies moral ugliness. Decorum, in short, encompasses analogies that rest on dichotomy as well as similarity, and every hyperbole in this episode is implicitly ironia.

Spenser can focus and organize this ironic inversion of praise and blame in one-word tropes as well as more elaborate figures, particularly in the evocative *epitheta* "goodly" and "faire." Through repetition goodly attracts into a pattern Lucifera's palace, the actions of Vanitie and those who blindly admire Lucifera, and, most significantly, the "vngodly" participants in Lucifera's procession of Seven Deadly Sins: "vngodly" directly inverts the *paronomasia* on "good" and "God" thrice-repeated in the four stanzas introducing Caelia's House of Holiness (I.x.1.9; 3.9; 4.4), eulogistic counter-exemplum to Lucifera's castle. These ironic puns exemplify *antiphrasis*: by placing a term of moral approbation within a series of morally corrupt contexts, the device organizes an antithetical field that reverses the evaluative connotations of that term. "Faire" undergoes a like process of transformation. Applied to Lucifera, her court, her courtiers, the procession of Deadly Sins, and Duessa, it functions dyslogistically. Applied, at the beginning of the episode, to Una (2.1), it evokes by allusion the normal significance of "faire" outside the aegis of Lucifera's court. "Faire" accounts for two of every three epitheta modifying "Una" in Book I, and since Una's ethos represents a fixed standard of goodness within the moral flux of Faeryland, "faire," like "goodly," is normally a term of moral approbation. "Faire" composes a one word allegoria labelling the coalesced categories of desirability which Una invests as a single object of desire, veiled through most of the Book until revealed as a "celestiall sight" to signal resolution of both erotic and transcendent estrangement (I.xii.23). Thus the *antiphraseis* associating "goodly" and "faire" with Lucifera's palace and its inhabitants "keep decorum": they extend a pattern of analogy from the level of single words to the cluster of figures that demonstrate the misperception and misconception misguiding Redcrosse to court Lucifera.

That pattern extends to encompass even the apparently isolated icons of Lucifera's "vngodly" counsellors: their constituent elements repeat those of the episode generally. Antitheses are prevalent, and usually demonstrate false appearance. Idlenesse carries a "Portesse" that "much was worne, but therein little red" (19.2), and refuses to work "for contemplation sake: yet otherwise, / His life he led in lawlesse riotize" (20.3–5). Lechery "clothed was full faire / Which vnderneath did hide his filthiness" (25.1–2). In some cases the antithesis indicates not merely false appearance in accidence but duality in essence, and is charged with topoi of failed reason. Gluttony's "mind in meat and drinke was drowned so, / That from his friend he seldome knew his fo" (23.4–5). Avarice is characterized by a cluster of related schemes: a conduplicatio on "wretched," a repetitio on "who" and its grammatical variants, a number of antitheses, and a final oxymoron (28.9–29.5). In concert, these clustered elements assert with emphasis the ultimate unreason of his ruling passion: "Who had enough, yet wished euer more." Similarly, Wrath who "through vnaduized rashnesse woxen wood" demonstrates a duality opposing will to reason (34.6–9), while Enuie "euery good to bad he doth abuse" (32.5) for "death it was, when any good he saw" (30.7).

Perhaps this phrase, "euery good to bad he doth abuse," might stand as synecdochal epigram to the depictions of all the counsellors; or, indeed, of all the inhabitants of Lucifera's castle. Having willfully embraced the material world as their highest, and only, "good," they become dupes of its inherent duality, uncertainty, and moral indecorum: Fortune's fools. Lucifera and her counsellors differ from the other inhabitants of the court only in degree, not in kind. They are extreme cases, or caricatures in the mode of comic hyperbole, depicting human types excessively, even exclusively, idle, gluttonous, lecherous, avaricious, envious, and wrathful. Lucifera ostensibly "leads" them but processionally "follows" them, creating a closed loop emblematic of the reciprocal identity of courtier and courted. Neither princess nor counsellors interacts directly with Redcrosse, but they demonstrate through hyperbolical exempla the effects of commitment to a materialistic ethos and constitute metonyms, objectified and ritualistically simplified, of the complex moral dangers dramatically encountered by Redcrosse in the form of such villainous exempla as Errour, Archimago, Orgoglio, Duessa, and Despaire.

This analytical sample from a representative episode illustrates both the complex dynamics of Spenser's elocutional decorum and why I must deal only occasionally and in summary form – when the motive of "justice" especially demands it – with analysis of Spenser's elocutio; it is easy to lose sight of his dispositional structure while engulfed in the astonishing intricacy of the analogical patterns constituting his elocutional detail. Spenser's strategies of elocutio, whether simple or elaborate, in their detailed copia disciplined by decorum, enrich the ethos (eulogistic and dyslogistic) of his exempla. These exempla carry the demonstrative burden of his distributio, the dynamic structure through which he courts our recognition of deep moral import in this ostensibly secular fable of adventure.

5   PROOF BY NARRATION

Dispositio, or "arrangement," is the office in classical rhetorical practice concerned with the organization of the elements of inventio to present their most persuasive form of argument. Spenser's "argument" is plot, the sequence of narrated action comprising his "leg-ende," and its dispositio involves persuasive strategies of narration that complement those of elocutio. Narrative, like structure, is a focus of current investigation in structuralist and postmodernist theory and of some controversy, especially among theorists and practitioners of the novel.[9] My interests in this essay touch theirs only tangentially. My concern is not primarily with such specific issues as appropriated voices, perspectives, *mise en abime*, reliability, privilege, durations, or focalization, but with the less choate, more elementary rhetorical dispersion from which these issues precipitate: the function of narrative as a method of proof.

Narrative is a sequential construct, and the very act of sequencing implies both analogy and decorum. X and Y in sequence signal the presence of an attractor that selected and so ordered them, and X in narrative sequence becomes a criterion of selection for Y. In Spenser's dispositio, sequence and the juxtaposing of sequences through *digressio*, as in the subplot creating separate narratives for the estranged Redcrosse and Una, demonstrate implied enthymemes, usually by logos. Such demonstration complements the mode of proof by pathos preponderant in his elocutio which seeks, as Alpers notes, "in any given stanza ... to elicit a response – to evoke, modify, or complicate feelings and attitudes."[10] The effectiveness of narrative sequence as an instrument of rhetorical proof depends upon an habitual and usually unexamined ritual conspiracy of immemorial antiquity between storytellers and listeners to accept logically distinct patterns of "priority" as analogous, even identical. Thus Spenser, in conven-tionally supplicating Clio, the Muse of history, addresses her as "chiefe of nine" because she is the eldest (I.pr.2.1). Like all rhetorical proofs, this variant of logos is alogical, although (in common with many rhetorical strategies) a simplified version of it tends to find space in elementary logic texts, impressively labelled in this case "post hoc ergo propter hoc," to illustrate illogical or faulty reasoning. Yet, as James Carscallen puts it, whatever "expository scheme" might influence Spenser's dispositio, it must be amenable to assimilation with "the temporal nature of a story."[11] Unless we conspire to accept that linear priority in space and time – the sequential order in which narrated events present themselves, or occur (first x then y) – implies causal priority (because x then y), most narrative would lose its dynamic contours, its virtual direction, motivation, and characteristic rhythm of complication either leading to resolution or creating the anticipation that it should. Disruptions or dislocations in serial con-tinuity may have pathetic effects, satisfying or frustrating condi-tioned expectations of coherence,[12] but my focus here is on the logos of sheer contiguity antecedent to continuity. That Y is contiguous with and "follows" X must signal the presence of an attractor generating a process of organization. Without this alogical logos of priority the organization of events would be arbitrary, "a-narrational": X would not condition the selection and contiguous placement of Y. Thus any sequential decorum would provide no lines of possible inference from distributio to inventio. Artists creating narrative, of course, may violate this decorum, or postmodern theorists may urge them to do so, but such violation is the decorous expression of an inventio, and a line of inference exists back to that inventio by way of the "prior" conventional principles of decorum that it transparently violates.

Inference is a process of logic. Applied to the analysis of narrative, it manifests a third and final component in the fusion of priorities. Narrative invites inference because sequential distributio constitutes the analogue of a discursive or argumentative inventio, and the suasive function of narrative sequence involves deductive as well as inferential processes of organization. These characteristics will remain undetected or appear simply paradoxical only if we forget the antistrophic nature of rhetoric and logic. Logos mimics logic. By extension of analogous patterns, causal priority must in its turn imply deductive or "logical" priority (because x therefore y $\rightarrow$ if x therefore y) to give narrative structure the demonstrative potential inherent in logical predication: events leading to an end become derivative attributes of that end, and sequence thereby "proves" them to be both necessary to and subsumed by it. The historical order, as Spenser himself notes, serves analytical, not annalistic, purposes. "For the Methode of the Poet historical is not such, as of an Historiographer. For an Historiographer discourseth of affayres orderly as they were donne, accounting as well the times as the actions, but a Poet thrusteth into the middest, euen where it most concerneth him, and there recoursing to the thinges forepaste, and diuining of things to come, maketh a pleasing Analysis of all."[13]

6   SEQUENCE AND "KINETIC" DECORUM

Dispositional sequence in narrative thus implies consequence: placement in time and space for an event asserts both causal and logical significance. Decorum, in this case, gains its affect by syntax rather than precedent: its rules of organization are those of grammatical structures where meaning is determined by position in an order, and the kinetic sequence of narrative signals the projection on a horizontal plane of the static, vertical hierarchy customary in structural figurations of causal inference and logical deduction. However distressing, indeed dangerous, it may be in the rational conduct of life not "to get our priorities straight," the conventional confusion, or fusion, of these particular priorities is fundamental to the rituals of storyteller and audience, to both the making and the "making-something-of" narrative art.

Perhaps these speculative reconsiderations of decorum, proof, and sequence will help to explain why I find Burke's theory useful in response to their problematics and consider its application to Spenser's text valid for reasons more intrinsic than Spenser's collateral dependencies on the Tudor court for preferment and the Arthurian court for legend. In narrative distributio, the rhetorical analyst accesses the structural analogue of a discursive, hierarchical inventio and works within the operational assumption that analogous structures, by definition decorous, generate from a common attractor or motive such as holiness in Book I or, I will argue, justice in *The Faerie Queene* as a whole. Burke's theoretical notion of courtship provides an adaptable model for rhetorical analysis because it incorporates both aspects of the analogy: the courtier's sequence of action in time and space serves as the agency of his ascent or descent on a hierarchical structure, be it social, erotic, aesthetic, or transcendent.

2 Redcrosse as Courtier; Narrative as Argument

Stripped to its rudiments, Spenser's principal sequence of distributio in Book I exhibits topoi of fabula common to romance, "legende," and fairy tale.[1] An untutored farmboy in borrowed armour undertakes a hazardous quest to rescue the parents of a mysterious princess whose castle is besieged by a giant dragon. Surviving encounters with monsters, wizards, witches, trolls, giants, and assorted other villains, he discovers his true identity as St George, the patron saint of England, completes his mission, and is betrothed to the princess. Such tales are the stuff of daydream, self-pleasing and uncritically optimistic. For the purpose of moral enthymemes, the topoi of fairy tale are seldom effective as ethos or logos, although they exert a timeless pathos, tending to captivate rather than persuade. Like Sidney's poet in *The Defence of Poetry*, they "give so sweet a prospect into the way, as will entice any man to enter into it." To entice the attention and sympathy of an audience is the first task of dispositio for the orator in his *exordium*, and these rhetorical elements of fabula allow Spenser to focus sympathetic attention on Redcrosse, who begins his quest as an exemplum, not of holiness or unholiness but of the daydream-self in Everyman: well-meaning, caught up in marvellous adventure, upward bound to success by dint of his good intentions and physical prowess alone.

Once his status is established by tactics of pathos, Redcrosse accumulates attributes that progressively render him capable of proof by ethos and logos. Unlike other exempla, he is not static in character but dynamic: neither saintly nor depraved, capable in potential of holiness or unholiness, he thus attains the function of surrogate for general humanity even as, indeed because, his ethos as a hero of fable is discredited by the manifest inadequacy of his good intentions and prowess over the first nine cantos. The narrator's *epiphonema* (summary moral) drawn from these cantos states as a discovered conclusion the enthymeme they seek to prove:

> What man is he, that boasts of fleshly might,
> And vaine assurance of mortality,
> Which all so soone, as it doth come to fight,
> Against spirituall foes, yeelds by and by,
> Or from the field most cowardly doth fly?
> Ne let the man ascribe it to his skill,
> That thorough grace hath gained victory.
> If any strength we haue, it is to ill,
> But all the good is Gods, both power and eke will.   (I.x.1)

Spenser's argument for this assertion proceeds through a sequence of dramatic demonstrations, in each of which the audience's surrogate exemplum, Redcrosse, takes on a dyslogistic exemplum: "takes on" in both the dramatic sense of encountering as antagonist and the structural sense of cumulatively manifesting the unholy aspect each exemplifies. He is enmeshed in Errour, deluded by Archimago, wounded in his worldly pride by Lucifera, seduced by Duessa, conquered and endungeoned in darkness by Orgoglio, bested in oratorical conflict and persuaded to self-destruction by Despaire. Equally demonstrative of the enthymeme are sequences wherein Redcrosse takes on the countervalent eulogistic exempla, being comforted, rescued, healed, guided, and taught by Una, Arthur, the dwarf, the stream and tree in Canto xi, and the figures of Canto x whose names compose a lexicon of religious terms: Caelia, Fidelia, Speranza, Charissa, Humilta, Zele, Reverence, Obedience, Patience, Amendment, Remorse, Repentance, Mercie, Contemplation.

These names, like other devices of elocutio, mark the presence of allegoria that coalesce with generic topoi of heroica and fabula in Spenser's inventio and serve to universalize both the exempla and the syntax of their relationship with Redcrosse. Allegory asserts analogy between narrative sequences. As the knight takes on successive exempla he simultaneously moves toward the end of his quest: thus the structure of narrative sequence, by its very nature, "proves" through logos that each exemplum is necessary to, and has a place in, the attainment of that end. Following Redcrosse, and the narrator, through this sequence, we arrive, after-the-fact, at Spenser's point-of-departure – the generative point of his dispositio – and so infer a principal enthymeme in his inventio on the subject of holiness: to accept the inefficacy of "fleshly might" against "spirituall foes" is a prior necessity for the attainment of grace.

The narrator, therefore, is in many ways as much our surrogate exemplum as is Redcrosse. He takes an initial posture identical with the untutored farmboy in borrowed armour, appearing as a rustic "in lowly Shepheards weeds" undertaking a mission for which he is unqualified and ill-equipped: "enforst a far vnfitter taske, / For trumpets sterne to chaunge mine Oaten reeds" (I.Pr.1). A locus of varied and often complex rhetorical strategies throughout the epic,[2] the narrator sometimes paces our understanding and sometimes lags behind with ironic effect, but Spenser projects the narrative dramatically through a puzzled, probing, often naively ingenuous consciousness within which telling and experiencing the story are synchronous acts. This concurrence of telling and experiencing is in turn simultaneous with the reader's synchronous "hearing" and experiencing. The narrator's functional demeanor as rhetor thus resembles that of an advocate who both presents evidence for his client before a jury and reacts to that evidence as a means of entraining and so controlling the response of his audience. Unlike an advocate, however, Spenser's narrator is clearly not rehearsing a story whose meaning, and ending, he already comprehends: he is more apprentice than advocate, his relationship to Spenser strategically similar to that of Dante's wanderer in the *Commedia* struggling in the midst of a journey that Dante the poet has already completed. Structurally, therefore, the narrator is not privileged: he occupies a position relative to Spenser coincident with that of the reader, estranged from Spenser's vision and struggling to infer from its dispositio the inventio informing that vision in the story he tells. His posture is that of courtier: in effect, he courts identity with his estranged creator while reciprocally, through him, his creator courts us.

Each episode in the narrative demonstration composing the "legende" of Redcrosse marks a step in this reciprocal process of mutual courtship. Equally, each episode in sequence is at once dramatically a step towards the goal of grace courted by the knight, and logically a derivative attribute of that goal: hence, structurally, it is an intermediate level in a hierarchical model with the goal at its apex, or ultimate term. As each exemplum accumulates, through elocutio, attributes derived from religious, historical, and literary topoi, it becomes a constituent common to more than one such hierarchy. Thus Redcrosse, in completing his fairy-tale quest by killing the

Dragon, at the same time reaches the analogous apices of erotic, social, and transcendent configurations, achieving identity as the betrothed of Una, a true knight of Gloriana, the patron saint of England, and recipient of salvation through grace.

Temporal simultaneity implies structural coincidence: all ultimate terms touch at the same point of convergence, demonstrating a variant decorum not of precedence or syntax but of homology. Spenser prefigures this narrative point of convergence in graphic form as the physical summit of Contemplation's mountain. Mountains provide a commonplace analogue for hierarchical structure from natural topography and serve Spenser as a fundamental device of suasion by structural homology reiterated throughout *The Faerie Queene*. Here a topothesia using elaborate *paraphrasis* identifies the place as Sinai (x.53), the Mount of Olives (x.54), and Parnassus (x.54), whose summits figure topoi of inventio for justice by invoking associations with, respectively, Moses and the Old Dispensation of Law, Jesus and the New Dispensation of Mercy, and the classical Muses, transcendent source of poesis. Contemplation's mountain thus illustrates with unusually graphic clarity the potential noted earlier for allegorical interpretation generated by analogous structures, but, however variously we may construe this episode allegorically, its rhetorical effect is to assert the identity of three apparently diverse mountains, making them analogous manifestations of a single entity. As Redcrosse climbs the mountain, led by Mercy towards discovery of his identity as St George and his vision of the "new Hierusalem" (x.55), both his quest for the summit and his function as courtier to Gloriana undergo an elaboration of ethos parallel to, indeed recapitulating, the accumulation of significance from his successively taking on eulogistic and dyslogistic exempla in narrative encounters. Similarly, the narrative sequences culminating in the Dragon's death, by virtue of their common constituent exempla, the common figure of Redcrosse as courtier, and the coincident point of their ultimate terms, become, despite their apparent diversity, analogous manifestations generated from a single hierarchical structure of courtship.

2   THE PARADIGM OF REFUTATIO: DESPAIRE

As both locus of culmination for the narrative sequence and focus of accumulation for its dyslogistic topoi, the Dragon undergoes an elaboration of ethos that complements that of Redcrosse and is synchronous with it. Dyslogistic exempla located in the narrative sequentially prior to the Dragon cumulatively demonstrate its topoi and transform a commonplace of fairy-tale villainy, dangerous simply because large and fierce, a gigantic threat to "fleshly might," into a *metonymia*[3] of the unholy, a universalized "spirituall foe" embodying the ultimate threat to salvation. Despite, or more accurately because of, its "culminating" position in the narrative sequence, Redcrosse's battle with the Dragon is dramatically anti-climactic. By the time that, and at the point where, Redcrosse engages the beast, he has already taken on its constituent attributes in the sequence of prior encounters with the anti-exempla of holiness.[4]

Hence the dramatic climax of these encounters occurs not at their ultimate hierarchical point occupied by the Dragon but at the penultimate point occupied by Despaire, where the ethos of evil retains dramatic pathos. Despaire's position in the sequence argues, by the logos of priority, that this highest of the Dragon's subsumed attributes poses the greatest danger to the contemplative man, and the ethical implications of that threat are largely unqualified by fairy-tale topoi of villainy. Alone of all the major dyslogistic exempla Redcrosse takes on before the Dragon, Despaire is without disguise. Neither the topothesia describing his cave nor the prosopographia describing his person is indecorous with his nature (ix.33–6). The cave is "darkesome" and "hollow" like that of Errour, it is surrounded by signs of suffering and death like the nether parts of Lucifera's castle and the dungeon of Orgoglio's, but no wooded maze, cunning cosmetic, or inviting fountain obfuscates its danger. Furthermore, the knight's senses confirm not only the evidence of past encounters but also the direct testimony of Sir Trevisan (ix.371–2). After and (by sequential implication) because of his reunion with Una and redemption from Orgoglio's dungeon by Arthur in a transparent allegoria of "heauenly grace," the knight's vision no longer carries an elocutio of distortion or dazzled amazement: he seems at last to have emerged from the "maze" of Errour's wood.

While Redcrosse now recognizes evil when he sees it, the topoi of his response nevertheless argue a continuing benighted state of rational indecorum. He still misdeems physical prowess as the decorous reaction to spiritual danger and advocates the imperative of "to kill" as the idiom of righteous justice (ix.37.4–9). In the temporal order of incidents Redcrosse is free of Errour's maze and reunited with Una for the first time since deserting her at the hermitage of Archimago; in the structure of hierarchical courtship, however, he remains effectively at its base, still under the aegis of Archimago. "How may a man (said he) with idle speach / Be wonne, to spoyle the Castle of his health?" (ix.31.1–2): the knight's allusive interrogatio demonstrates his failure to discern from experience with Archimago the vulnerability of physical prowess to the power of rhetoric. The ethical implications of this allusive elocutio multiply in the successive answers to the question. First Trevisan evokes Despaire's persuasive power by linking that rhetorician's "subtill tongue" not only to the playing waters of Archimago's "sacred" fountain but also to the drizzling water in the cave of Morpheus and, more particularly, to the enervating waters of the fountain where Redcrosse consummates erotic courtship with Duessa and aborts his transcendent courtship by falling under the thrall of Orgoglio (vii.2–12). Second, of course, is the oration of Despaire itself, which validates the decorum of Trevisan's allusive metaphor: Despaire's "subtill tongue" inverts Redcrosse's courtship, persuading him to abort again his quest for grace and transpose the imperative of to kill mandated "by righteous sentence of th'Almighties law" (i.50.4) from active to reflexive.

The strategies whereby this speech achieves such a transformation have been extensively treated by Spenser's commentators, as have its figures of elocutio; indeed, perhaps no other passage in the epic has been the object of such systematic rhetorical analysis, and to rehearse this analytical detail here would be both redundant and indecorous.[5] Of importance to this study is not the elocutio of Despaire's speech but the relationship between its dramatically climactic location and its function in Spenser's dispositio. This function, like the homologous decorum focused in Contemplation's mountain, establishes a vital suasive presence by reiteration throughout the epic.

In the arrangement of orations, rhetorical theory urges both *confirmatio*, consisting of all arguments supporting the speaker's case, and *refutatio*, acknowledging opposing arguments in order to discredit them. Despaire's speech functions as refutatio to Spenser's, and the technical brilliance the poet lavishes on his creature's oration demonstrates, like its sequential position in the distributio, the ethos of despair in Spenser's inventio as the ultimate danger to Everyman courting grace.

Etymologically, despair derives from the privative of "to hope" (Lat. *espere*); theologically, deprivation of hope denies the possibility of salvation since the fundamental condition of transcendent grace is faith in its possibility. Rhetorically, despair might be defined functionally as a state of frustrated courtship: all arguments for despair assert a primal enthymeme denying the efficacy of all courtship. Since Spenser defines his questing knights by a virtue and its courtship, this primal enthymeme denies, in effect, the very foundation of his epic. Perhaps the most economical literary assertion and disposition of the enthymeme occurs in the generally minimalist context of Samuel Beckett's protagonists as they wait for and upon Godot.

Vladimir: Question of temperament.
Estragon: Of Character.
Vladimir: Nothing you can do about it.
Estragon: No use struggling.
Vladimir: One is what one is.
Estragon: No use wriggling.
Vladimir: The essential doesn't change.
Estragon: Nothing to be done.[6]

This is not the tragic manifesto "character is destiny," but its dyslogistic opposite, a call to capitulation not heroic action: "no use struggling." Its quick, witty, stichomythic structure gives to the static interchange of repetitious homily a spurious impression of logical progression.

A virtually identical progression underlies the argument of Despaire, and his version of the primal enthymeme, "nothing to be done," while couched in the serpentine paraphrase that characterizes his general rhetorical method, calls for an ultimate capitulation through suicide to the tyranny of determinism, demonstrating the metonymic decorum of absolute stasis with the status quo as absolute: "The lenger life, I wote the greater sin, / The greater sin, the greater punishment;" "Death is the end of woes; die soone O Faeries sonne" (ix.43; 47). This gradatio parodies the burden of sequential logos in Spenser's narrative structure for Book I, and paraphrases the summative sententia from Spenser's own enthymeme, expressed by his narrator as an inference from the evidence of Redcrosse's actions in the sequence leading to the encounter with Despaire: "If any strength we haue it is to ill, / But all the good is Gods, both power and eke will" (x.1.8–9). Hence Despaire co-opts not only Spenser's enthymeme but also his exempla as the substance of a counter-argument in refutatio:

> All those great battels, which thou boasts to win,
> Through strife, and bloud-shed, and auengement,
> Now praysd, hereafter deare thou shalt repent:
> For life must life, and bloud must bloud repay;   (ix.43)

> Is not enough, that to this Ladie milde
> Thou falsed hast thy faith with periurie,
> And sold thy selfe to serue Duessa vilde,
> With whom in all abuse thou hast thy selfe defilde?   (ix.46)

Neither we, nor Redcrosse, have any cause to impugn the accuracy of Despaire's evidence.

Despaire's selective exempla of the knight's malefactions, however, provide proof by logos only of the conditional enthymeme "you have sinned," not the absolute "you are sinful" asserted indirectly in such locutions as "thy euil life," "the lenger life … the greater sin" and directly in the exclamatio "O man of sin." The leap from conditional to absolute parallels that of Beckett's clowns and follows the course of a suppressed, loosely syllogistic progression that might be represented in general terms as follows:

Effect follows cause,
My condition now is an effect;
My condition has a cause.
My actions are the cause;
My condition is the effect of my actions.
Action is choice;
My condition is the effect of choice.
Choice is volitional;
My condition is volitional.
Volition is character (I am what I will);
My condition is determined by my character.

Both Despaire and Beckett's courtiers to Godot make selective adaptations from this basic series and all seem to accept its validity. Redcrosse does not dispute it. (Nor indeed would Spenser, although Beckett would and does through his creatures.) For Spenser it is culturally unconscious, part of the unexamined mental-set of Renaissance humanism before David Hume awoke Immanuel Kant from his dogmatic slumber with devastating proof that causality is a rhetorical enthymeme of probability, a psychological fiction based on experience, not a logical premise.[7] If the principle of causality and the doctrine of free-will are accepted as premises, however, the conclusion of the series has the force of logical certainty.

Since Spenser writes for an audience schooled in classical rhetoric, he could expect it to recognize that Despaire appropriates the certainty of the conclusion illegitimately, retaining the conclusion as a hidden, implicit enthymeme while denying the premise of free choice on which it depends: "Is not enough thy euill life forespent? / For he, that once hath missed the right way, / The further he doth goe, the further he doth stray" (ix.43.7–9). If the will is free to choose morally, it cannot also be determined by previous choice: the right way, once missed, may be recovered by a new act of volition. As Redcrosse's awakened sense of inadequacy and repentant guilt demonstrate, his character is a locus of redemptive as well as corruptive potential. Ironically, it is the very source of this redemptive potential, his stricken consciousness of guilt, that blinds him to the fallacious inconsistency of Despaire's argument and leaves him vulnerable to its pathetic suasiveness (ix.49); guilty fear, not reason, accepts exempla of past sins as proof of their future inevitability. Spenser's narrator compares Redcrosse, in the aftermath of Despaire's eloquence, to one "charmed with inchaunted rimes" (ix.48), and certainly a hypnotic idiom of spellbinding incantation decorous with his mesmerizing strategies whispers through Despaire's soporific alliterations, open-vowelled assonance, and balanced periodicity, entraining the processes of thought in its cradling rhythms and suspending critical awareness.

He is no sorcerer, however, merely a verbal conjurer, manipulating perception by misdirection through language. Unlike Spenser, Despaire suppresses any refutatio to his spellbinding confirmatio: using *pysma* he serially accumulates interrogatives without pause for response to generate a spurious impression of sequential reasoning. Thus Una's one-line, mimicking interrogatio, "In heauenly mercies hast thou not a part?" (ix.53.4) undercuts with sudden, comic peripeteia the suasiveness of Despaire's entire elaborate 200-line superstructure of argument by supplying a suppressed constituent of divine justice that distinguishes it from righteous vengeance. Redcrosse, in short, is the object of courtship by pathetic proof, and in Despaire Spenser has created the quintessential propagandist whose function as refutatio and methods of appeal establish the allusive model for a sequence of exemplars with analogous, and equally crucial, dispositional roles in subsequent books: Acrasia and Mammon in Book II, Busirane in Book III, the giant demagogue with scales in Book V, and Mutabilitie in Book VII. Sequence invests a logos of consequence, and its culminating members imply that this sequence of functional analogues is consequential to Spenser's inventio of justice: thus Acrasia and Mammon, although extrinsic to the nominal dispositio of justice involving Britomart and Artegall, warrant attention in rhetorical analysis of Spenser's inventio simply because they are part of a consequential pattern of demonstration and must not be fragmented from it. In fact, they anticipate some topoi of Artegall's dispositio and display variations from Despaire in techniques of refutatio that will repay brief consideration.

3   ACRASIA AND MAMMON: THE "PLACES" OF REFUTATIO

In Book II, Spenser's subject is "temperaunce," and the legend of Sir Guyon constitutes a dispositio proving his inventio. Both Mammon

and Acrasia use variants on Despaire's enthymeme and his hyperbolically elaborated structures of misdirection by pathetic proof to
counter Spenser's case for temperance. Unlike Despaire, however,
they manipulate material appearances rather than language. Each
demonstrates a contrary inventio to Spenser's through literal structures of argument comprised in the sequenced chambers of Mammon's "house of Richesse" (II.vii.passim) and the "staged" artifice
(both sequenced and stage-managed) of Acrasia's Bower of Bliss
(v.29–34; vi.10–13; xii.42–83). Like their eulogistic complement in the
house of Alma (ix.21–58), both Mammon and Acrasia state their case
in their dwelling: topothesia composes dispositio. Acrasia's Bower
exceeds Lucifera's palace, "or Eden selfe, if ought with Eden mot
compaire" (xii.52.9), as a hyperbolical compendium of seductively
attractive topoi, while Mammon's house, "like an huge caue, hewne
out of rocky clift" (vii.28.2), is contrastingly dyslogistic, its topoi
heavily allusive of Despaire's cave (2.8–9; 3.1–5; 30.6–9). Despite these
differences in elocutio, each is decorous with its suasive purpose:
Mammon's dispositio like Acrasia's "art striuing to compaire / With
nature" constructs an artificial Eden courting identification with its
inventio by promising to bridge the primal estrangement of lapsarian
Man from God and Nature: "Loe here the worldes blis, loe here the
end, / To which all men do ayme, rich to be made: / Such grace now
to be happy, is before thee laid" (vii.32.7–9). Mammon and Acrasia
are equally adept at creating illusions of social and erotic potency
respectively: Mammon misrepresents social courtship – as Acrasia
misrepresents erotic courtship – to be transcendent, and Acrasia's
seduction is no less an echo of Despaire's enthymemes than Mammon's temptation.

   Acrasia's argument supplements the Bower itself with generic
topoi of *carpe florem* (xii.74–5) sung by "some one" to her "new Louer"
Verdant (xii.75.6–9). Echoing the advocacy of Despaire and Phedria
(vi.16–18) while anticipating Mutabilitie's in a "sentimental evocation
of the great theme of mutability,"[8] Acrasia's lullaby, like the dispositio
of her Bower, argues that the "lap-sarian"[9] state, with its subjection
to mortal transience, is an absolute: her ostensible alternative, like
the selection of lethal instruments Despaire tenders Redcrosse
(I.ix.50), parodies the free choice its idiom and inconsistent gerund
pretend to offer in the time-bound "equall crime" of loving and being
loved (xii.75.9). "Nothing to be done," in short, is the enthymeme
actually proven by the one doing she advocates. Her reduction of
alternatives to one, denying choice, is characteristic of propaganda,
as is the misdirection effected through the indecorum between
enthymeme and ornament in her Bower of Bliss, a hyperbolically

overloaded elocutio of sensation befogging any powers of critical distinction: "That all things one, and one as nothing was, / And this great Vniuerse seemd one confused mas" (xii.34.8–9). Chaos stills the dance of reason: it is a-decorous.

Verdant's posture in response to Acrasia's lulling art replicates that of Cymocles with Phedria, "laying his head disarm'd / In her loose lap" (vi.14). The homology argues that Verdant is simply Acrasia's "old louer" Mortdant in potential, situated at a median point of descent on the chain of being from human to inert matter sequentially equivalent to the station of a beast:

> ... These seeming beasts are men indeed,
> Whom this Enchauntresse hath transformed thus,
> Whylome her louers, which her lusts did feed,
> Now turned into figures hideous,
> According to their mindes like monstruous.   (xii.85.1–5)

The Odyssean allusion here to Circe enriches through classical topoi the significance as ethical exempla of Guyon, Guyon's quest, and the anti-type he takes on in Acrasia. Acrasia may be a "witch" and "enchauntresse," but by borrowing topoi from Circe Spenser gains for his creature the ready-made (as it were) ethical transformation already effected by Homer of a villainous commonplace from fairy tale into a figure of epic stature.[10] Indeed, the entire episode in canto xii presenting Guyon's voyage to the Bower of Bliss and his engagement there with Acrasia's seductive rhetoric draws considerable allegorical resonance from Spenser's copious borrowing of topoi for its elocutio from *Odyssey* and *Aeneid*.[11]

4   "STRUCTURE" AND "INTRINSIC" DECORUM

Acrasia's functional analogies with Despaire, however, like the sequence of counter-advocates in which both participate, illustrate a complementary source of allusive resonance within and among Spenser's own exempla. As the sequence of his dispositio develops through later books, so does the relative rhetorical significance of this internal source. Through iteration and reiteration of dispositional function, elocutional detail, and homologous patterns, by echo and anticipation, "recoursing to the thinges forepaste and diuining of thinges to come," later episodes build upon earlier. Spenser's dispositio, in short, is radically self-fashioning: it evinces the presence of a strong attractor which progressively conditions his choices for selection and order, making them contingent upon prior choices. Commentary tends to neglect or fragment this substantial intrinsic decorum in favour of extrinsic influences and sources, thereby contributing significantly to the imbalance in commentary on Spenser's rhetorical practice that I seek to redress. My focus on this autogenetic aspect of dispositio neither confirms New Critical topoi nor refutes New Historicist alternatives: its decorum is conditioned by the need to compensate for a disequilibrium derived from procedural indecorums too general for attribution to any particular theoretical inventio. Spenser's sequenced steps of recapitulation and amplification are particularly important in tracking an inferential path to the motive of justice: they cobble the narrative road to Arlo Hill and compose an iterative scaffold justifying my use of the metaphorical term "structure" to label the product of Spenser's dispositional decorum in *The Faerie Queene*.

For structural analogy, as for other forms of analogy, such iteration or repetition with variation, makes the presence of an attractor available to the analyst and establishes logos through sequence. Mammon's "mountaines" of gold coinage (vii.8), for instance, represent both a parodic analogue of the Mount of Contemplation and an inversion of Mammon's cave-like habitation, the "hollow earth" of which the mountains are, literally and figuratively, the abstracted core. Since Philotime and the Garden of Proserpine occupy the deepest third room of that habitation (vii.40ff) at the source of Mammon's "ample flood" of worldly "goods," by schematic analogy their hierarchical position is equivalent to the highest point of Mammon's mountain and antipolar to the summit occupied by Contemplation. Viewed from above, the apex of a conic form schematically centers its circumference, and Philotime's location at the source of Mammon's "ample flood" occurs in narrative sequence prior to, and so by logos becomes a derivative component of, the grove centering Proserpina's garden (vii.51.9–52). These co-locations, in turn, are homologous with the locus occupied by Acrasia at the center of the Bower of Bliss (xii.60–2). Thus Guyon's journey into the core of Mammon's habitation takes on ethical resonance – and provides a rich source of allegorical potential – from both its structural inversion of Redcrosse's ascent to Contemplation and its structural reiteration in Guyon's voyage to the Bower. Topological analogy and narrative sequence argue in concert by logos that the attributes of Mammon's house are subsumed by Acrasia's Bower: thus to take on the former is a necessary prior condition of engagement with the latter.

Such logos in the refutational sequence containing Despaire, Mammon, and Acrasia is easily eclipsed if we isolate one element from the series and focus exclusively on ethos or pathos. Commentary bears manifest witness to the effect of so isolating Acrasia: readers find it difficult to reconcile the attractive pathos of her Bower, "the faire aspect / Of that sweet place," with the ethos of its dismantling by Guyon, and consider the deconstructive "tempest of ... wrathful-nesse" (xii.83) motivating the principal exemplar of temperance to be indecorous with the virtue he demonstrates.[12] Hamilton, however, warns against judging the incident in isolation from its context: "the moment remains painful only for readers who regard the end of the Book as the end of the poem ... Guyon's response to the Bower has initiated an action that requires the rest of the poem to resolve."[13] My contention is that Guyon's action echoes as well as anticipates and may seem less preeminently a matter of pathos, painful or otherwise, if recognized to be part of a process of logos both resolving and complicating by elaboration prior issues raised through Despaire and Mammon.

Decorum resides not in Guyon's action but in the relationship between that action and the rhetorical structure that forms its context as an element of proof. Rhetorically, Acrasia's Bower composes her argument against temperance. Its pleasing pathos is simply a eulo-gistic version of Mammon's dyslogistic house; indeed, since Acrasia as an exemplum structurally assumes the prior attributes of Mam-mon, her argument enfolds Mammon's within itself. The Bower's "faire aspect," however, disguises its "foul" substance, including the incorporated attributes of Mammon's house: it constitutes a treacherous antiphrasis allusive of Duessa, Lucifera, and Despaire. Acrasia's dispositio is a physical structure as hyperbolically over-elaborated as Despaire's verbal structure; hence, precedence and homology require it be overturned just as suddenly, not by words as in Una's undermining of Despaire but by refutative physical action: Guyon dismantles Acrasia's argument and discovers, like Arthur with Duessa, the "fowlest place" underlying "the fairest" (xii.83.9). In transfiguring "the fairest" into "the fowlest," Guyon invents ("now made") an elocutio decorous with the enthymeme of the Bower, an enthymeme which Acrasia's "fairest" elocutio dissembles.

Indeed, this physicality of Guyon's response to Acrasia's Bower echoes the climactic death-faint he suffers immediately upon emerging from Mammon's house (vii.65) and, in turn, the failure of "fleshly might" in Redcrosse. By analogy, Guyon's physical collapse becomes a device of ethos buttressing his highly platitudinous verbal responses to Mammon's tempting argument; it demonstrates an agony of endur-ance sustained in resisting Mammon's advocacy "So goodly [to] beguile the Gyler of the pray" (64.9). Thus his action to beguile the guileful and beguiling Acrasia of her "pray" echoes Redcrosse's "anti-climactic" struggle with the Dragon and anticipates Britomart's three-day passion in Busirane's house: it too is invested with the ethos of prior analogues, and the superficial ease with which Guyon resists the seductions of Acrasia's rhetoric asserts an antiphrasis of agony, one expressed appropriately, like his faint, as a dramatic physical exemplum, a climactic "tempest of ... wrathfulnesse." Narrative sequence makes his reaction to Acrasia the consequence of his exhausting struggle with Mammon, and its violence measures Acrasia's power rather than Guyon's prudery. The knight's rhetorical function is to demonstrate an inventio of temperance not of tolerance, and his destruction of the Bower involves proof by logos and ethos as well as pathos. Thus our simply regretting (or applauding) the destruction of Acrasia's beguilements is surely asymmetric with Spenser's argument: his dispositio courts recognition both that those beguilements and their constituent lures of wealth and power are exceedingly difficult to resist and that "temperaunce" requires such resistance.

5   INVENTIO OF TEMPERANCE; TOPOI OF JUSTICE

It is primarily in these "constituent lures," particularly those composing Mammon's refutatio, that issues of temperance presage those of justice, and in so doing raise vital questions of decorum. What common issues of inventio warrant the sharing of dispositional topoi by echo and anticipation between temperance and justice? This question is obviously implicated in a larger problematic: what inventio of justice warrants, as I claim, its subsuming dispositional topoi from all of Spenser's other virtues, "priuate" as well as "polliticke"? If justice has such hierarchical priority why does it lack sequential finality: why is "courtesy" subsequent in the narrative to justice? Why does Artegall require Calidore to assume his mission? I will engage these general questions directly as analytical evidence develops a context for them, but the specific question of why temperance and justice share topoi adumbrates some components of that engagement.

Certainly one answer lies in the epiphonema Guyon draws from a synecdochal exemplum of disordered passion in the account of Acrasia's victims, Amavia and Mortdant; he expresses a primary enthymeme of temperance in Platonic topoi:

Behold the image of mortalitie,
And feeble nature cloth'd with fleshly tyre,
When raging passion and fierce tyrannie

Robs reason of her due regalitie,
And makes it seruant to her basest part.   (i.57.2–6)

This Platonic *metalepsis* of just order in psyche and state provides authoritative topoi also to Spenser's inventio of justice. Socrates' characterization in *The Republic* of the polis as the psyche writ large seems initially to be a synecdoche, merely a model of the part in the whole, but as the dialogue develops it becomes clear that the point of the linkage is its causality: the just state requires just souls as a prior condition, and Guyon anticipates a principal generator of rhetorical development in succeeding books when he defines cupiditas as the "roote of all disquietnesse," producing the dystopic order of "wrongfull gouernment" in both the public and "priuate state" (vii.13.9–14.2). While thus conceding that Mammon does indeed "kings create" (11.6), Guyon casts his tempter's proof of ethos into the dyslogistic mode: his catalogue of tropes condemning the social consequences of intemperance might with perfect decorum equally serve to indict the "sacred hunger of ambitious mindes, / And impotent desire of men to raine" (V.xii.1) characterizing the private motives of injustice:

> ... realmes and rulers thou doest both confound,
> And loyall truth to treason doest incline;
> Witnesse the gultlesse bloud pourd oft on ground,
> The crowned often slaine, the slayer cround,
> The sacred Diademe in peeces rent,
> And purple robe gored with many a wound;
> Castles surprizd, great cities sackt and brent:
> So mak'st thou kings, and gaynest wrongfull gouernement.   (II.vii.12)

Similarly, a recurrent Ovidian topos identifies intemperance and injustice as common descendents in the modern world of moral decay through time from a state in "the antique world" characterized by Guyon in Book II as one of uncorrupted decorum between human appetite and nature's "gifts of soueraigne bounty" (II.vii.16–17) and by Spenser's narrator in Book V as one of "peace vniuersall" characterized by a pandemic courtship of the goddess Iustice "high ador'd." Here justice merges with sovereignty, twin products of Providential Will derivative from the ultimate term of ultimate terms: "Most sacred vertue she [Iustice] of all the rest, / Resembling God in his imperiall might" who "doth to Princes lend" the "soueraine powre" to dispense justice and "rule his people right." Sovereignty and just order become coincident at the ultimate term of social and transcendent hierarchies (V.Pr.9–11).

Guyon confronts in Mammon a figure who claims ethos as "God of the world and worldlings" in tropes allusive of Fortune not Providence (vii.11.6–9). Mammon thereby anticipates by perversion and inversion the principal topoi and hierarchical structure of justice defined in Book V, and prefigures the giant with scales and Mutabilitie in presuming to usurp the hierarchical position and function of "Iustice." His title, with its implied ethos, invites social courtship under the guise of transcendent; his strategy, like those of Phedria and Acrasia, represents service and subjection as sovereignty. He offers "commaund" atop mountains of gold coinage if Guyon should "deigne to serue and sew," expecting the appeal to pathos in manifold wealth to conceal the indecorous logos of service as command.

Here rhetoric courts suasive "union" only through subjugation, and so parodies the rhetorical ideal of "persuasion without advantage," a state wherein the dependent acts of persuading and being persuaded remain a reciprocal dynamic with neither party absorbing the identity of its necessary complement. Estrangement is resolved through mutual participation within an equilibrium of complementarities, not the appropriation of one singularity by another. This ideal and its violations will require elaboration in the analysis of later books, but even here in the exposition of a "priuate" virtue its topoi raise issues of reciprocity in the "polliticke" realm of courted and courtier. Mammon and Acrasia rule only by subjection, and among their functions in the legend of Guyon is to act as agents of "wrongfull gouernement." Guyon accumulates ethos as exemplar of temperance, this "priuate" virtue, by refusing the role of courtier in their service, and particularly demonstrates eulogistic topoi of both temperance and justice by rejecting Mammon's temptation to marriage with Philotime, who merges the temptations of her father and Acrasia of both social and erotic power (vii.44–8). Thus Guyon, on awakening from his death-faint, swears fealty to Arthur, "My lord, my liege" (viii.55.5), who in turn cites their common fealty to a higher ultimate term in a trope evocative of justice: "Are not all knights by oath bound, to withstond / Oppressours powre" (56.4–5). The opening stanzas of Canto ix immediately succeeding make that common ultimate term explicitly identical with Gloriana: "My liefe, my liege, my Soueraigne, my deare" (ix.4.5).[14] In the posture they consequently assume as common questers subordinate to a common ultimate, "so goodly purpose they together fond" (viii.56.7), Arthur and Guyon resolve Mammon's paradox of ruling by service: their service as courtiers to Gloriana involves a free act of self-governance in subordination to a figure who herself exemplifies a Platonic decorum among psychic and social orders (ix.3).

My point is not to deny topoi of allegoria in Spenser's inventio of temperance or question the validity of reading this "polliticke" narrative allusively as psychomachia. Rather I wish to cast a stronger light than is usual on the "polliticke" component of the allegoria. Already tacit in Guyon's legend are tropes symptomatic of preoccupation with the court as a hierarchical ultimate term and center of power where the reciprocal dynamic of private motives among courtiers and the prince affect public policy and hence the common wheal. Acrasia and Mammon as dyslogistic exempla argue a contrary eulogistic ideal of sovereignty that would configure prince and courtier, ruler and ruled, in a reciprocal equilibrium exactly cognate with the rhetorical ideal of "persuasion without advantage." Spenser's inventio thus supplements the classical authority of Platonic and Ovidian sources with topoi from a more contemporary political discourse common to Machiavelli, Erasmus, More, and, preeminently, Castiglione. Since Burke's model for the elision of rhetoric with courtship derives from the same source, I hope my contention that Spenser's rhetorical practice attracts Burke's theoretical topoi decorously will seem less arbitrary than it might initially appear: it stands upon considerations of historical as well as formal analogy.

Spenser's initial agents of refutatio in *The Faerie Queene*, particularly Mammon, his excavated kingdom, and his daughter, thus provide a conjunction of topoi common to issues of justice and temperance that demonstrate both the agency of Platonic and post-Platonic inventio in Spenser's vision, modeling the corporate state on the individual psyche, and the consequent indecorum, even in the earliest books, of any dispositio isolating "priuate" from "polliticke" virtues. Figured synecdochally in the parallel histories of Faeryland and England, which iterate essence through sequence to prove by logos rightful sovereignty in the "chronologos" of Elfin emperors and Briton kings (II.x), Spenser's own "famous antique history" (II.Pr.1.2), his dispositional sequence of narrative in *The Faerie Queene*, iterates the essence of virtue through metonymous private and public idioms within a single discourse. His topos of praise to Elizabeth identifying her as the original, the ideal historical exemplum of this essence "mirrhour[ed]" in his art (II.Pr.4), becomes for Spenser's audience (including Elizabeth Tudor) a topos of challenge. We are positioned as quester-in-common with the knights: like Arthur and Britomart, we court the original of that image in Spenser's "faire mirrhour." For the mirrored original of justice, Britomart is the decorous choice as our surrogate quester, and the dispositio of her courtship marks the analytical path I follow in Parts 2 and 3 of this essay.

PART TWO

Iuris Comitatus

3 Britomart Ascendant and Venus Transcendent

1 LOVE AND ITS POET ON TRIAL

Commentators tend to treat Book IV as an extension of Book III because the erotic courtships of Belphoebe by Timias, Marinell by Florimell, Amoret by Scudamour, and Artegall by Britomart continue from one to the other; indeed, C. S. Lewis terms them "a single book on the subject of love."[1] The core of Spenser's dispositio in these books, however, is the narrative of Britomart and Artegall that extends through Book V. Britomart courts Artegall, Artegall is the knight of Justice, and Justice is a transcendent object of courtship: "most sacred uirtue ... resembling God" (V.pr.10). Britomart's motive comes to structural resolution only when she and Artegall achieve identity at the ultimate term of the hierarchy of Justice, an achievement delayed for her until she reforms Radigund's "commonweal" at V.vii.42–3 and for him until his aborted reform of Grantorto's corrupt tyranny at V.xii.26–7. For the rhetorical analyst, therefore, Spenser's narrative strategy requires an examination of structure treating all three Books as the dispositio of a common inventio. Rather than simply extending Book III to closure, Book IV, "Of Friendship," extends a transitional sequence between the book of chastity and the book of justice.

My purpose in this chapter and the next is threefold: to examine that narrative of transition as a structure of argument; to illustrate protocols of analysis more systematically and in greater detail than my introductory use of Redcrosse and Guyon allowed or warranted;

and to consolidate within this systematic context existing commentary on Books III and IV where it reflects partial, unsystematic, or incidental application of rhetorical theory.

Spenser encapsulates his transitional *dispositio* at the outset of Book IV by establishing in its Proem a dramatic atmosphere of forensic rhetoric in which love appears seeking justice. His narrator opens with a spirited defence of "looser rimes ... praising loue" and "magnifying louers dear debate" against the disapprobation of "Stoicke censours" in high civil authority, "The rugged forhead that with graue foresight / Welds kingdomes causes, and affaires of state" (IV.pr.1). What corrugated the grave and serious brow of this senior courtier was the thought of "fraile youth" led to folly by "vaine poemes weeds," youth "that better were in vertues discipled." Evidently those striving for identification with the ultimate term through social courtship, then as now, found it politic to take a stern public view of erotic courtship, or at least the depiction of its strategies. Whether this passage refers to William Cecil and concerns *Amoretti* or *Colin Clouts Come Home Again*, both published the preceding year, or indeed whether the passage is occasioned by any actuality outside the poem has little impact on its rhetorical effect. Spenser's placement of this defence as the Proem to Book IV makes Book III the immediate and dominant focus of reference for the seriatim reader and discredits the attack as ludicrously misguided for anyone who has just been "discipled" through 684 stanzas in the virtue of chastity, with temperance and holiness as prologue. Any further defence would seem to strangle subtlety in redundancy.

Yet advocacy here is anything but subtle. The bardic voice launches an *ad hominem* attack on the credentials of his critics, whose "frosen hearts" make them "ill iudge of loue, that cannot loue," proceeds to claim the ethos of "those wise sages" unnamed, but hinting at Homer and Virgil, calls on "the father of Philosophie" as witness in an untypically muddled allusion to Socrates' teaching Critias "of loue full manie lessons" while "shaded oft from sunne," and ends by going over the "rugged forhead" of her minister to Elizabeth herself who, unlike the "Stoicke censours," locks the "treasures of true loue" in her "chast breast" and is a fit judge: "To her I sing of loue, that loueth best" (pr.2–4). Indeed, Elizabeth is the ultimate term not only of the social hierarchy but of the erotic and transcendent as well: "The Queene of loue, and Prince of peace from heauen blest" (pr.4.9). Seldom has a larger advocatory club been used to squash a smaller gnat.

Judged as referential and organic to the poem, however, rather than simply as a response to some external occasion, the passage demands criteria of decorum more complex than those of courtroom debate. Situated as proem not only to Book IV but also to Spenser's move from nominally "priuate" to "polliticke" virtues in the second half of his epic, this advocatory passage functions as a strategy of transition. An attack on the probity and value of love poetry by a person of authority, whether actual or fictional, provides a dramatic incident that calls for an advocate to defend the poet of love by asserting the transcendent value of his subject: "love" is not a weed, but "the roote" of "honor and all vertue" in which youth should be "discipled," and it "brings forth glorious flowres of fame, / That crowne true louers with immortall blis" (IV.pr.2). "Honor" and "immortall blis" add social and transcendent tonalities to the erotic connotations of "loue" in an accumulation of ethos both recapitulating the rhetorical evolution in Book III of Britomart's erotic volition to court Artegall and anticipating its further development. Appropriately, in evoking the heroic exploits depicted by "wise sages" to give his defensive enthymeme high ethical proof, the advocate-narrator simultaneously evokes the ethos of *The Odyssey* and *The Aeneid* as an allusive context for the exploits of Britomart and Artegall. Odysseus and Aeneas also welded "kingdomes causes, and affaires of state," ordered or founded nations, established laws. The comparison dwarfs the authority of "Stoicke censours" and provides a eulogistic demonstration of love as the volitional source of justice and concord: Odysseus courts simultaneously a just social order in Ithaca and concord in marriage with Penelope, while Aeneas crowns his destined quest, like Britomart and Artegall, by not only founding a dynasty and empire through marriage but also seeding the universal concord of *Pax Augustus*.

The muddled appeal to Socrates is equally resonant, despite its failure to clarify a specific dialogue. "Shaded oft from sun" suggests the setting for *Phaedrus* in the shade of a plane tree, but Critias is not an interlocutor in that work and a consensus of editorial opinion holds that Spenser erred in the allusion. Spenser's choice of the name Critias from among Socrates' recorded disciples, however, allows etymology, as it does for him so often, to make a point with economy.[2] Critias implies, against the claims of authority, a youth not "fraile" and easily "to folly led" but one critically discerning who shares with Elizabeth fitness to judge (*kritikos*), and suggests that Spenser's allusion is not simply to *Phaedrus* or any other specific work but to their general *inventio*, the Platonic structure, in which the state is the individual writ large, private and politic virtues are causally interdependent, and the concord derived from rational love in the soul figures metonymically justice in the state and in the order of nature.

The dialectical continuum of love-concord-justice in Socrates' philosophy, as in the evolving narrative quests of Odysseus and Aeneas, mirrors the structural progression of Books III, IV, and V from chastity through friendship to justice, and the Proem to Book IV epitomizes the transition. Considered as "drama," the passage hails the private virtue of Book III into the public realm. Love appears in court to answer unjust charges brought by authority unfit to render judgment, and only through appeal to the highest authority, Elizabeth, can love obtain or attain to justice.[3] In this dramatic configuration, therefore, Elizabeth already appears as the embodiment of ideal justice, anticipating her transcendent structural status depicted in the Proem to Book V (V.Pr.11). The ultimate terms of love and justice merge in Elizabeth, attracting into resolution both poles of the transitional structure in Book IV: she demonstrates through emblematic exemplum their mutual dependence and anticipates the narrative transition provided by Britomart's courtship of Artegall. Britomart accordingly becomes the instrument of transition when the narration resumes immediately subsequent to the Proem: she begins Book IV as she ends Book III in the 1596 edition, escorting Amoret in search of Scudamour while herself still seeking Artegall.

Since Spenser's *inventio* of justice thus draws so fundamentally upon topoi of chaste love, his conception of justice depends heavily for its persuasiveness upon the ethos of Britomart: both Artegall, her object of courtship, and the concept he exemplifies gain stature in direct proportion to the demonstrated worthiness of their courtier. Her rhetorical significance at this complex pivotal point of structure in the Proem to Book IV is, in turn, dependent upon ethos accumulated in her function as the principal exemplum of Book III. In this chapter I focus analysis on Spenser's dynamic tension of *refutatio* and *confirmatio* composing the primary contours of that cumulative structure, and I adduce its constituent topoi from recurrent detail in specific episodes, particularly the three-part incremental reappearance of Venus.

2 BRITOMART'S ETHOS

Unlike Redcrosse and Guyon, Britomart's stature does not develop primarily through a sequential structure of encounters and knightly exploits. She takes on as opponents in battle Guyon, Malecasta's knights, Malecasta herself, Marinell, Paridell, Ollyphant, and Busirane. She is slightly wounded in her side by Gardante's arrow (III.i.65) and Busirane's knife (III.xii.33), and is unhorsed along with Paridell in the fury of their collision (III.x.16), but she emerges otherwise unscathed and ever-triumphant from all encounters. Her battles seldom consume more than one stanza; even at Busirane's castle she passes through the flames in three lines (III.xi.25) and in thirteen lines easily subdues Busirane himself (III.xii.32–4).

Britomart's invulnerability presents Spenser with a problem of epic ethos similar to those he confronts with Guyon and Calidore, but here perhaps more demanding than anywhere else in *The Faerie Queene*. Chastity must prove invulnerable to every exemplum of unchaste topoi, yet invincibility is a commonplace of fairy tale, not epic heroism. Britomart's martial exploits, therefore, cannot of themselves reconcile the demands of both logical and ethical proof.

To resolve the conflict Spenser uses the dispositional strategies noted by most commentators on Book III: multiple heroes and multiple interlacing plots or, as Spenser terms it in the letter to Raleigh, "intermedled" adventures. Britomart disappears from the narrative after leaving Marinell for dead on his "rich strond" in III.iv.18, reappears briefly at Malbecco's castle in Canto x, and becomes an active protagonist again only in Canto xi. Within this frame, in the middle cantos that comprise fully half of Book III, Spenser argues his inventio of chastity through characters whose actions and descriptions have sequential consequence for the suasive affect of Britomart's encounters in the framing cantos. Belphoebe and Amoret, Scudamour and Timias, Marinell and Florimell, all function schematically as exempla of incomplete or vulnerable chastity, occupying various stages of becoming below the ultimate term of chastity occupied by Britomart. Her right to occupy that apex, and by extension her ethos to court identity with justice, depend upon Spenser's ability to offer suasive proof through similarity and contrast that she does indeed both subsume and transcend the virtues exampled by the other protagonists.

Florimell's topoi, for instance, are asymmetric with Britomart's but not dislogistic: she epitomizes the ambiguous tension between estrangement and identity generic to analogy. From encounters with the Foster (III.i), Witch (III.vi), Spotted Beast (III.vii), fisherman (III.viii), and Proteus (III.viii), Florimell emerges uniformly non-triumphant except insofar as she successfully flees all but the last of her antagonists. Flight is to Florimell what fight is to Britomart, a reaction to threat as fundamental as instinct in both immediacy and consistency. Exempla of unchaste topoi, however, pose the common threat to which both respond, thereby identifying the two protagonists as exempla of the same virtue. The demonic false Florimell, not Britomart, is Florimell's antithesis. Indeed, Florimell's similarities to Britomart complement her contrasting reaction to the enemies of

chastity and provide her major rhetorical impact. Florimell, like Britomart, courts a knight who has arbitrarily forsworn women, and her
continuous posture of flight from friend and enemy alike is actually
motivated as a quest toward Marinell, the report of whose death at
Britomart's hand draws her from the safety of Gloriana's court, as
the image of Artegall in Merlin's glass draws Britomart from her
father's court.

In Spenser's rhetorical structure, such devices of identification and
contrast function to locate Florimell and Britomart relatively in an
hierarchical model of courtship. "Britomart," as Berger puts it, "has
a Florimell within."[4] She includes Florimell's attributes as a chaste
erotic courtier but transcends her in both rational discernment and
courage, and their specific relationship exemplifies Spenser's strategy
in Book III generally. Spenser embodies each stage of ascent toward
the ultimate term of chastity in a separate protagonist with Britomart
as the apical exemplum. Through comparative devices of *dispositio*
and *elocutio*, Britomart takes on, without encountering as antagonists, each of the protagonists below her: logically, their attributes are
derivative from her. Experienced by the reader as a kinetic process
of interlacing plots, this static hierarchical structure accumulates
ethos for Britomart by creating the effect not of a fairy-tale hero who
is chaste *sui generis* but of one who has become the embodiment of
chastity by transcending the stages of becoming exemplified in her
co-protagonists. Spenser's eulogistic exempla in Book III are more
complex than those of Books I and II, both because of their number
and status as co-protagonists, indicating the complexity of Spenser's
inventio, and because no matter how virtuous their qualities and
actions, each both falls short of and defines an attribute of the ultimate term embodied in Britomart. Ethical ambiguity is thus built into
the co-protagonists and exactly how each, particularly Belphoebe and
Amoret in addition to Florimell, both resemble and fall short of
Britomart has been the focus of considerable and diverse allegorical
interpretation. My interest here, however, is to position them relative
to Britomart as components of metonymia, not contest or adjudicate
their function as elements of allegoria.

Belphoebe's rhetorical function, as the variety of her interpretation
testifies, in some ways presents the most considerable of puzzles and
will repay a closer look. Her initial prosopographia in Book II
(II.iii.21–31) is not only the longest in *The Faerie Queene* but also un-
stintingly eulogistic; its topoi of praise recur extensively in Book III.
She is "vpbrought in perfect Maydenhed" by Diana (III.vi.28),
defined as *"the* Mayd" (III.v.36, my emphasis) functioning as an
instrument of "prouidence heauenly" (III.v.27) in the saving of

Timias; she is "the highest staire / Of th'honorable stage of woman-head" (III.v.54). Spenser's use of the superlative in these devices of elocutio identifies Belphoebe as an ultimate term: she is to heroic virginity what Britomart is to heroic chastity.

The two hierarchies, however, illustrate the need to recognize ambiguity within analogical structures, including allegoria. While her compassion for and succour of Timias exemplify love in one of its aspects, as a response to the accidental vulnerability of "mortall wights ... bound with commun bond of frailtee" (III.v.36), the love she demonstrates falls short of the topoi composing Britomart's commitment of herself as potential victim to redeem Amoret in the house of Busirane (III.xi.18). Similarly, the topothesia of Belphoebe's deep-forest dwelling (III.v.37–40) is paradisiac (40.5) but lacks the topoi of fruitful generation stressed in the juxtaposed topothesia of the Garden of Adonis immediately succeeding (III.vi.30–50), a lack also in marked contrast with the fruitful generation of a royal dynasty central to Britomart's ethos as a courtier. Indeed, Spenser's depiction of the scene in the remote forest glen where Belphoebe aided by her woodland "Damzels" carries Timias, "that goodly boy, with blood / Defowled ... in deadly case"(III.v.38), to her remote forest bower "With mountaines round about enuironed" (v.39) to treat his wounds, provides a virtual re-enactment of Cymoent, aided by her sea-nymphs, finding Marinell "al in gore / And cruddy bloud enwal-lowed ... in deadly swound" (III.iv.34) and taking him for treatment to "her watry chamber ... Deepe in the bottome of the sea, her bowre ... built of hollow billowes heaped hy" (iv.41–3). Such detailed elocutional similarities place Belphoebe and Cymoent in equivalent postures, a juxtaposition contiguous with their identity in common dedication to celibacy as an absolute, a posture which mortally wounds both Timias and Marinell psychically, in each case without intent to injure, despite the care each takes of her patient physically: "Oh foolish Physick, and vnfruitfull paine, / That heals vp one and makes another wound" (v.42).

Spenser, like Shakespeare in *Measure For Measure*, stresses through contrasting exempla a distinction between physical and spiritual states: neither "unchaste virgin" nor "chaste non-virgin" is an oxymoron. The apparent discrepancy between Belphoebe's ethos in her prosopographia as the ideal of virginity in the book of temperance (II.iii.21–31) and her conditional, less eulogistic ethos here in Book III is a matter of decorum: attributes appropriate to the ultimate term in one context are not appropriate to the ultimate term in another. Belphoebe informs an absolute: since one cannot be a little bit virginal or in the process of becoming a virgin, she necessarily retains the invulnerability of fairy tale and enhances Britomart's epic stature by contrast. The qualifying of Belphoebe's ethos serves rhetorically not to discredit her but as a strategy to position her metonymically relative to Britomart in the hierarchy of chastity.[5] Britomart contains or takes on Belphoebe's attributes of martial skill and enmity to the wild beasts used habitually by Spenser as commonplace exempla of lawless passion, but transcends the celibacy demanded of virginity as an absolute value in order to fulfill her quest in a wider, more complex world than Belphoebe's forest. Britomart's is a treacherous world defined by topoi of sea and court, respectively the natural and artificial loci of Fortune, where the ethical demands of chaste love require both personal integrity and the vulnerability of commitment to another.

Spenser elaborates the exacting nature of this vulnerability in Belphoebe's twin and complementary exemplum, Amoret, who is vulnerable where Belphoebe is invulnerable. As with the "fairest" Florimell and the ideal Belphoebe, Spenser's prosopographia of Amoret uses the superlative mode to define her as an ultimate term: "Of grace and beautie noble Paragone," introduced by Venus "To be th'ensample of true loue alone, / And Lodestarre of all chaste affectione" (III.vi.52). "To be" confuses priorities in this passage; Venus represents Amoret as being already what she must come to be. Spenser's dispositio of Amoret and Scudamour proves the enthymeme inherent in Amoret's prosopographia by testing, through the agency of Busirane, her status as the "Lodestarre of all chaste affectione" and Scudamour's status as the exemplum of erotic courtship guided by that star. Their courtship effectively begins with *the denial* of their physical consummation – at the point where conventionally the estrangement engendering suasive erotic devices is bridged. Indeed, in the succeeding Book IV Spenser subsequently intensifies the demonstrative value of this moment by identifying the effective inauguration of courtship with the celebration of marriage (IV.i.2–4) and by cancelling the consummation effected through Britomart's rescue of Amoret from Busirane (III.xii.45–6:1590). I will address in the next chapter some rhetorical implications of this radical departure from "an Historiographer's" temporal priority in the extended dispositio of Amoret and Scudamour, but my point here is that Busirane's abduction of Amoret in Book III prevents a resolution of estrangement through physical consummation, a resolution that would prove by logos not simply an enthymeme equating chastity with sexual gratification but also, as a corollary, that the courtship of chastity is exclusively erotic, without either social or transcendent components.

That Spenser's inventio of chastity involves all three components is evident in its principal exemplum: Britomart erotically courts the embodiment of justice, a virtue both social and transcendent (V.pr.10), to procreate a line of kings. Elaborating this distinction, Spenser deviates significantly from the elocutional tactics used with Florimell and Belphoebe. He locates Britomart in the hierarchy of chastity relative to Scudamour and Amoret by including her directly in their narrative structure. She takes on by substitution both Scudamour in the role of rescuer and Amoret in the role of captive victim. Scudamour's topoi of despair engendered by frustrated erotic courtship (III.xi.8–10) echo Britomart's in her initial reaction to the envisioned Artegall (III.ii.43–4), while the "mighty rage" and "fiercenesse" stimulated by his inability to follow Britomart through Busirane's flames (III.xi.26) recreate the "fierce furie" of Britomart's attack on Marinell (III.iv.16) driven by the unresolved "passions of distroubled sprite" (iv.12.7) imaged in her complaint (iv.8–10). By passing through the flames Britomart transcends as rescuer Scudamour, whose "greedy will" and "envious desire" defeat him, a narrative exemplum proving by logos that she has transcended the Scudamour within herself. Once inside the flame Britomart becomes functionally identical with Amoret, not immediately in her role as victim of Busirane, but as his audience and therefore his victim in potential.

3   BUSIRANE: CHASTITY AND JUSTICE IN REFUTATIO

Busirane, like Archimago, Despaire, Mammon, and Acrasia, is a master spellbinder and propagandist. Spenser's tripartite topothesia of his house progresses with Britomart through the Arachean tapestries of a thronged public room (III.xi.29–46) to an unpeopled gallery etched with "monstrous formes" of "false loue" (xi.51–3), the empty theatre where Busirane stages his Masque of Cupid (xii.7–15). Masque and decorations comprise a rhetorical argument presented to the "fraile," "amazed," and "dazed" senses of Britomart (xi.49). Busirane's subject is Spenser's subject: chastity. His method of advocacy, however, depends entirely upon exempla uniformly dyslogistic and pathetic. With the distorting selectivity and relentless repetition of demagoguery, in a hyperbolic glut of exempla occupying thirteen stanzas, Busirane's tapestries reverse the dynamic of both transcendent and erotic courtships. Through reductive selection from the rich copia of Ovidian myth, Busirane's Olympian gods appear merely as agents of bestial lust, as the superhuman courting hierarchical identity with the sub-human, and the female objects of erotic courtship appear only as victims of lawless power. Since it is the metaphoric catalyst of these inversions, sexual passion appears appropriately first in the gilded bas-relief as an elocutio of the "monstrous," mutating through "a thousand formes," and subsequently in the broken weapons and garlands of triumph "troden to dust with fury insolent." This "monstrous" passion thus becomes the source of inversions in the social hierarchy of noble achievement, exemplified in "mighty Conquerours and Captaines strong, / Which were whilome captiued in their dayes / To cruell loue, and wrought their owne decayes!" (xi.52). Finally, displacing all former ultimate terms, the golden statue of Cupid with Minerva's dragon, the protector of chastity, blinded and submissive, tail enfolding left foot to form one continuous figure of appetitive passion united to conquered chastity, becomes the sole object of social courtship, levelling all other hierarchical distinctions:

> Kings Queenes, Lords Ladies, Knights and Damzels gent
> Were heap'd together with the vulgar sort,
> And mingled with the raskall rablement,
> Without respect of person or of port,
> To shew Dan Cupids powre and great effort.   (III.xi.46)

Transcendent inversion follows metonymically from social: "And all the people in that ample hous / Did to that image bow their humble knee, / And oft committed fowle Idolatree" (xi.49).

Busirane's tapestries and etchings court Britomart's acceptance of their implied reductive enthymeme (love is destructive lust) by pathetic proof that appeals to fear of both her violation as a woman and the ruin of her noble achievement as a warrior. More specifically threatening to Britomart, however, is the summation of these pathetic proofs in the figure of Cupid, which embodies chastity conquered by a perverted image of justice. Cupid presents an ultimate term of inverted social and transcendent hierarchies, a "cruell," "mercilesse" figure of "fury insolent," a "Victor of the Gods" commanding obeisance through "powre" in anticipatory parody of the statue in Isis church (V.vii.5–7) and the vision it inspires (V.vii.13–16). The courtship of Artegall, Busirane's dispositio argues, will lead not to fulfillment of chastity in justice but to enslavement and tyranny.

The Masque of Cupid constitutes, in its processional form, a narrative re-statement of the argument. Courtship appears first as a succession of twelve paired exempla from the generic topoi of Courtly Love, described, like Lucifera's counsellors, through *icon*, with their dress, manner, the emblems they carry, and allusive similes of description all attracted to their abstract names: Fancy and Desyre, Doubt and Daunger, Feare and Hope, Dissemblance and Suspect, Grief and Fury, Displeasure and Pleasance. None is an exemplum of rationality, and in concert they depict courtship as "following" Fancy, chaotically subject to wide, sometimes polar, swings between emotions paired to create a totally self-reflective enclosure, isolated in estrangement with no outlet for positive courtship. The Masque thus presents a narrative of courtship antithetical to Spenser's and (like Despaire's primal enthymeme) denying its very possibility. Busirane's strategy addresses the emotional vulnerabilities of his audience, both recreating the tempestuous topos of Britomart's complaint (III.vi.8–10) and evoking her despairing self-identification with Narcissus (III.ii.44). Courtship, he argues, leads only to the state of Amoret, who follows next in the procession (xii.19–21), bleeding from an "entrenched" knife in her bared breast and literally "dis-heartened" (xii.21).[6] Her posture parodies the ideal reciprocity of courtier to sovereign, and her triumphant captor figures an ultimate term "That man and beast with powre imperious / Subdeweth to his kingdome tyrannous" (III.xi.22), anticipating and perverting ethical topoi of Artegall who begins his mission by imposing justice "vpon wyld beasts ... with wrongfull powre oppressing others of their kind" until "euen wilde beasts did feare his awfull sight" (V.1.7–8). Busirane thus courts Britomart's identification of herself and Artegall with Amoret and Cupid, depicting resolution of erotic estrangement as debasement and victimization by tyrannous power and predicting that her completed quest will issue not in the line of kings and just order prophesied by Merlin but in a "rude confused rout" of progeny as chaotic and dyslogistic as the courtship itself (xii.25).

Like Despaire's eloquence, Mammon's mine, and Acrasia's Bower of Bliss, Busirane's house functions rhetorically as refutatio, acknowledging contrary arguments in order to discredit them. Indeed, Spenser grants Busirane the longest refutatio in the epic until Mutabilitie appears on Arlo Hill, and provides his opponent with many of his own rhetorical weapons, including topoi of myth, allegoria, and romance expressed in vivid, allusive, and powerfully evocative strategies of elocutio and dispositio to support enthymemes antithetical to his own. While the care and space Spenser devotes to Busirane's advocacy recognizes a significant danger to chastity in the attitudes he represents, Spenser's method discredits such attitudes as irrational misrepresentations. As readers, we are one with Britomart in constituting an audience for Busirane's advocacy; unlike Britomart, we are free of her emotional vulnerability. Conditioned by the preceding ten cantos of Spenser's argument, we recognize both the reductive distortions in the principles of decorum governing Busirane's selection of exempla and the comparative weakness of proof dependent entirely upon pathos. The fact that Britomart, lacking the reader's advantages, overcomes her emotional vulnerability to resist enthrallment signifies the completion of her ethical evolution in Book III as both exemplar of rational love and an heroic surrogate, like Redcrosse and Guyon, of common humanity. Her quick defeat of Busirane in battle, like Guyon's of Acrasia, becomes not the daydream exploit of fairy tale but a confirmation in action of the nightmare struggle she wins by triumphant endurance through a long, harrowing passion as Busirane's audience – a struggle, in effect, for life since Busirane, like Redcrosse's tempter Despaire and Guyon's tempters Mammon and Acrasia, counsels self-annihilation by withdrawal from the very quest that defines the knight-exemplar's identity. By forcing Busirane to unbind his spell, thus freeing Amoret (xi.33–8), Britomart effectively duplicates Spenser's refutation of Busirane's "spell-binding" rhetoric and confirms her status as ultimate term, including but transcending Amoret, who appropriately falls "prostrate" before the "noble knight" in a redeemed posture of reciprocal courtship: "I your vassal, by your prowess freed" (xii.39).

4   CONFIRMATIO: THE ETHOS OF VENUS

To prepare a context disputing the grounds of Busirane's refutatio, Spenser constructs a confirmatio that anticipates his opponent's erotic topoi from Ovidian myth, and anchors the structure of its dispositio in three ethically diverse, even contradictory, appearances of Venus: dyslogistic in Malecasta's tapestry, more ambiguous in debate with Diana, and unequivocally eulogistic in the Garden of Adonis. Such iterative repetition signals the presence of an organizational topos central to Spenser's inventio and warrants analytical attention.

The topothesia of Malecasta's Castle Ioyeous (III.i.31–2) provides both the first appearance of Venus, in tapestries depicting her as the erotic courtier of Adonis, (III.i.34–8) and the setting for Britomart's first encounter with dyslogistic exempla. Malecasta's rhetorical use of mythical images clearly anticipates Busirane's, but some differences are significant. Venus, like Busirane's deities, is motivated by sexual passion to court a mortal, with disastrous consequences: Adonis is "engored of a great wild Bore." Despite the image of brutal violation, however, Venus is not herself depicted as brutish; it is the mortal, not the deity, who metamorphoses, and into a flower not a beast (i.38). Far from a figure of tyrannous power, Venus in Malecasta's tapestry takes the role of supplicant in a social hierarchy. Suffering "bitter balefull stowers," and smitten in "her tender hart" with "many a feruent fit" (i.34), she "wooed" Adonis with "girlonds," "ambrosiall kisses," and flowered baths (i.35–6). Malecasta's strategic use of mythic exempla here differs diametrically from Busirane's. By causally isolating the wounding of Adonis from the wooing of Venus, Malecasta's tapestry echoes an enthymeme from Phedria and Acrasia, arguing that violation is the consequence not of sexual passion but of its denial to seek heroic action, "to hunt the saluage beast" (III.i.37).

In her attempted seduction, Malecasta courts Britomart's pathetic identification with Adonis by herself taking the role of the suffering Venus (i.53). Britomart's immunity to the ploy carries none of the ethical implications of her resistance to Busirane's fearsome strategies, for she is not immune to the pathos of Malecasta's "inward fire" and ironically identifies herself with Venus and her would-be seducer, not with Adonis (i.54). She "inly deem[s]" Malecasta's "loue too light, to wooe a wandring guest" (i.55), but her judgment goes no further than such conventional prudence, failing to penetrate the "malengine and fine forgerie" of Malecasta's hyperbolic rhetoric (i.53) or heed the warning of her castle, itself a study in excess of "sumptuous array" and "exceeding cost," the "image of superfluous riotize" (i.32–3). It's topoi evoke allusively the topothesiae of Acrasia's Bower and Lucifera's House of Pride, but only for the reader: our perspective develops ironic distance from Britomart's. Her disarming and escape from care in sleep (i.58) become exempla of irrational response, antithetical to the depiction of her armed wakefulness in Busirane's castle (xi.55). Thus Spenser treats her actions on awakening to danger as a parody of heroic action in the strategies of bedroom farce: a resonant comic paradigm of mistaken identity. Britomart simultaneously takes on Malecasta in battle and takes on her enemy's emotional extremism (i.62). Spenser projects the scene from the perspective not of Britomart but of the knights, "rashly" awakened and justifiably confused, thereby stressing the two stances – Malecasta in a swoon and Britomart in a nightgown armed and threatening – as equal and opposite over-reactions, an ironic use of hyperbole reinforced in Britomart's uncontrolled, flailing response to being "lightly rased" by Gardante's arrow: "Here, there, and euery where about her swayd / Her wrathfull steele" (i.66). Gardante is the first of six knights whose catalogued names provide a short narrative of courtly seduction in simple prosopographia (i.44–5), reproduced in action by Malecasta, and merely sketching the fully elaborated narrative progression in Busirane's Masque of Cupid. Gardante's ability to "gore her side" (i.65) complements the strategies of farce to qualify ironically the ethos of Britomart's second easy victory over Malecasta's knights by adding identification with Adonis to her self-identification with the Venus both portrayed and portraited by Malecasta.

Malecasta's depiction of Venus in the posture of ministrant to the wounded Adonis anticipates the tableaux of Belphoebe with Timias and Cymoent with Marinell, their homologous postures identifying the three juxtaposed ministering agents. That both Belphoebe and Cymoent promote celibacy as an absolute makes this formal identification with Malecasta's Venus function rhetorically like an oxymoron, analogously casting Venus in the role of Diana. Such a collision of polar extremes generates an exemplum to argue that opposite and equally restricted attitudes toward sexual passion issue in a common result: Timias and Marinell duplicate Adonis in his posture of erotically wounded victim.[7] In canto vi Spenser brings the implications of this structural oxymoron to specific focus by introducing Venus and Diana as characters. He frees them from the passive context of the topothesia, transforming elements of elocutio into elements of dispositio, to give their words and feelings the same authority as those of other characters, an ethos of performance rather than reputation. He thereby creates a touchstone to judge the validity of their interpretation by Malecasta and Busirane.

In this second appearance Venus again functions as a courtier. As a means of completing the quest for her missing Cupid, she seeks to bridge the estrangement between herself and Diana – not the estrangement of sex, but that of polar extremities in values.

> As you in woods and wanton wildernesse
> Your glory set, to chace the saluage beasts,
> So my delight is all in ioyfulnesse,
> In beds, in bowres, in banckets, and in feastes.   (III.vi.22)

Here Venus does not court Diana's capitulation to her own values as she does with Adonis in Malecasta's tapestry. Rather she courts Diana's acceptance of their equal validity as complementary components of a transcendent order encompassing them both: "We both are bound to follow heauens beheasts, / And tend our charges with obeisance meeke" (vi.22). In the inventio of Venus's petition, neither holds the social status of ultimate term in the hierarchy of love; neither can advocate their extreme position as definitive of love; both are subordinate to a higher, transcendent principle. The factors undermining the ethos of Venus in Malecasta's tapestry, her pathos and tactical elocutio of "sugred words and gentle blandishments" (vi.25), here advantage her ethos, and she "wins" the debate insofar as she persuades Diana to join her in the hunt for Cupid. Since she does not seduce Diana to abandon the "chace" of "saluage beasts," as Malecasta's Venus does Adonis, her victory does not discredit celibacy. Neither courted nor courtier loses the integrity of her individual identity: their estrangement is bridged by each subordinating her individual values to the value they hold in common. In consequence, as companion questers seeking the same goal, Venus and Diana gain allusive ethos from the analogous union of Guyon with Arthur in Book II and actually realize the triadic schema envisioned by Venus in the inventio of her appeal to Diana, with the committed and vulnerable love of mother for child at the apex transcending both sexual passion and celibacy. Functioning as an exemplum, therefore, Venus in her unconventional characterization that merges both voluptuary and distraught mother, and in her role as rhetorician, mediates between conventional extremes, resolving the apparent oxymoronic polarities in Spenser's juxtaposed tableaux of Malecasta's Venus with Belphoebe and Cymoent into the congruence of metonymia to prove the enthymeme that love is a hierarchical complex of elements, and to discredit the notion of chastity as a choice between the extremes of voluptuousness and celibacy.

Belphoebe and Amoret, foster children of Diana and Venus respectively, as twin offspring of the same mother by immaculate conception (vi.3–4), provide a complementary exemplum again in the schematic form of Venus's triad with the transcendent term at its apex. Their separation from each other and from their mother inverts the exemplum of congruence represented in the common quest of Venus and Diana, proving Spenser's argument by the logos of consequence. Both Belphoebe and Amoret become adequate exempla of chaste love only when the narrative sequence projects their common identification with and transcending by Britomart.[8]

This second appearance of Venus also establishes Cupid's ethos against the misrepresentations of Busirane's propaganda. Venus's account of the search for her wayward son dwells on his reputation in "Court" (vi.13), "Citties" (vi.14), and "country" (vi.15), a reputation consistent with his depiction by Busirane: "cruell," "wicked," "foule," "the disturber of all ciuill life, / The enimy of peace, and author of all strife." Venus ends the recital of these charges, however, by smiling (vi.15.9), an enigmatic, ambiguously placed response that may refer to the sweet complaints of "gentle shepheard swaynes" immediately preceding or to the whole litany of complaint culminating in the conventional topoi of a pastoral genre. In either case, her smile invites ours. The very repetition of commonplaces, regardless of courtly, urban, or rural context, creates the effect of unexamined cliche, the comic stock response, which dilutes ethical and pathetic suasiveness in the charges. Viewed from the perspective of Venus that Spenser maneuvers us to share, that of a mother whose "little sonne" has run away from home after a tiff (vi.11), the attacks on Cupid seem hyperbolical and self-serving, used reflexively to disown responsibility for the consequences of irrational passion. Dyslogistic characterizations of Cupid and his mother alike become invalid when measured against the actuality of their depiction in canto vi. By this touchstone Spenser preemptively brands Busirane's characterization in the Masque of Cupid a misrepresentation.

Retroactively he tinges with irony the ethical and pathetic significance of the love-complaint, whose topoi recur not only in the shepherds' verse "sweetly heard" by Venus but also in Britomart's lament to the sea, Cymoent's lament over Marinell, and Arthur's lament to Night, all, as in Venus' account, coming in thick succession (iv.8–10; iv.36–9; iv.55–60). None blames Cupid for their state in these passages, but any resort to the rhetorical genre itself, irrespective of content, ironically associates the speaker with an exemplum of irrationality once the positive ethos of Venus has established the association in canto vi. Spenser's narrator is the earliest locus of this irony in his application to Britomart of the cliched tropes as justification for her lovesick state: he attributes her condition to the tyranny of "imperious Loue" (ii.23) and a "wound" inflicted by the "false Archer" (ii.26). Furthermore, Britomart herself uses not only the form but also its discredited tropes during her subsequent dialogue with Glauce in canto ii (35–8), a species of complaint as duet, culminating in her self-identification with Narcissus (ii.44). Her use of these topoi defines her potential vulnerability to the misrepresentations of Busirane's rhetoric and ironically qualifies the superficial ethos of her martial victory over Marinell, just as Spenser's topoi of farce ethically qualify her victory over Malecasta and the knights of Castle Ioyeous. She takes on Marinell in combat and conjunctively takes on his irrationality (iv.12; 15).

Britomart's early feats as knight-militant in borrowed armour (iii.58), like those of Redcrosse, are fairy tale exempla. Her physical prowess and affecting love-sickness for the handsome knight seen in a magic mirror provide strategies of exordium "enticing" pathetic identification of the daydream self in Everyman with her adventurous quest and its passionate motivation. Again as he did with Redcrosse, by qualifying Britomart's early fairy tale heroics ironically, Spenser implicitly asserts the requirements for epic heroism. Exploit and ironic qualification together superimpose two images of the protagonist: what she is and what she must become, contrasting the elements of chastity she informs with those she must acquire. Britomart's extreme reaction to, and easy conquest of, two figures exemplifying physical indulgence, sexual in Malecasta and material in Marinell, identify her fairy tale heroism with the austere militancy of Diana in the paradigm structure of canto vi. To transmute into an instrument of logical and ethical proof from mere fairy-tale pathos, to become fully exemplary of Spenser's inventio, she must take on the qualities of Venus as well as those of Diana: she must accommodate and transcend both.

Spenser establishes her potential to do so in Redcrosse's eulogy on Artegall (ii.9–10) in response to Britomart's manipulative dyslogy (ii.8.6–9), and in Merlin's prophecy concerning the "most famous fruits of matrimoniall bowre" consequent on her union with Artegall (iii.22–50). The first, supported by the demonstrated ethos of exemplary holiness, identifies the object of her erotic courtship with the ultimate term of "gentle knighthood" (ii.9) and embodiment of transcendent virtue, "soueraine honour raisde to heauens hight" (ii.14). The second, Merlin's prophecy, identifies the goal of erotic courtship with the fulfilment of the ends of providential will in history (iii.24). In schematic form, Merlin's vision projects sexual union as the apex of a triad from which subtends the causal series of progeny deriving through time and culminating in Elizabeth. Thus he provides historical exempla in proof of an enthymeme asserting transcendent purpose. Merlin, "th'Enchaunter" (iii.17) is the antithetical exemplum to Busirane "the vile Enchaunter" (xii.31), as Contemplation is to Archimago: he is the source of true vision, and Britomart must accept Merlin's vision in order to reject Busirane's enchanting countervision. Her irrationality, therefore, in the encounters with Malecasta and Marinell, in her duet-complaint with Glauce, and her complaint to the sea, signifies a disordered hierarchy of will and passion insubordinate to reason; Redcrosse's eulogy and Merlin's prophecy establish the implications of that disorder for analogous social and transcendent structures.

Since they are analogous, their ultimate terms are coincident, and to achieve identity with one ultimate term requires that Britomart achieve identity with all. To do so she must first subordinate her individual will and passion to the supremacy of reason, as the willful Diana and passionate Venus accept subordination to the demands of a common cause. Coincident terms, however, require equivalent postures. As a transcendent courtier she must subordinate her celibacy to the procreational will of Providence; as an erotic courtier she must subordinate her individualism to union with Artegall. Britomart's motives as protagonist-courtier, therefore, must be sacrificial, not acquisitive.

5   THE GARDEN OF ADONIS: PERSUASION WITHOUT ADVANTAGE

Busirane, of course, plays on anxieties projected in Amoret and Britomart as responses to the prospect of such subordination. Surrender of body and will to another, he argues, threatens identity, and sacrificial motives invite victimization. Countering Busirane, Spenser's topothesia of the Garden of Adonis (vi.30–50) includes Venus in her third appearance and Adonis in his second as exempla for a model of love in which the motives of courtier and courted are mutually and reciprocally sacrificial, not acquisitive. Estrangement is bridged by neither the absorption of one into the other nor the mastery of one over the other but by the generation of closure through perfect equilibrium, the ideal rhetorical equilibrium of persuasion without advantage. Here the momentum of persuading and being persuaded becomes suspended at a fulcrum, the moment of exact complementarity. Courtship becomes a gerund of perpetual motivation, of becoming, with subject and object interchangeable in a reciprocal dynamic of court-ing: "Ioying his goddesse, and of her enioyed" (vi.48). Like the lovers in perpetually balanced tension on Keat's Grecian urn, Venus and Adonis remain discrete yet indivisible within the system they compose, a system at once always stable and ever dynamic, simultaneous and reciprocal. Mechanically, such a system generates a closed loop; rhetorically, persuasion without advantage; geometrically, a circle, the track described by points at centre and margin in polar opposition constantly striving toward each other but held apart at a fixed distance.[9]

Centred like Contemplation in Book I, Venus and Adonis occupy the topographical apex of the Garden, on a "stately Mount" located "Right in the middest of that Paradise" (vi.43), and the cyclical dynamic of their "courting" epitomizes with decorum Spenser's topothesia of the Garden as a whole, the "first seminarie / Of all things that are borne to live and die" (vi.30), which informs an eclectic merger of topoi attracted from myth, Platonic philosophy, and scripture. Homeric and scriptural topoi characterize the setting, like its central inhabitants, as a reciprocal equilibrium: "There is continuall spring, and haruest there / Continuall, both meeting at one time" (vi.42). The processive cycle of life (vi.32–3), "so like a wheele," is Platonic, again circumscribing accidental change within essential constancy: "The substance is not chaunged, nor altered, / But th'only forme and outward fashion" (vi.38). Venus is "great mother" (vi.40) and Adonis "the father of all formes" (vi.47), himself "eterne in mutabilitie, / And by succession made perpetuall" (vi.47). Their procreation of all living things from sexual union proves by mythic exempla the Socratic enthymeme in *Symposium* that progeny provide a source of immortality for mortal man and fulfills the expression of providential will in Genesis: "the mightie word, / Which first was spoken by th'Almightie lord, / That bad them to increase and multiply" (vi.34).

The garden is lapsarian, its generations subject to time and death (vi.40); it concedes the conditions of mortality and within them asserts a redemptive inventio of love and metamorphosis contesting Busirane's propaganda of despair. Rhetorically, therefore, Spenser's topothesia of the Garden argues Merlin's providential enthymeme using mythic rather than historical exempla. It constructs a topographic and biological hierarchy with Venus and Adonis depicted as ideally reciprocal lovers, their ethos sanctioned by Platonic and scriptural allusions, constituting an ultimate term coincident with the analogous position of Britomart and Artegall at the generative apex of their progeny envisioned in Merlin's prophecy. This structural identification of Britomart with Venus in the central canto of Book III marks the eulogistic antithesis of the dyslogistic identifications forged by Malecasta's misrepresentative, irrational use of myth in canto i and invited by Busirane's in the closing cantos.[10] Indeed, the evolution of Venus in narrative sequence from dyslogistic to eulogistic exemplum, from destructively irrational seductress *of* Adonis to advocate of rational concord *with* Diana, leading, by implication causally, to the transcendent, productive co-principle of life *in* Adonis provides a mythic paradigm that anticipates the stages Britomart must ascend to attain identity as the social, erotic, and transcendent exemplar of chaste love, an ascent demanding that she demonstrate motivation sequentially from acquisitive to sacrificial.

6   *ENUMERATIO* ON VILLAINY

Thus "villainy" in the inventio of Book III attracts to its exempla analogically symmetric demonstrators, composing erotic motives for courtship that are uniformly acquisitive, never sacrificial. Following Malecasta and leading to Busirane, these antitypes of chastity include the Foster, Argante and Ollyphant (incestuous, demonic twin antitheses of Belphoebe and Amoret), the witch and her son, the fisherman, Proteus, Satyrane, Hellenore, and Malbecco. Although Britomart encounters only Malecasta, Satyrane, and Ollyphant directly, she contains the confrontations with villainy of the supporting protagonists whom she transcends structurally, and actively takes on the corporate metonymia of all prior villains in Busirane's court, where Spenser's depiction of villainy finds allusive summation. Like all seducers, kidnappers, and rapists among Spenser's villainous exempla, Busirane acts from acquisitive and appetitive motives to possess love by coercive force: "the vile Enchaunter sate, / Figuring straunge characters of his art, / ... And all perforce to make her him to loue. / Ah who can loue the worker of her smart?" (xii.31). These lines evoke by echo Britomart's elocutio in her first encounter with exempla of acquisitive courtship, the six agents of Malecasta who attempt to compel Redcrosse's renunciation of his love for Una: "then bene ye sixe to blame, / To weene your wrong by force to iustifie; /... Ne may loue be compeld by maisterie" (i.25). Ironically, Britomart proves her enthymeme by "maisterie" of arms in that opening episode; in the closing episode, by contrast, against Busirane, "Where force might not auaile, there sleights and art / She cast to vse" (xii.28). Reiterating Malecasta's agency against Redcrosse, Busirane distorts the anatomy of chaste courtship to force Amoret's renunciation of her pledge to Scudamour, "To whom her louing hart she linked fast / In faithfull loue, t'abide euermore" (vi.53), a pledge that informes Amoret's potential to achieve with Scudamour the state of ideal courtship epitomized mythically in the total reciprocity of Venus and Adonis at the apex of the Garden of Adonis.

By inserting Britomart into the position of Amoret, Spenser defines the status of Britomart's antagonist in the rhetorical structure of Book III. Busirane's refutatio seeks to persuade Britomart to negate her potential for reciprocity with Artegall at the ideal point of erotic, social, and transcendent coincidence figured in the Garden of Adonis, Redcrosse's eulogy, and Merlin's prophecy. He thus occupies the position of ultimate term in a symmetrically inverted, ethically "demonic," mirror image of those triadic hierarchies established in Spenser's dispositio. He incorporates and transcends all the antagonists of chaste love in his argument, just as Britomart encompasses and transcends all the protagonists in Spenser's. Their confrontation in its final cantos is a dramatic *enumeratio*, or recapitulation, of the issues argued by Spenser's dispositio in Book III. Busirane is the ultimate object of acquisitive, as Artegall is the ultimate object of sacrificial, courtship. Britomart's rejection of the former asserts her acceptance of the latter, thereby justifying her ethos as the champion of chastity and simultaneously asserting by logos implicit topoi of chaste love that justice must reciprocate: their union requires both to be rational, sacrificially motivated, free of "maisterie," and sanctioned by providential will.

4 Proof by *Digressio*: A Rhetoric of Marriage

1 BRITOMART AND THE DECORUM OF CLOSURE

When narration resumes in Book IV, immediately subsequent to the dramatic transition placing love and its poet on trial in the Proem, the narrator, too, becomes an instrument of transition by alluding back to the sufferings of Amoret and Florimell in Book III (IV.i.1) and forward in the dispositional sequence of their courtship to an event temporally past in their history: the scene of Scudamour's struggle for Amoret in the Temple of Venus recounted in canto x. Again anticipating canto x (53–7), and again demonstrating the distinction between historical and dispositional sequence, the narrator then devotes two stanzas (i.3–4) to Amoret's seizure by Busirane, adds the new attribute that it occurred on her wedding night, and recapitulates her imprisonment and rescue by Britomart from Book III. The immediately succeeding entrance of Amoret in company with Britomart, still searching together for Scudamour, reinforces the narrator's stress on the separation of Amoret from Scudamour and represents a significant reversal of the original conclusion to Book III in the 1590 edition that depicted the lovers in "sweete rauishment" of "long embracement," their estrangement as male and female transcended in the Ovidian figure of Hermaphroditus (III.xii.45–6:1590). Hermaphroditus thus functions identically with the triad of reciprocal love incorporating Venus and Adonis in III.vi as an emblematic exemplum of ideally resolved erotic courtship.[1] Spenser recast this ending for the appearance of Books IV, V, and VI in 1596 to have Scudamour desert his post outside Busirane's castle before Amoret's rescue, succumbing to "despaire" through a failure of reason in his "misdeeming" of Britomart's chaste powers (III.xi.45:1596).

For Goldberg,[2] who gives narrative itself the status I give justice as Spenser's subject, Spenser's dispositio is a text about the production of text. His interpretation of rhetorical function therefore differs here from mine: he treats the "revisionary gesture" (144) that opens Book IV and the change in Amoret's status to married (73 ff) as a focal exemplum in proof of an enthymeme asserting the indecorum of narrative closure: "the narrative structure in *The Faerie Queene* is not closed and complete, but instead describes a kind of loop, moving ... from 'perfect' to 'to be perfected'" (6). I agree with Goldberg insofar as I contend that the conditions of courtship are estrangement and its mystery: the motive force of narrative can be sustained, therefore, only by constantly regenerating estrangement from its resolution. I cannot agree, however, that every disruption and discontinuity in temporal or historical sequence, or every addition of attributes to the topoi located in a character, functions so univocally as Goldberg assumes to present invariably an exemplum in proof of an enthymeme about narrative "closure." Rhetorically, story-closure and dispositional closure involve distinct principles of priority and decorum. Spenser resolves his inventio by means of his dispositio: sequential proof is independent of the Historiographer's temporal order, and Spenser obtains closure at the point where, and to the extent that, his dispositio invests his inventio.

By linking this rewritten ending for Book III with the narrator's introductory recall in Book IV of Amoret's abduction by Busirane, intensified with its wedding-night elaboration, Spenser identifies the rhetorical functions of the two episodes: both propose, then deny, physical union between Scudamour and Amoret. As Busirane's abduction opens up the issue of erotic courtship to social and transcendent overtones, so the rewritten ending re-opens the issue in Book IV by rescinding its closure in Book III. As the source of union between Amoret and Scudamour in the original closure, Britomart's function in the narrative structure corresponded to the emblematic function of Hermaphroditus. Such identification does not simply confirm Britomart's subsuming of both Amoret and Scudamour, the lodestar and star-lover of "all chaste affectione": it also proves an implied ancillary assertion that, with her victory over Busirane, Britomart has resolved metonymically the analogous estrangement between herself and Artegall by containing both the male and female components of her own courtship in ideal union. Such a union would give her transcendent status as the exemplar of justice as well as chastity. By rescinding Britomart's structural identification with Hermaphroditus in the new ending to Book III, Spenser is denying not her implied potential to attain this ideal union but rather the conclusive significance of her victory over Busirane.

It is here that the rhetorical analyst must depart from interpretations that follow the influential work of Lewis and Roche in assessing Book IV to be primarily the second of two books on the subject of love. Rhetorically, Britomart is the courtier not of chastity but of justice "through" or "by way of" chastity: it was never the "end" of her mission to defeat Busirane and rescue Amoret – she must fulfill the prophecy of Merlin in fruitful marriage with Artegall. Against Busirane she demonstrates attributes of the identity she courts: rational control and sacrificial motivation are requirements for the resolution of her quest, not proof of its completion. Scudamour's failure of reason, his "despaire" and "misdeeming," becomes identical with Busirane's villainy in its consequences and Britomart begins Book IV facing those consequences as if, effectively, her victory over Busirane had never occurred: she has resolved neither the estrangement between Scudamour and Amoret nor the analogous estrangement between Artegall and herself. Furthermore, I will argue, diverging from a substantial consensus, these estrangements remain unresolved at the end of Book IV.[3]

Spenser re-establishes Britomart as the principal vehicle of his dispositio in the opening cantos of Book IV, using the narrative continuation of Book III to create an elaboration, not a simple extension, of its argument. Britomart functions as an agent of amplificatio, not repetitio, in her evolving exemplification of chaste love. Rhetorically, Book III and Book IV are less Lewis's "single book on the subject of love" than two of three books on the subject of justice melded through Britomart, who functions, like the emblematic figure of Elizabeth in the Proem to Book IV, as a common focal exemplum to demonstrate progressively that the rational order of the individual psyche, concord among individuals, and just order in the state manifest a common principle.

Britomart's first exploit in Book IV is symptomatic of this nexus: she defeats in combat an "unlawfull" knight who challenges her for Amoret, making him "repent, that he had rashly lusted / For thing vnlawfull, that was not his owne" (IV.i.11). Not content with trial by combat, she then calls upon "the Seneschall" to judge between the claimants for Amoret (i.12), seeking to reconcile the conflict without rancour and restore "goodly fellowship" (i.15). The incident depicts lust as the cause of "vnlawfull" acts, and justice as the source of fellowship. By defeating "vnlawfull" lust, Britomart repeats her role in Book III, but here the context of her action undergoes elaboration:

she is identified as a force of lawful order in victory and a supplicant of merciful justice in forging concord. This initial incident in Book IV thus exemplifies a central enthymeme from Book V where the narrator asserts "licentious lust" to be the enemy of justice:

> Therefore whylome in knights of great emprise
> The charge of Iustice giuen was in trust,
> That they might execute her iudgements wise,
> And with their might beat downe licentious lust,
> Which proudly did impugne her sentence iust.   (V.iv.2)

Chastity, fellowship, and justice face a common foe in lust, and the incident identifies the championing of chastity with the demonstration of justice; Britomart's first exploit in Book IV, like the rescinding of her status as Hermaphroditus, functions to recapitulate and re-contextualize her exploits from Book III in order to incorporate them allusively by the decorum of precedent as exempla for Spenser's inventio of friendship in Book IV. They serve, as it were, double duty; indeed, like Britomart herself, triple duty, since the argument they prove extends through Book V.

With the same allusive decorum of precedent, and for the same purpose, Spenser also incorporates as elements of proof in his dispositio of friendship Britomart's metonymic analogues from Book III: Scudamour and Amoret, Belphoebe and Timias, Marinell and Florimell. Venus, too, makes a sequential reappearance, extending her evolution in Book III to achieve the status of Hermaphroditus, "Both male and female, both vnder one name" (IV.x.41) and conjointly, as the object of supplication by "great sorts of louers" having "cause of good or ill," to become an exemplum combining topoi of love and justice (x.43). Like "loue" and the poet of love summoned to trial in the Proem, therefore, Britomart and the co-protagonists she contains are subpoenaed to appear in Book IV to justify in a public forum their ethos as chaste lovers. Less figuratively, Spenser argues in Book IV that chastity and friendship are ultimate terms of analogous hierarchies, and constructs his dispositio accordingly with Britomart as the locus of contiguity, the analogical "attractor," reiterating with amplification her function as courtier in both contexts.

2   BRITOMART AND THE INVENTIO OF FRIENDSHIP

The pattern from her first exploit, combat followed by reconciliation, recurs in the central canto of Book IV, where Britomart unhorses

Scudamour (vi.10) and battles Artegall (11–19) until a "wicked stroke" shears away the front of her helmet, revealing her "diuine" beauty. Immediately both antagonists become supplicants. Artegall "of his wonder made religion" and "pardon her besought his errour frayle" (vi.22); Scudamour "did worship her as some celestiall vision" (vi.24). Glauce petitions her "To graunt vnto those warriours truce a whyle" (vi.25). Britomart's "wrathfull courage" and "haughtie spirits" begin "meekly to adaw," however, only when she recognizes Artegall"s face from Merlin's glass and hears his name (vi.26–9).

The scene is the fulcrum of both narrative and argument in Book IV: "climactic" in the narrative and a crux of dispositional proof. Britomart's beauty is the physical exemplum of her chastity, and its effect on her antagonists merges chastity with ethical topoi of both justice and divinity. Britomart assumes a configuration and transcendent status recreating the structural posture of Elizabeth in the Proem and anticipating those of both the Hermaphroditic Venus in canto x and Isis in the central episode of Book V (vii.5–7). Spenser thus creates a momentary, purely emblematic multiple identification demonstrating analogous ultimate terms coincident in the same figure. Furthermore, the configuration is social and erotic as well as transcendent. Positioned at the apex of a triad, Britomart stands in relation to the suppliant Artegall and Scudamour as sovereign to socially inferior courtiers. Scudamour's shift from belligerent to supplicant posture necessarily configures Britomart's superiority, and signals his recognition that the rational control she embodies is both essential to chaste love and lacking in himself. Analogy here isolates against a ground of similitude the "lack" or absence of identity; an ethical or hierarchical estrangement projected in narrative sequence as causal. In the account of Scudamore's exploits it "accounts for" his frustrated courtship of Amoret, his inability to penetrate Busirane's flames, his consequent despairing misjudgment of Britomart's ability to do so, and his vulnerability to the discord sown by both Ate (IV.i.49–53) and Care (IV.v.40–5). For Artegall the same shift signals his recognition of chaste love as essential to the "salvage knight" of justice (vi.31). He courts identity in Britomart with rationality and sacrificial motives whose lack "accounts for" his defeat at her hands in Satyrane's tournament (IV.iv.43) and his consequent discordant, and unjust, passion for revenge (IV.vi.6).

Erotically, this emblematic moment also marks the convergence of Britomart and Artegall, like Venus and Adonis in the garden at the corresponding core of Book III, as reciprocal courtiers; indeed, as the moment passes they configure a separate hierarchy superimposed on the first, a triad defined by an apex outside time subventing attributes of itself in time-past and time-future, with the transcendent Britomart at the apex retaining both male and female aspects in suspended courtship by subsuming the beauty-smitten Artegall before (vi.21–3) and the equally smitten Britomart after (vi.26–9). Britomart also becomes structurally coincident with Amoret as the object of Scudamour's courtship, complementing her formal coincidence with Scudamour at the point in the initial episode where she "wins" Amoret from the "unlawfull" suitor. This identification with both erotic courtier and erotic courted completes a momentary reinstatement of her status as the Hermaphroditus figure (III.xii.46:1590) rescinded by Scudamour's irrationality (III.xii.45:1596).

At the centre of Book IV and of the chastity-friendship-justice sequence, therefore, Spenser provides a paradigm of his *inventio*: the emblematic figure of Britomart represents the ultimate term of erotic, social, and transcendent hierarchies and combines the cognate qualities of chaste love, concord, and justice respectively. Projected into dispositional sequence these emblematic motifs become causal motives: it is love that mitigates Britomart's just wrath to permit the concord of reconciliation with Artegall and Scudamour. Spenser conscripts, as it were, the Britomart and Artegall of Books III and V respectively to meet in mutual recognition and reciprocal courtship at the centre of Book IV, thereby "proving" by narrative *logos* the same assertion posited in his *elocutio* of emblematic triads: Friendship is a concept that merges the qualities of chastity and justice; rhetorically its *inventio* draws upon no independent *topoi* and its *dispositio* presents no independent advocate in *refutatio*.

3   ANATOMY OF "THE PROTAGONIST"

Decorum, both precedential and syntactical, thus makes the *dispositio* of Book IV contingent on this *inventio* of interdependency, and the inclination of commentators to focus solely on *topoi* conscripted from Book III to the exclusion of those from Book V may account for the evident situation noted by Hamilton that readers seem to find Book IV "the least interesting," and confirm Murrin's suggestion that this dislike and consequent neglect by modern, formalist critics arises from their perception of a "messy plot" that resists analysis of "the poem as object."[4] Yet Spenser's dispositional structure is no more disordered here than in Book III or Book VI, although the apparent lack of a single protagonist and the atypical use of the *digressio* as a fundamental rather than supplemental element of argument make its principles of decorum less easily adduced than those generating the "intermedled" patterns of courtship in the legends of chastity and courtesy. Once topoi from Book V are granted equal status with those from Book III, however, the dispositio of friendship derives just as contingently from its inventio as those of any other virtue. Since the ideals of chastity, social concord, and justice are ultimate terms of analogous hierarchies, their component qualities are interdependent and the courtier questing for identity with one must attain identity with all. This aspect of inventio dictates the decorum of Spenser's dispositional choice to divide the function of protagonist between two courtiers, Britomart and Arthur, and to locate the division in narrative sequence at this critical juncture in canto vi. He thereby constructs a narrative that, while too discontinuous for the "Historiographer's" particular topoi of coherence, distributes an argument highly symmetrical and, perforce, hardly "messy."

When Britomart finds Artegall and Scudamour, she loses Amoret (vi.36); Arthur finds Amoret (viii.19) and assumes Britomart's role as her protector. Each is identified with Amoret as a heart-yearning companion in a common erotic quest (Britomart in IV.vi.16; Arthur in IV.ix.19). Up to canto vi Britomart encounters exempla of discord whose motives stress the erotic rather than the unjust: the "iolly knight" (i.10–15), Blandamour (i.36), a host of challengers to the knights of Maydenhead at Satyrane's tournament, including Artegall in "saluage" disguise (iv.43–5), and the false Florimell (v.20), all preface the summative encounter with Scudamour and Artegall (vi.10–19). Subsequent to this crucial point in canto vi, Arthur encounters exempla of discord in whom unjust motives eclipse the erotic: Sclaunder (viii.23–33), Corflambo, and his daughter Poeana (viii.35-ix.16). Britomart and Arthur finally join forces against Druon, Claribell, Blandamour, and Paridell, chaotic exempla of discord "in friends profest" (ix.27) and parodic exempla of reciprocal commitment (ix.21–37). Britomart and Arthur also share the two synecdochal exemplars of friendship between them: the tale of Cambell and Triamond (ii.35-iii.52) forms a digressio within the dispositio of Britomart; that of Amyas and Placidas (viii.50–62) a digressio within the dispositio of Arthur.

The functional continuity between Britomart and Arthur derives contingently from their functional identity in Book III where their duplicated topoi of chaste courtiers and visionary motivation make one redundant as a vehicle of proof; thus Arthur makes no appearance in Book III. In Book IV, however, once Britomart finds her object of courtship, they embody complementary topoi of chastity and justice, not identical topoi of friendship. Thus Amoret, despite her fear, is "as safe as in a Sanctuary" with Arthur, as safe as she is with

Britomart (i.15–16), because he "goodly learned had ... [t]he course of loose affection to forstall, / And lawlesse lust to rule with reason's lore" (ix.19), and we are not invited, as Goldberg contends, to concur in Amoret's dyslogistic perception. Goldberg reads "sanctuary" as synonymous with "ark or reliquary," since all represent loci where treasure is protected. "Hence," he argues, "it is no wonder that Amoret can read Arthur's protection as menacing, for the same configuration can be found in the figure of Lust, the privy figure, who stores 'the relickes of his feast, / And cruel spoile (vii.60).'"[5] Surely, however, if the term "sanctuary" invites juxtaposition of Arthur's protection and Lust's incarceration, the rhetorical figure involved is not metaphor but antiphrasis, the strategy to highlight differences against a ground of similarity. Amoret's "reading" of Arthur is Busirane's and so anticipates, as I will argue subsequently (chapter 6, section 5), Britomart's "dream-reading" of Artegall in Isis's Church. Arthur becomes the champion of friendship because he combines the topoi of Britomart and Artegall; conversely, Britomart ceases to be an appropriate exemplar of friendship at the point where she finds Artegall, because at that point the topoi of chastity and justice become poles of reciprocal courtship apportioned between herself and Artegall.

While Britomart and Arthur function as the actual protagonist in Book IV, they are not its titular heroes, and judging by Spenser's practice in other books Britomart and Arthur should each feature in a digressio complementing or supplementing the exploits of Cambel and Telamond, the ostensible champions of "Friendship." Instead, the decorum of Spenser's inventio relegates them to a digressio within the exploits of Britomart. Telamond resembles a shadow character in drama, a name with no corresponding actor on stage: Triamond appears, evidently in Telamond's stead, as co-exemplum with Cambel. One can agree with Goldberg that this treatment of the nominal heroes of Book IV constitutes "a radical disturbance of narration" typical of the work generally without agreeing that it is a "slip or error of naming," like Redcrosse for Guyon in the versicle to III.ii, or accepting his "implication" that no principles of functional decorum distinguish heroes, that "any hero is all heroes, all heroes are the same hero."[6] Triamond is a sort of literalized metonymia: he literally enfolds the essence of his brothers Priamond and Diamond. In their turn, Cambel and Triamond join Scudamour and Artegall as eulogistic exempla whom Britomart takes on in combat, thus taking on and transcending through victory their topoi in her ascent to the ultimate term she figures emblematically in canto vi. That ultimate term seems to coincide structurally with the locus represented by "Telamond," which Roche renders etymologically as a barbarism for "perfect world" [G. *teleios*; L. *mundus*], arguing that the brothers' story "constitutes an allegory of the harmony of the world."[7] Hierarchically, Telamond subvents Priamond, Diamond, and Triamond as constituent derivatives.

In their subsequent encounter Britomart assumes the corporate ethos of not only Cambel and Triamond but also Canacee and Cambina, the male and female components in a species of ritualized courtship dance. This dance begins in bloody discord so hyperbolically irrational as to mark "the dreddest day that liuing wight / Did euer see vpon this world to shine" (iii.3), and proceeds through repetitiously detailed, thrice-repeated trials by combat before evolving to absolutely rational domestic concord, social and erotic: "In perfect loue, deuoide of hatefull strife ... That since their days such louers were not found elswhere" (iii.52). The superlative mode of the narrator complements the supernatural topoi of an exemplum dominated by the marvels of fabula: Cambel is invincible by virtue of his sister Canacee's magical ring (ii.39); Triamond invests successively the souls and battle-skills of Priamond and Diamond, his brothers, as they fall mortally stricken by Cambel (iii.13; iii.22) in fulfilment of a bargain struck by his mother Agape with the Fates (ii.52). Their enmity, "the fellonist on ground," is resolved by the intervention of Cambina, Triamond's sister, "learned ... in Magicke leare" in which "she farre exceld all other" (iii.40), who enters in a "wondrous" chariot drawn by "two grim lyons" (iii.38–9) and reinforces her tearful plea for peace by smiting the combatants with "her powerfull wand" and giving each a draught of Nepenthe:

> Of which so soone as they once tasted had,
> Wonder it is that sudden change to see:
> Instead of strokes, each other kissed glad,
> And louely haulst from feare of treason free,
> And plighted hands for euer friends to be.
> When all men saw this sudden change of things,
> So mortall foes so friendly to agree,
> For passing ioy, which so great maruaile brings,
> They all gan shout aloud, that all the heauen rings.   (iii.49)

Indeed, the "change" to "foes so friendly" is oxymoronically sudden, emphatically so by repetition in lines 2 and 6; a "wonder" and a "maruail" from fairy tale. "Ioyous feast" and the double marriage of

Cambel and Triamond to their respective sisters complete the hyper-bolically conventional symbolism of concord and anticipate the pre-dictable coda: they lived "happie" and "long," if not ever after (iii.52).

This digressio defines friendship as the social antithesis of enmity and "cruell war" (iii.50): it provides eulogistic and dyslogistic devices of pathos to prove the superiority of concord over discord – to prove, in short, the obvious. By asserting this conventional definition through blatant topoi from fairy tale, devices accentuated not dis-guised by the narrator, Spenser provides a narrative amplificatio on Chaucer's tale but accentuates one of its elements, the magical, to a point of dominant focus. He stresses with hyperbolical elocutio the dependence of friendship for its realization in the tale on magic. Accordingly, while the exemplum of discord magically transmuted to concord carries the suasive power of pathos, its protagonists are limited to the status of fairy tale heroism. They remain agents of magic, not of chaste love and justice, the component sources of social concord in Spenser's anatomy of friendship. Cambel and Triamond prove an enthymeme dissociated from the central inventio of that anatomy: they demonstrate only the affective consequences not the systemic cause of social enmity and its antithesis. Hence their deco-rous isolation from its central dispositio in a digressio. They remain so isolated because the very source of their amity precludes move-ment from fairy tale to epic ethos: any act of friendship on their part demonstrates the influence of magic, not rational volition. Even their generous effort to award each other the second day's prize at Satyrane's tournament takes on the rhythm of a comic turn (IV.iv.36). A further blow to their epic ethos occurs on the third day when their prowess is overshadowed by Artegall; all three, of course, are over-matched in turn by Britomart.

Spenser's dispositional strategy thus renders epic ethos unattain-able to Cambel and Triamond and imports Britomart, already pos-sessed of epic stature attained in Book III, to be the champion of friendship in their stead. This departure from Spenser's structural treatment of titular heroes in other books asserts through strategic contrast the dependence of his inventio of friendship on topoi from the virtues which bracket it. In the evolution of her ethos, Britomart takes on (assumes and transcends) the titular exempla of Book IV to make friendship a derivation from chaste love. Thus Britomart and the "iolly knight" in the opening episode schematically duplicate Cambel and Triamond in their fairy tale exemplum, and Amoret, as the prize of combat, duplicates Canacee. Britomart also assumes Cam-bina's function as the instigator of reconciliation; her instrument how-ever is justice, not magic. Symmetrically, in the closing episode of her role as champion of friendship in canto vi, she finds within herself the motive for reconciliation with Scudamour and Artegall, acting from chaste love, not reacting to a magic wand and taste of Nepenthe. In Britomart, rational and sacrificial motives (the motives of chastity) displace magic as the source of social concord; like her co-protagonists in Book III, the nominal heroes of Book IV function in their digressio as instruments of proof by ethos and sequential logos: they justify through contrast Britomart's status as exemplary quester.

Arthur's portion of this dispositio in Book IV contains the symmetrical digressio of Amyas and Placidas, whose friendship is tested and confirmed without the agency of magic. Placidas, from sacrificial motives replicating those of Britomart at Busirane's castle (viii.55), offers himself in place of Amyas, imprisoned by the tyrannous Corflambo and "wooed" by the tyrant's daughter Poeana. Aside from the physical identity of the two friends (viii.55.9), which makes the substitution possible, nothing in Placidas's action depends upon topoi from fairy tale, and the narrator explicitly cites this digressio (ix 3.1–4) as an exemplum in proof of his enthymeme asserting the superior ethos of love between friends (measured against love between men and women or among kindred) on the grounds that such love, like justice, confronts the moral indecorum of Fortune:

> For naturall affection soone doth cesse,
> And quenched is with Cupids greater flame:
> But faithfull friendship doth them both suppresse,
> And them with maystring discipline doth tame,
> Through thoughts aspyring to eternall fame.
> For as the soule doth rule the earthly masse,
> And all the seruice of the bodie frame,
> So loue of soule doth loue of bodie passe,
> No lesse then perfect gold surmounts the meanest brasse.   (ix.2)

Amyas and Placidas, the narrative interjection confirms, exemplify friendship as a species of chaste love. Their oppressor, Corflambo, as anti-exemplum of friendship, exhibits "lustfull fire" of the unchaste, but his acquisitive motives issue in acts of social injustice (viii.48). The "maystring discipline" of friendship finds its dyslogistic antithesis in Corflambo, who seizes treasure and dominion "by wrong / And tortious powre, without respect or measure" (ix.12). Arthur "ymp[s]" the giant's severed head to his body in a ruse to breach Corflambo's keep (ix.4), but the head would serve displayed on a pole just as aptly as Pollente's does to emblemize Artegall's warning against incontinent appetite as a source of injustice:

To be a mirrour to all mighty men,
In whose right hands great power is contayned,
That none of them the feeble ouerren,
But alwaies doe their powre within iust compasse pen.   (V.ii.19)

Thus villainy, like heroism, demonstrates the accommodation of topoi from chastity and justice in Spenser's inventio of friendship. Corflambo attracts topoi from such anti-exempla of justice as Pollente (V.ii.5–6) and Grantorto,[8] and from the anti-exemplum of chaste love, "greedie" Lust (IV.vii.5–7), Busirane's echo, who abducts Amoret and Aemylia in a digressio from the actions of both Britomart and Arthur but one which bridges both. Britomart loses Amoret to Lust; Belphoebe, her subsumed co-protagonist from Book III, kills the villain; Arthur rescues and befriends Lust's victims, thereupon assuming Britomart's function as Amoret's protector. In the parallel episode against Corflambo, Arthur combines the roles of destroyer and rescuer he shared with Belphoebe against Lust, demonstrating in this configured analogy that the qualities of both heroism and villainy are derivative in common from topoi of chastity and justice. The parallel also defines the ethos of Arthur in Book IV: his enmity to both inchastity and injustice makes him a decorous champion of friendship.

Arthur's immunity to Sclaunder demonstrates the same ethos while stressing more directly its attributes of justice. Like Corflambo, Sclaunder bears a close resemblance to enemies of justice: Arthur and his companions are "vniustly blamd, and bitterly reuilde" (IV.viii.28; 35) in anticipation of Artegall's treatment by Enuy, Detraction, and their Blatant Beast (V.xii.38–43). She cannot break the concord among Arthur, Amoret, and Aemylia because Arthur exemplifies the virtues of the "antique age" in the narrator's Ovidian trope of decline (viii.29–33); he embodies the discipline "goodly learned ... of yore" that is common to chastity, friendship and justice: "The course of loose affection to forstall, / And lawlesse lust to rule with reasons lore" (ix.19).

4   JUDGING SCUDAMOUR'S CASE: PRIORITY AND PROOF

This stress on topoi of justice in the dispositional strategies establishing Arthur's ethos makes it appropriate that he, and not Britomart, should control the closure of their common mission to reunite Amoret and Scudamour. Hamilton evidently represents a consensus among readers in assuming the reunion takes place at the end of canto ix: "one must assume, [Arthur] resolves the theme of 'maistrie' in

Books III and IV by presenting Amoret to the assembled company at the end of Canto ix so that she may freely choose, and, of course, choose Scudamour."[9] In his gloss to ix.38, Hamilton notes: "Though Amoret is with Arthur, she is not present until he chooses to present her, as apparently [Spenser] may have intended him to do between stanzas 39 and 40."[10] Since there is no textual evidence for it, Hamilton's assumption, while reasonable, obfuscates the compelling rhetorical problem of why such a narrative lacuna should exist. We need not assume authorial inadvertence or printer's miscue. This apparent fracture in the story-line produces no discontinuity within the structure of argument it projects if we accept that Arthur withholds presentation of Amoret and delays any union at the end of canto ix pending Scudamour's account of his courtship. That account, comprising the whole of canto x, presents testimony to make a case for his just "right" to Amoret (ix.38.8). Both champions of friendship "hear" Scudamour's "case," and Britomart "did him importune hard" to make it (ix.41.2), but it is Arthur who has assumed the guardianship of Amoret after Britomart lost her to Lust while surrendered to "fearelesse" sleep in "shadow myld" (vi.36), a situation with erotically ominous precedents in her encounters with Malecasta and Busirane. Arthur, therefore, exercises the effective power to grant or deny Scudamour's claim.

Furthermore, he does not render a decision. Spenser freezes Scudamour's courtship at the crux of success or failure without narrative resolution of the crisis, and suspends Arthur in the posture of judge, thereby accenting in sharp relief his stature as a figure of justice. The strategy has significant rhetorical affects; it identifies the reader's perspective with Arthur's and isolates the issues of Scudamour's courtship from its narrative dynamic, leaving the reader, like Arthur, to judge whether unification or continued estrangement would preserve decorum with the evidence of Scudamour's ethos adduced in his statement of claim. That we know the outcome only intensifies the rhetorical purpose. The sequential end for Spenser's *dispositio* of Amoret and Scudamour is the sequential beginning of their history: Spenser's narrative strategy isolates causal from temporal "ends" and so focuses the issue of motive. Their marriage is given sequentially prior to this point in Spenser's *dispositio*, but it functions less as an event in time-past that determines consequence than as a prior given to be tested, and the issue at stake in Scudamour's advocacy becomes not whether they are, were, or will be married, but whether they ought to be.

Thus Spenser configures an argument with intense social resonance for Elizabethan sovereignty by giving issues of ethos logical and causal priority over and before their political consequences. "Marriage is a form of power," notes Goldberg, and "the single most important feature in international diplomacy during the Renaissance,"[11] but Spenser's strategy forces re-examination of any notion of marriage as simply the imposition of power. Indeed, such imposition, at first sight, makes Scudamour's claim seem ill-founded. He gains entry to the temple of Venus by force, defeating the twenty knights who guard its access (x.10), wins the "shield of Loue" emblazoned with Cupid's "killing bow / And cruell shafts" (x.55), and, as "Cupids man" (x.54), abducts the unwilling Amoret by force. The postures of abductor and victim recall the central tableau in Busirane's Masque of Cupid, and the accidental pattern of this courtship conforms to the villainies of Lust and Corflambo. In defence of actions so fraught with topoi of inchastity and injustice, Scudamour testifies about his motivation and cites Concord and Venus as supporting witnesses of high ethos. Cupid's shield was the "prise" and Amoret the "spoil" to prove Scudamour's worthiness as a knight, "to winne me honour by some noble gest" (x.4), and Concord favours his courtship, granting him safe entry to the temple and safe exit with the captive Amoret (x.57).

Concord's prosopographia, in keeping with her abstract name, displays strategies of allegoria to epitomize her stature as an exemplum. It depicts her at the apex of three analogous triads. One is social, with Concord as the mother of twin offspring Peace and Friendship (x.34); one is erotic, with Concord the Medina-like controlling mediatrix between the half-brothers Love and Hate whose "contrarie natures" she "well ... tempred both" (x.32–3); one is transcendent, with Concord anticipating Dame Nature (VII.vii) as deputy to the "Almightie maker" in maintaining balance in the ordained natural order between cosmos and chaos (x.35). Her prosopographia recapitulates by abstraction the common derivation from rational control of friendship, chastity, and justice respectively. Its analogous triadic structures thereby identify Concord's ethos and component attributes with those of the emblematic Britomart in canto vi, who tempers love and hate not only in herself but also in Scudamour and Artegall, and with those of Arthur, who now mediates Scudamour's courtship of Amoret as Concord did.

As both judge of Scudamour's claim and adoptive protector of Amoret, Arthur also stands surrogate for Scudamour's second witness, Venus, whose "laugh" signifies her "favour" of Scudamour's "sacrilege" in her temple (x.53; 56). Spenser's prosopographia of her statue (x.39–43) depicts Venus as a juridical figure, judging "cause of good and ill" in petitions brought by "great sorts of louers" (x.43), in a eulogistic antithesis to the topoi depicting Cupid's statue in Busirane's castle (III.xi.47–9) which commands idolatrous submission to power. As eulogistic emblems of justice and knightly honour, Venus's statue and Cupid's shield here complete Spenser's refutation of the dyslogistic misrepresentation of their nature in the art of Malecasta and Busirane, and Venus presides over a setting of ideal friendship whose eulogistic topoi of art and nature accord with those of the Garden of Adonis and invert those of Malecasta's Castle Ioyeous, Busirane's house, and Acrasia's bower (x.23–70). She functions rhetorically like Concord as a recapitulating exemplum to epitomize the distributio of Britomart and Arthur: she occupies the ultimate term in a structure of social harmony whose ethos assumes concomitant attributes of both justice and, as the hermaphroditic creator of the world (x.41,47), transcendent chastity. Hence, in claiming to court Amoret under the approving aegis of this figure, Scudamour asserts identity with Britomart and Arthur, who court the erotic, social, and transcendent ideal of friendship.[12]

Scudamour is a failed courtier, however, and his defence in canto x contextualizes the source of his unresolved estrangement from Amoret. Like Britomart and Arthur he seeks "honour" by "noble gest," and like Britomart he is "bold," but Scudamour's is the boldness of "young mens thoughts" (x.4) untempered by the rational control central to the ethos earned by Britomart and conceded to Arthur. His erotic motives are appropriately acquisitive, not sacrificial, producing an indecorum between the inventio and dispositio of his courtship that is reflected in the inconsistent topoi of his defence. Amoret is the "spoile" of conquest, and Britomart proves her ethos in Book III as the champion of chastity by acting sacrificially to free Amoret from bondage as the "spoile" of Busirane, whose miasmic, corrupting rhetoric functions as the actualized exemplum of Scudamour's misconceived enthymeme. By delaying Scudamour's account of the genesis of his estrangement from Amoret until Book IV and juxtaposing it against a potential resolution under the aegis of both Britomart and Arthur, Spenser again recapitulates his argument. From an irrational hindrance to chaste love in Book III, Scudamour's untempered acquisitive motivation evolves in significance, like the ethos of Britomart and Arthur, to preclude, as they include, justice and friendship in common with chastity, and his courtship of Amoret is dependent for the success or failure of its resolution in friendly love precisely on the chastity and justice of his motivations.

Scudamour is not a villain: he demonstrates Spenser's inventio not by informing a fixed set of dyslogistic topoi as villains do but by evolving through active experience from a locus of dyslogistic to one of eulogistic topoi, in the process discrediting the former and accrediting the latter. Concord and Venus, by favouring his abduction of Amoret, set it antithetically against Busirane's and assert Scudamour's potential for such evolution. The change in his perception of Amoret from "spoile" to "my lifes deare patronesse" (x.28) provides evidence for their assertion. Arthur, their surrogate, weighs, with the reader, the justice of his case.

Scudamour's concluding identification of himself with Orpheus in his heroic but failed courtship of Eurydice, and his resuscitation of "spoyle" (x.58) as an epithet for Amoret, provide ambiguous exempla of ethos evidencing either recognition of culpability or continued delusion, an ambiguity unresolved by Spenser's narrative. For Scudamour is the narrator of this episode, and we literally have only his word to go on: "So ended he his tale, where I this Canto end" (x.58). Direct narration and unresolved ambiguity complement the rhetorical strategy of Arthur's unrendered decision. Both court the audience to share Spenser's perspective by enticing participation in the process of argument: to recognize in an act of judgment unmediated by narrative authority that chaste and just motivation determines the resolution of estrangement into friendship.[13]

5   "MARRIAGE" AS NARRATIVE CLOSURE

Two exempla of such resolution immediately follow Scudamour's account and conclude Book IV: the wedding of the rivers Thames and Medway (IV.xi.8–53) and the reunion in betrothal of Florimell and Marinell (IV.xii). Their conclusive placement and sustained celebratory tone create the effect of a summative peroration, locating marriage at the structural apex of friendship, just as Merlin's vision established it at the apex of chastity. In their contrast to the unresolved estrangement of Scudamour and Amoret, both these exempla of successful courtship accentuate topoi of justice: they function as refutatio to "unlawfull" topoi in Scudamour's courtship.[14] The Medway consents to marriage with the Thames by free choice, unconstrained by coercion (xi.7). Florimell escapes coercive courtship as the "spoile" of Proteus by the "warrant" of Neptune in response to Cymoent's petition for justice against "a cruell Tyrant" (xii.29–33), and becomes a Eurydice reclaimed from death by the reciprocal love essential to chastity.

Rhetorically, the order of nature has ethos equivalent to scripture: it is an ordained hierarchy generated from an apex coincident with Divine Will. Spenser progressively asserts analogy among this order and the hierarchies of chastity, friendship, and justice by making their ultimate terms coincident in mythic exempla. Venus and Adonis in the Garden of Adonis (III.vii), like Concord and Venus in the Temple of Venus (IV.x), stand surrogate for the source of ordained generation and natural order, anticipating the transcendent position of mythologized Justice in Spenser's Proem to Book V, the "dread Souerayne Goddesse ... resembling God" who "all his workes with Iustice hath bedight" (V.Pr.10). The resulting formal homology asserts through mythic topoi a Platonic metalepsis with Friendship as the social manifestation of a common source generating just order in the individual soul, the state, and nature.

Neptune is a recapitulating exemplum of this inventio. A figure of justice in resolving the estrangement of Florimell and Marinell, he appears first as the progenerative ultimate term of a hierarchy that is both social and natural, structuring "in order as they came" (xi.9) the declension of sea-gods and their progeny (xi.11–53). Spenser's elocutional device of *distributio*, or "epic catalogue," in this tour-de-force imposes symmetry and cohesion on an inchoate body of mythic lore representing the most chaotic, fortune-charged of natural elements, the sea; thus strategy and subject, art and nature, merge to epitomize concord in celebration of one marriage and prologue to another.

In the trope of marriage, Spenser provides an idealized point of resolution appropriate to dispositio by narration. It is a goal or end of quest, made coincident by mythic devices of elocutio (prosopographia, topothesia, catalogue) with an abstract point of generation, allusively Platonic, common to structures of chastity, friendship, and justice, and identified in turn with the ordained source of natural order. Marriage, so transfigured, becomes an ultimate term whose courtship resolves erotic estrangement in a social institution within which courtier and courted exhibit, by a reciprocal procreative equilibrium of commitment without coercion, essential topoi of both chastity and justice.

6 DIGRESSIO AND DECORUM

Allegorical interpretation of Book IV tends to focus primarily on the orders of chastity, friendship, and nature in this collocation of analogues, and to exclude the order of justice. Consequently such interpretation takes the re-established natural order coincident with the union of Florimell and Marinell to represent the resolution of the argument Spenser begins in Book III: "With this powerful image of Marinell that suggests a reviving Adonis or, more exactly, a restored Verdant, the larger patterns of Books III and IV would seem to be resolved."[15] Goldberg provides an important voice of dissent as part of his speculations on analogies between Spenser's fictions and those that sustain power in Elizabeth's court.[16] He reads Neptune's procession as political allegory. "A translation into contemporary political terms is readily apparent; the rivers represent an imperialistic fantasy (139)." Hence for Goldberg the procession anticipates unresolved issues of power and its exercise in the civil order.[17]

Goldberg gives recognition to a component of allegoria suppressed by selective rhetorical focus, but he is no less inclined than other commentators on allegoria to fragment Spenser's dispositional rhetoric: his study isolates Book IV and so fractures it from Book III as well as Book V. For the rhetorical analyst, however, Spenser's dispositio is a function of Britomart's courtship of Artegall, and the development of that dispositio remains unresolved at the conclusion of Book IV. Indeed, the concluding three cantos of Book IV (the episodes of Scudamour and Amoret, Thames and Medway, Marinell and Florimell), like those of the titular heroes Cambel and Triamond and their co-exemplars of friendship Amyas and Placidas, are all digressions within the dispositio of Britomart's courtship. The extraordinary prominence of the digressio in Book IV signals, in a device of dispositional structure, the conceptual dependence of friendship on topoi of chastity and justice in Spenser's inventio. These digressions act in concert progressively to wed the ethos of justice to Britomart's ethos of chastity, imported from Book III, and anticipate the goal of her quest, union with Artegall: marriage, the ideal of friendship, thereby becomes itself a wedding of chastity and justice. Furthermore, the estrangement of Scudamour and Amoret stands unresolved on a issue of justice, and the courtship of Florimell and Marinell proceeds episodically from separation in a digressio of Book III, to reunion in a digressio of Book IV, to marriage in a digressio of Book V. Rhetorically, the closing cantos of Book IV, like its Proem, function not as a resolution to the argument begun in Book III but as a transition to its continuation in Book V.

PART THREE
Civilitatis Causa

5 Ovid's Cone and the Rhetoric of Law

1 "OVID'S CONE"

If the seasonal cycle coincident with Florimell's revitalization of Marinell (IV.xii.34) represents a point of resolution, it is structurally a highly unstable and fleeting one. The congruence of natural and human orders providing such an harmonious coda to Book IV dissolves into a sharply dissonant chord with the Proem to Book V.

> Right now is wrong, and wrong that was is right,
> As all things else in time are chaunged quight.
> Ne wonder; for the heauens reuolution
> Is wandred farre from where it first was pight,
> And so doe make contrarie constitution
> Of all this lower world, toward his dissolution.   (V.Pr.4)

Spenser moves from resolution to "dissolution" in barely five stanzas, producing a disjunction virtually oxymoronic and a consequent qualification, less ironic than poignant, of Florimell and Marinell as exempla. The irony does not undermine their ethos – it invites revaluation of the enthymeme they prove. Indeed, Spenser's prelude to the legend of Artegall, I will argue, retrospectively qualifies and revalues all precedent champions and their co-protagonists. Like their heroic synecdoche, Arthur, all belong to the antique world and exemplify its virtue, but their world and virtue are suddenly recontextualized within an abruptly expanded perspective of time and moral variability.

Here, in the disjunctive transitio from Book IV, Florimell, Marinell, and the other exempla of concord stand revealed not as the coda to friendship left them, at the regenerative turning point of seasonal cycle, but at the starting point for a dynamic of degeneration which that cycle becomes in the overture to Book V: "Me seemes the world is runne quite out of square, / From the first point of his appointed source, / And being once amisse growes daily wourse and wourse" (V.Pr.1).

Spenser's tropes here suggest not simply the linear metamorphosis through time from golden to iron ages that he borrows from Ovid, but an elaboration of the Ovidian topos in which that line of descent defines the vector of a centrifugal dispersion, an entropic spiral spawned from natural cycle "runne quite out of square." For ready reference I have affixed the label "Ovid's cone" to this structure because, considered schematically, its dynamic spiral freezes into a static cone, with natural and human concord at the apex, the "first point" of an "appointed source," broadening through a dispersion of ordered unity into chaotic discord, like Yeats' widening gyre, at its base.

In the second half of the Proem (9–11) and Canto i, Spenser erects an homologous structure fixing "Iustice ... high ador'd with solemne feasts" at the apex in a state of transcendence, sovereignty, and concord, where "Peace vniuersall rayn'd mongst man and beasts" (Pr.9). From this apex the order of "Iustice" and "Peace vniuersall" again disperses to "the sient base" of disordered growth sprung from "wicked seede of vice" (V.i.1). Furthermore, by metonymic extension Spenser conventionally involves the structure of the state (itself a conical hierarchy) in this congruent merging of orders, since its ultimate term, the sovereign, functions as God's surrogate, embodying "his imperiall might" to fulfill the cause of justice in the civic order:

> That powre he also doth to Princes lend,
> And makes them like himselfe in glorious sight,
> To sit in his owne seate, his cause to end,
> And rule his people right, as he doth recommend.   (V.Pr.10)

Thus the anti-exempla of justice, the villains of Book V, are agents of civic "dys-order" by force and fraud; their actions offer proof by logos to support Spenser's identifying the dynamics of injustice in the state with the Ovidian, and allusively Dantesque, spiral of natural and moral degeneration into chaos.[1]

That this Ovidian construct has focal significance in Spenser's general rhetorical structure for *The Faerie Queene* is evident from the fact that its elaboration in the Proem to the legend of Artegall represents a culmination and contextualizing of unelaborated precedents in each of the previous books (I.xii.14; II.vii.16–17; III.i.13; IV.viii.29–33). Thus it signals the presence of a powerful "attractor," in the sense of that term adduced earlier both to signify the point of organization into contiguous sequence of discrete elements and to elucidate thereby a procedural notion of structural decorum. Taken together, elaboration and recapitulation focused in Ovid's cone invite a pause for retrospective examination of characteristics in the Ovidian pattern that might justify Spenser's preoccupation with it at this point in the dispositio of his epic, characteristics of rhetorical structure rather than those of apocalyptic theology or historical allegory which tend to dominate interpretation of the trope.

Starting from Kenneth Burke's "principle of courtship" in rhetoric as "the use of suasive devices for the transcending of social estrangement,"[2] I have consistently treated the social model, hierarchically triadic in two-dimensions or conic in three, as the pattern for analogous structures generated by erotic and transcendent estrangement. The static architecture of Spenser's degenerate spiral is, of course, directly analogous to the hierarchical conic form of courtship structures in each of Books I through IV, but this formal identity would not in itself warrant devices of elaboration and placement suggesting a crux in, not the mere extension of, a series. It is through the dynamic rather than the static character of the Ovidian cone that Spenser brings to focus elements latent but unstressed in these analogous courtship structures, and retrospectively intensifies both their resonance and their cohesion. As the spiral unwinds through time, from past to present, its vector of degeneration and dissolution is moral, moving from what ought to be to what is. Narrative, of necessity, is also a temporal mode of sequential organization, but the legends of Holiness, Temperance, Chastity, and Friendship tell of knights whose quest invariably procedes against the moral flow of Ovidian degeneration: the history of their quest records a movement through time from what each is to what each ought to be, from actual to ideal, from fairy tale to epic ethos. Yet only when he reaches the knight of Justice does Spenser draw specific attention to this counter-valent characteristic of heroic courtiers, identifying Artegall with Bacchus and Hercules among those who, "inspired with heroicke heat," periodically establish justice by cropping the strangling thicket of vice (V.i.2); a metaphor which, significantly, leaves the "wicked seede of vice" still viable, awaiting (in dyslogistic parody of the trope "resolving" Book IV) seasonal regeneration. Artegall must take up the cause of justice against the spiralling tide of a world abandoned by his patroness and teacher Astraea, and fallen from "perfection" into "all filth and foule iniquitie" (V.i.5): the metaphor of a fallen garden infested with seeds of vice, ever in need of weeding, predicts the limited success of his mission (V.xii.27).

More significantly, the Proem to Book V retrospectively qualifies the success of the analogous missions in Books I through IV, because Spenser's Ovidian spiral renders the temporal designator "now" into a relative term. Until the beginning of Book V, readers experience the history of each quest as a succession of immediate events in the now of fictional narrative. Abruptly, with the Proem to Book V, those "histories" become history, relegated to the "antique age" long removed from the "age of stone" that corresponds to the actual present of both Spenser and his reader. Spenser locates us at the degenerate base of the unwinding spiral. Thus Artegall himself becomes a figure in which both apex and base of Ovid's cone inhere; he belongs, in a kind of double-vision, to both the now of story-time, a figure of the antique age, and to the chaotic now of historical sequence degeneratively derived from that age, an age whose virtues he is now charged to court. He both is and was what he courts as our surrogate: yet in Spenser's most radical dissociation of temporal from structural priority, the Proem precludes the success of Artegall's mission "before" its legend begins.

Several commentators have noted this disorienting fusion, and confusion, of historical, hierarchical, and narrative priorities, this "mirroring that turns antique narrative into a speculation on the historical 'present'" (to borrow Miller's nice phrasing), without engaging in speculation on its rhetorical significance.[3] As with the seasonal cycle closed in Book IV by the union of Florimell and Marinell only to be re-opened, the rhetorical effect of this sudden recontextualizing of all previous quests as prologue to Book V is to redefine the enthymeme each proves by re-opening the apparent closure of their successful courtships into an expanded dimension of argument. However great the achievements of Redcrosse, Guyon, Britomart, and the synecdochal Arthur in the fulfilment of their spiritual potential as individuals, Spenser's Proem to Book V asserts their inefficacy against the tide of degeneration in the general civil order since the antique age. While every book subsequent to the first uses previous books as one source of allusive exempla to build a rhetorical structure, the strategy here functions with exceptionally inclusive and summative effect. Spenser's purpose is clearly not to undermine the proven ethos of prior quests but to incorporate their attributes in his inventio of justice and enhance the ethos of Artegall's mission, a mission against the very tide of civil degeneration left unstaunched by the singular achievements of his predecessors. The structural placement and elaboration of the Ovidian spiral in the Proem to Book V thus imply an inventio of justice which includes and depends upon previously established topoi of holiness, temperance, chastity, and concord. Such topoi, however, while necessary, are not sufficient constituents of justice. The topos of divinely delegated cosmos in the state (V.Pr.10) completes and complements these constituents and adds an equally implicit enthymeme as corollary asserting Justice to be not simply another virtue in the series but the culmination and completion of previous virtues.[4] It is capable of realizing their private potential in the public realm; of justifying, in the Miltonic sense, their private ethos to the corporate good of man as a creature of the polis.

Despite cultural differences in the selection of their component virtues, Spenser's inventio reflects Plato's in this reciprocal dependency among justice and its constituents: the just state requires the just soul. One just soul, however, or even a few of heroic proportions cannot make a just state. Justice requires a reciprocal dynamic of "priuate morall" and "polliticke" virtues. Such reciprocity is total at the apex of the Ovidian cone, the temporal point of ideal past marking "Saturnes ancient raigne" when "all the world with goodnesse did abound" because "all loued vertue." Justice, in consequence, enjoined universal courtship, "sate high ador'd with solemne feasts, / And to all people did diuide her dred beheasts" (V.Pr.9). As a locus of such total reciprocity, the Ovidian apex resonates by structural analogy with the "middest point" of the "stately Mount" in the Garden of Adonis, participates with that locus in its analogy to the summit of Contemplation's mountain, and functions in antiphrasis with the disordered court of Busirane's idolatrous Cupid (III.xi.46ff).

The Ovidian apex thus defines an ethical antipode to Busirane's house. Its tropes evoke precedents juxtaposing Iustice and Busirane as antitypes through allusive, descriptive devices of elocutio and give particular rhetorical status to the interdependency between justice and those of its constituent topoi represented by Britomart. Britomart's defeat of Busirane placed her at the hierarchical apex of chastity, its ultimate term. Her position now becomes coincident with that of Iustice insofar as both embody ultimate terms diametrically opposed to the same dyslogistically ultimate exemplum represented by Busirane. Furthermore, the idealized absolute of Concord coincides with the universal courtship of justice when "Peace vniuersall rayn'd mongst men and beasts" (Pr.9.6). Since Britomart co-championed this virtue with Arthur, and the nature of her interaction with Redcrosse and Guyon at the outset of Book III engrafted their ethos to hers,

Britomart herself takes on sufficient of their attributes to serve as principal or delegate for all virtues contained metonymically in Spenser's inventio of justice. Her still-unfulfiled need for completion in the reciprocal dynamic of marriage with Artegall provides a narrative motive for the dispositio of Book V, demonstrating an enthymeme implicit in that inventio: for their complete realization in the civil order, justice and all previous virtues are mutually dependent.

2   ELIZABETH TUDOR AS HISTORICAL EXEMPLUM

These natural, moral, and civil hierarchies evoked in the Proem also attract into their congruence Merlin's envisioned cone of progeny, expanding through time and dependent from an apex locating the hypothetical point of union between Britomart and Artegall. That ordained descent of descendents also moves from ideal past to actual present, and its principal vector, the line of Briton kings, ends with Queen Elizabeth.[5] This very structural congruence, however, engenders a rhetorical strategy to preserve decorum which has troubled commentators who focus on the historical allegory of Book V. Particularly troublesome are the transparent identification of Elizabeth herself with Queen Mercilla (V.ix.27.9; x.3) and of Elizabethan policies with Arthur's subsequent exploits on behalf of Belge and Artegall's exploits on behalf of Burbon and Irena. Whatever may have motivated Elizabeth's domestic policy regarding Mary, and her foreign policy in the Netherlands, Spain, France, and Ireland, it was not the abstract principles of ideal justice. Those who interpret these passages as history distorted to serve political polemic can scarcely be blamed for their disapproval: good propaganda seldom makes good art. For the rhetorical analyst, however, these episodes are neither methodologically inconsistent nor the occasion for aesthetic dismay. In every book Elizabeth serves as a historical exemplum of the ultimate term engendering each virtue, and while her justice may be more easily questioned on the basis of documentary evidence than her holiness, temperance, chastity, or friendship, such evidence only enhances her rhetorical function. Spenser, no more than Virgil, attributes eulogistic topoi to a sovereign for the purpose of verisimilitude: their rhetoric of praise celebrates what ought to be and just possibly, should their courtship succeed persuasively, what might be, not what is.[6] Ovid's myth of degeneration from golden to iron ages mocks the utopian pretensions invested in an imperial mythology of *pax Augustus* as it does any Elizabethan successor to that myth. It is not the fragmented "Spenser" courting only Elizabethan preferment but the complex, multivalent poet courting a union of minds on a concept of justice with his audience, itself multivalent, who invites rhetorical analysis of his exempla from topical history and the suasive strategy they accommodate.

Spenser's Proem carefully establishes the concept of history operative in Book V, an a priori concept which interprets current events only insofar as it contextualizes them unconditionally and indiscriminately within a universalized spiral of natural, moral, and civic degeneration moving from past to present. Thomas Cain is surely on solid ground rhetorically in arguing that such a preface to Book V "puts, in advance, a construction on those episodes in the second half of the book which allegorize in ideal terms certain events drawn from 'state of present time.' There any Elizabethan would recognize familiar events depicted as they had not occurred and in the discrepancy would sense political comment."[7] Any event in the now of Spenser and the audience he addresses, including, of necessity, the actualities of Elizabethan policy, becomes perforce a dyslogistic exemplum of his historical enthymeme. Far from distorting those actualities, Spenser's rhetorical strategy in the closing cantos of Book V takes advantage of their assumption as a given by his audience. They permit proof by logos for his conceptual inventio of justice, providing implicit historical exempla of justice as it is upon which the fabulous exempla of justice as it ought to be (Mercilla's court and the exploits of Arthur and Artegall with Belge, Burbon, and Irena) establish their decorum and persuasive resonance. In Spenser's argument, proposals for what ought to be take relevance and validity from knowledge of what is, of concrete ills they seek to remedy. Artegall is unequivocally identified as a rhetorical device, "the instrument" of praise to the "great iustice" of Elizabeth who is addressed as "Dread Souerayne Goddesse" (V.Pr.11), and these exploits have an instrumental function as eulogistic exempla consistent with other exploits by Artegall or any of his co-champions. They differ from other legendary exploits only in the explicitness of their allusion to evidence from the reader's direct experience of a "stonie" age.[8] Furthermore, this rhetorically productive tension between actual and ideal Spenser both projects into episodic narrative and focuses emblematically in the figure of Elizabeth herself. She becomes, structurally, both the actual sovereign co-temporal with the age of stone, culmination of the historical vector of royal progeny descendent from Britomart and Artegall, and antithetically an ideal ultimate term, "Dread Souerayne Goddesse," of the antique age coincident with "Iustice ... high ador'd." Thus knowledge of the actual Elizabeth again lends suasive resonance to topoi of justice Spenser attributes to the ideal Elizabeth:

she embodies with incisive economy in a single, powerfully allusive exemplum the juxtaposed polarities, central to Spenser's inventio, of justice as it is and as it ought to be – the base and apex respectively of the Ovidian spiral.[9]

Topoi of praise are, by definition, always eulogistic, but as Erasmus's *Encomium Moriae* exquisitely demonstrates, faint is not the only sort of praise to damn, or at least blame, its object.[10] The dynamics of decorum dictate that the rhetorical effect of encomiastic topoi are contingent upon occasion and audience, and it is a committed advocate of justice, not a sycophantic apologist, who would confront his sovereign with idealized transformations of her actual policies before an audience who recognizes the transformation; an audience, moreover, which includes the sovereign herself. If merely to curry favour were Spenser's purpose in the closing cantos of Book V, then simple prudence would enjoin his silence on Elizabethan policy, not its atypically, therefore emphatically, transparent allegorization. We must assume a very foolish Elizabeth indeed who would mistake Spenser's trans-figuration for a self-portrait. Demonstrably, neither sovereign nor poet was a fool.

I dwell at such length on this issue of interpretation not to discredit the arguments of historical allegorists but to place their evidence in its rhetorical context, lest a narrow focus on Spenser's contemporary exempla in Book V eclipse the strategy they serve and an accomplished advocate of justice be mistaken for an indifferent historian. Such selective perception accounts, at least in part, for a critical tendency to devalue the significance of Book V: "While Book IV arouses the least interest, Book V has been judged the simplest and remains the least liked."[11] Yet Spenser, on the evidence of rhetorical structure in the Proem, conceived of justice as a virtue of primary, even pre-eminent significance, "Most sacred vertue of all the rest" (V.Pr.10.1), containing and completing all previous virtues. This discrepancy of evaluation between author and critic narrows perceptively in work on Book V examining moral and ethical issues, particularly the allegorical studies of Anderson, Aptekar, Bieman, Dunseath, and Fletcher. They tend to find more depth and complexity in Book V than historical allegorists precisely because their approach engages aspects of Spenser's inventio that fall outside the purview of strictly historical analysis. By choosing to treat justice as an entity compounded of interdependent virtues, not of statutes, processes, and instances, Spenser of necessity invokes moral topoi. He thereby preserves consistency of inventio with previous books. Concomitantly, by choosing to draw heavily upon allusive historical exempla as proof for his inventio of justice, he again accedes to an obvious decorum, acknowledging that this "polliticke" virtue evidences itself particularly in the dynamic of civic orders, both within themselves and amongst each other. Rhetorical analysis, therefore, offers no basis for privileging or precluding either the moral or the historical approach to Spenser's allegory: it can only caution against application of one to the exclusion of the other.

3   ARTEGALL'S ETHOS

Allegorical potential, available to either approach, inheres rhetorically in Artegall's quest, which carries the burden of dispositional proof in Book V. As the Proem announces at its conclusion, a place of emphatic prominence, Artegall is explicitly "the instrument" of praise whereby Spenser courts Elizabeth, adopting a stance of humble supplication, "thy basest thrall," before an object of ostensibly social but specifically transcendent courtship in her position as the deputed instrument of Divine judgment: "Dread Souerayne Goddesse, that doest highest sit / In seate of iudgement, in th' Almighties stead" (Pr.11.1–2). Her position, however, is one where "magnificke might" requires the significant addition of "wondrous wit" to render judgment "righteous" and warrant praise (Pr.11.3). To praise this carefully qualified, idealized Elizabeth is to praise justice, with whose deified prosopopeia Iustice she is made structurally coincident in the Proem.[12] As the instrument of praise, Artegall, through his exploits, anatomizes the constituent attributes of justice abstracted into the ultimate term occupied by Queen and Goddess. His quest in praise of justice demonstrates its topoi.

This model of Artegall's function as instrument, however, inverts the actual structure of demonstration in Book V. Like the other books, it is neither treatise nor encomium, but a secular fable: the conventions of quest involve a process of demonstration by the quester directly opposite to that of the orator, a process of inductive discovery, attribute by attribute, not one of deductive anatomization.[13] Spenser, in his persona as orator-narrator praising the Dread Souerayne Goddesse, begins with a fully comprehended inventio of justice that Artegall and the reader have yet to discover. Orator and quester, therefore, simultaneously court the same object, Justice; for the poet, however, both creatures (orator and quester) serve as the instrument whereby he courts a meeting of minds with his readers. The success of this courtship thus depends fundamentally on the ethos of Artegall, and those who judge Book V to be "simplest" and "least liked" characterize an unpersuaded reaction to "the Champion of true Iustice" himself (V.i.3) as well as to the historical allegory he facilitates.

"The basic problem of Book V is evident enough," summarizes Judith Anderson with admirable concision, "justice is the most inclusive and exalted moral virtue in *The Faerie Queene*; the Book of Justice is the most comprehensive Book, drawing together the central symbols and concerns of earlier Books; yet Artegall ... seems the most disappointing and ineffectual hero in the entire epic."[14]

Notwithstanding, his legend is no less charged with pathos than that of any other champion. It informs a mission replete with topoi from fabula. A child of the forest, unaware of his destiny to found a line of kings, nurtured by the goddess Astraea in the final days of her sojourn among mortals and trained by her "In all the skill of deeming wrong and right" (i.8), Artegall lives among wild beasts and practices his skills on brute creation until, arriving at manhood and charged by Gloriana to deliver the rightful kingdom of the fair Irena from usurpation by the giant Grantorto, he ventures forth to be tested in the human world accompanied by a magical helper, the invincible Talus, and equipped with Chrysaor, a super sword, like Talus, of divine manufacture. Divine armory, rustic origins, the nature and goal of his marvellous adventure, all exert pathetic enticement to identification with Artegall and enhance this pathetic appeal with ethos derived from allusive similarities to the "legende" of Redcrosse.

Indeed, a comparison of the two champions at the outset of their quests gives the ethical advantage to Artegall. He has training and experience backed by the authority of Astraea where Redcrosse has none, and he receives a recommendation in superlatives denied the fledgling knight of holiness from the narrator, who identifies Artegall with Bacchus and Hercules (V.i.2) and echoes the Proem in asserting justice to be an unexcelled virtue common to all honourable knighthood: "Herein the noblesse of this knight exceedes, / Who now to perils great for iustice sake proceedes" (ii.1). Furthermore, the Proem to Book V, unlike that to Book I, gives anticipatory ethos in its dramatic topology of cosmos-lost to a hero who would set himself to counter the momentum of such universal calamity "for iustice sake" by evoking a lively sense of the "perils great" he faces and the great issues at stake in the spiralling disintegration schematized by Ovid's cone.

Ethos functions persuasively in classical rhetoric either because of the respect due the source of an argument or because of the advocate's performance in presenting an argument; in the former case ethos is granted on the basis of reputation, while in the latter it is earned. Clearly, respect is due Artegall for the importance of his mission and his credentials to undertake it, but there is always a danger that his performance will fail to justify his glowing introduction, and those who find Book V simplistic, or unlikable, or both, reflect disappointed expectations. Artegall's performance fails to persuade such readers that either he or, in consequence, the concept of justice his actions argue warrants consent to the pre-eminent significance and moral authority Spenser asserts to be their due. Disappointed expectations, however, are ambiguous evidence for the rhetorical analyst since they may be symptoms of a rhetor's indecorous execution or, equally, of an auditor's indecorous expectations. Such evidence begs the prior question of what expectations are, in fact, appropriate; a vexing, and alas far from simple, or simplistic, question in Book V.

The comparison Spenser invites of Artegall with Redcrosse initiates complexity. At the outset of their respective quests it favours Artegall ethically, but this advantage seems inconsistent with their subsequent development. Redcrosse gains ethos as an epic hero and surrogate for general humanity only because his topoi of good intentions and physical prowess as a hero of fable are discredited over the first nine cantos of Book I through their demonstrated inadequacy against the anti-exempla of holiness. If the comparison creates expectation of a parallel development in Artegall's legend, it is certainly disappointed, for his exploits, even his defeat by Radigund (V.v.12–15), do not discredit the efficacy of physical prowess, either his own or, more particularly, the power he commands through Astraea's creature Talus, a figure whose incorruptibility, invincibility, and immunity to human passions inform topoi more decorous to fabula than epic. The champion of justice, in short, contrasted against the champion of holiness, appears caged within the captivating pathos of fairy tale without access to the persuasive ethos of epic.

4   TALUS

Unquestionably, his melding of fabula with allegoria in the exemplum of Talus presents Spenser with strategic difficulties. "Talus" evokes by allusion Plato's Talos (*Minos* 320C), the brazen one who defends the integrity of laws inscribed in brazen tablets and thus both incorporates metonymously the letter of the law and enforces it. Lotspeich suggests that Talus represents the "testamentum" of law given, according to Comes (1616,II.ii), by Astraea before her departure.[15] He is styled "true guide of [Artegall's] way and uertuous gouernment" (viii.3) but his actions in the narrative demonstrate only the function of enforcement. He subdues Sanglier (i.23), forces entry to Munera's castle and executes her (ii.21–6), executes the giant demagogue and disperses his mutinous mob of adherents (ii.49,53), disperses the tormentors of Terpine (iv.24), wreaks such havoc in

Radigund's army that she is forced to seek vengeance through single combat with Artegall (iv.44,47), disperses Dolon's would-be assassins (vi.30), forces entrance to Radigund's city after her death and is prevented from working total slaughter on her people only by the "very ruth" of Britomart (vii.35–6), captures the elusive Malengin and flails him to death (viii.16,19), scatters the oppressors of Burbon (xi.47), routs the mob to rescue Burbon's lady (xi.59), forces an amphibious landing against Grantorto's army and scatters the counter-attack (xii.5–7), restrained from total slaughter this time by Artegall (xii.8), reveals "hidden crimes" in searching out lingering thieves and rebels "gainst lawfull gouernment" from Grantorto's toppled regime (xii.26), and is again restrained from taking vengeance on Envie, Detraction, and the Blatant Beast by Artegall (xii.42–3). Eulogistic attributes when applied to a code of law – and tolerable in the simplistic commonplaces of fabulous pathos who nightly advocate the Hollywood heroic on our flickering screens – topoi of incorruptibility, immortality, invincibility, and indifference to the flux of passion produce a highly unstable and ambiguous response when embodied dramatically in an exemplum instigating this catalogue of violence and destruction. Our response is particularly ambiguous given the context of allegoria demanding ethical judgment rather than its suspension to allow a vicarious release of primal emotions, however "law-abiding" their pretext.

Before concluding that his execution of the allegoria on Talus is indecorous, however, it is essential to recall that Spenser's subject in Book V is justice, not law, and Talus is not the champion of justice but his servitor. Justice entails, as the encomium to the "Dread Souerayne Goddesse" specifies, both "magnificke might" and "wondrous wit," with the former, by implication, in servitude to the latter. Talus corresponds in function if not in etymology less to the Talos of Plato's *Minos* than to a corporate synecdoche for the class of "Auxillaries" in *The Republic*,[16] who function in Plato's fabula on justice only to execute the wisdom of the Philosopher King. As a collective entity without individual purpose or advantage, they act not from reason but by conditioned reflex and their scope of action is limited to protecting the integrity of the just state (not simply enforcing its minimal law code) by reaction against those, unjust by definition, who threaten it from within or without. The elaborate schemes of indoctrination, training, genetic control, and communal economy that Plato concocts in *The Republic* (II 375A-IV 427A; V 457A-471B) to mould an entity that will react as one and to assure its incorruptibility, invincibility, perpetuation, and freedom from all acquisitive motive save that for honour, and all passion save unwavering courage,

Spenser accomplishes in a single stroke with Talus, the iron artifact. Talus has neither parent nor issue to favour, lacks acquisitive or appetitive needs, and is "programmed" only to react against male-factors with wrath and implacable force under the command and restraint of Astraea or her delegates.

By allusive identification with this ideal classical locus of law and its enforcement, Talus both takes on ethos and asserts more explicitly than either *Minos* or *The Republic* that the law-code is an artifact – and of iron, not gold or even brass – which may serve justice but only with proper safeguards and is therefore not identical with jus-tice. "The ideal," Fletcher notes, "is not laws codified into total uni-formity and rigor, but a flexible system always responsive to the promptings of man's deeper instincts toward equity."[17] Through the complementary narrative functions of Talus and Artegall, Spenser distinguishes both law from justice and "magnificke might" from "wondrous wit" and argues that the two pairs are cognate. Talus remains a fixed exemplar of law and might, but his fabrication gives Spenser room for Artegall to develop through narrative sequence as an exemplar of justice and wit by initially subsuming, then tran-scending, Talus to take on attributes of equity and mercy in his structural development as courtier to Britomart and Mercilla respec-tively. Narrative sequence thereby mimics logical consequence: the letter of law or "justice absolute" embodied metonymically in Talus is logically prior to equity and mercy, since the letter must exist before it can be ameliorated.[18]

This narrative constellation of power in servitude to wit again conforms to the Platonic model of the just state as a metonym of the justly ordered tripartite soul in which the spirited and appetitive elements function under control of their rational complement.

> O Sacred hunger of ambitious mindes,
> And impotent desire of men to raine,
> Whom neither dread of God, that deuils bindes,
> Nor lawes of men, that common weales containe,
> Nor bands of nature, that wilde beastes restraine,
> Can keep from outrage, and from doing wrong,
> Where they may hope a kingdome to obtaine.
> No faith so firme, no trust can be so strong,
> No loue so lasting then, that may enduren long.   (V.xii.1)

Spenser's narrator cites Burbon, Geryoneo, and Grantorto as exempla in proof of this enthymeme expressed as a discovered epiphonema (or summary conclusion), but any other villainous anti-exempla from the previous eleven cantos provide equal proof: the enthymeme is a principal assertion of Spenser's *inventio* on the subject of justice, encapsulating the burden of its Proem in the final canto of Book V. Injustice defies all sources of order: divine, civic, and natural. Arising from intemperance, it breaks continent controls that bind, contain, and restrain acquisitive appetites to destroy the principles of holiness ("faith" xii.1.8), chastity ("loue" xii.1.9) and friendship ("trust" xii.1.8), thus necessitating that justice encompass all previous virtues to counter their common antagonist. While unreason threatens any of these virtues and "wondrous wit" is their appropriate champion, the threat specific to justice arising from injustice lies in irrationality directing "magnificke might" toward the dissolution of civic order, the condition at the degenerate base of Ovid's cone. In turn, these topoi of injustice establish criteria for dramatic exempla of justice.

> Who so vpon him selfe will take the skill
> True Iustice vnto people to diuide,
> Had neede haue mightie hands, for to fulfill
> That, which he doth with righteous doome decide,
> And for to maister wrong and puissant pride.
> For vaine it is to deeme of things aright,
> And makes wrong doers iustice to deride,
> Vnlesse it be perform'd with dreadlesse might.
> For powre is the right hand of Iustice truely hight.   (V.iv.1)

The narrator echoes commonplaces of humanist ideology, likely derived from Pico della Mirandola's *Oration on The Dignity of Man*.[19] Any act of free will requires harmonious concert between the knowledge to act, the volition to act, and the power to act: the just man lacks freedom as surely as the unjust man enslaved to passion and unreason if his "skill" to "deeme of things aright" and his volition "to maister wrong and puissant pride" lack the "powre" to act accordingly. Faith, by contrast, need command no physical power to be free, nor need temperance, chaste love, and friendship. By inviting a comparison between the legends of Redcrosse and Artegall, Spenser sets this specific difference against the common ground among justice and its constituent virtues. Expectations produced by the comparison are thus indecorous if disappointed by the failure of the legend of justice to follow the legend of holiness in discrediting physical prowess. Modulation of "magnificke might" from an instrument of fairy tale pathos to one of ethos and logos results from contextualization rather than discreditation: Artegall's potential of wit and will requires Talus's power to actualize that potential in free acts of justice. That Talus cannot remain a creature of fairy tale is perhaps the most ominous spin-off from Ovid's spiralling cone.

5 ARTEGALL AS COURTIER

Talus is a static exemplum, a programmed artifact, whose suasive function on the subject of justice is limited to proving its essential need for an inscribed code of law and the power to enforce it. On Artegall, therefore, falls the major rhetorical burden of Spenser's demonstration. Like champions of the other virtues, he is not static but dynamic, and his legend, like theirs, provides a linear sequence of dramatic encounters that project a hierarchical structure of argument as courtship. Occupying the apex of the hierarchy are ultimate terms coincident with the goddess Iustice. These include not only Gloriana and Astraea, who make Artegall's courtship both social and transcendent, but also Britomart, object of erotic courtship, identified in the Proem with Iustice as the antitype of Busirane and surrogate for the virtues demonstrated in the four previous books.

Artegall has already assumed a position of humility and supplication before Britomart in emblematic tableau at the structural point centering the three books which chronicle their courtship (IV.vi.22–3), and they remain effectively frozen in their emblematic attitudes of courted and courtier until the beginning of Book V when Artegall reappears, embarked on the mission for Gloriana in service to Astraea which estranges him from Britomart and delays their marriage. His mission, therefore, re-animates the frozen tableau; Artegall's courtship of justice is one with his courtship of Britomart, and becomes by implication the pre-requisite condition for marriage with Britomart. Books III and IV establish marriage ideally as a locus structurally equivalent to the ultimate term of both chaste love and friendship. There courtship is resolved not by its termination with one party absorbing the other but by its perpetuation in a reciprocal dynamic of sacrificial motives between complementary equals, each retaining integrity as an individual: the reciprocal dynamic emblemized in the mythic allegoria of the Garden of Adonis (III.vi).

In its contrast with this emblematic configuration at the centre of Book III, the central tableau of Book IV, with Artegall prostrate in a posture of servitude before Britomart, anticipates graphically the imbalance which Artegall's quest must correct in Book V, and demonstrates that Britomart's finding of Artegall at the mid-point in Book IV does not mark the end of her quest. She finds the lover imaged in Merlin's glass but not the husband envisioned in Merlin's prophecy, the co-occupant of the apex from which depends an ordained issue of kings. To occupy that apex, Artegall must rise to equivalent status with Britomart as exemplar of his appropriate virtue. Thus the completion of Britomart's quest is dependent upon Artegall's successful completion of his and reciprocally, as the events of Book V demonstrate, again in its central cantos (vi and vii), the completion of his quest is dependent upon her.

This structure of reciprocal dependencies generates a highly complex, broadly resonant rhetorical dynamic focused in those central cantos on Radigund and Isis, and adequate examination of the argument it projects must await my next two chapters. My purpose here is to establish the precedents affecting Artegall's ethos at the structural crux where "Left to her will by his owne wilfull blame," Artegall succumbs to Radigund (V.v.20.2) in a failure of wit, not of might, which draws Britomart into his quest. Artegall's exploits in the sequence preceding this narrative crux constitute, at least superficially, successful exercises of wit and power. Thus apparently eulogistic demonstrations of justice in sequence lead to a dislogistic consequence, and the analytical problem is to infer a topos justifying this paradoxical logos. What is it that Artegall demonstrates in these episodes if it is not justice? What argument is projected in their paradoxical sequence?

Artegall begins his demonstration of justice and re-starts his courtship of Britomart with yet another echo from Book IV: he re-encounters Sanglier, his first opponent at Satyrane's tournament (IV.iv.40). Artegall and Sanglier give each other no recognition as former opponents, demonstrating by logos that the two encounters, although occurring in successive books, are structurally coincidental rather than dramatically sequential and mark the same point of Artegall's courtship. That point is homologous with the lowest stages of Artegall's countervalent ascent against the Ovidian vector of civil disintegration. Here the knight takes on his first attributes of regeneration by countering among "wyld beasts ... With wrongfull powre oppressing other of their kind" (i.7) the parody of justice expressed in the bromide "whatever serves the interest of the stronger," advocated by Thrasymachus in *The Republic* (I 338–9). Since Sanglier takes his motivation from the Thrasymachian principle and takes his name from the French for wild boar, Artegall's first exploit in the human world occurs structurally at the same level of ascent as his "experience / Vpon wyld beasts" (i.7). He transcends that level and transits fully out of the animal world by weighing and rejecting not only trial by combat, the human procedural equivalent of identifying right with might, but also "Sacrament" and "ordele" as means of resolving disputed claims because "ill perhaps mote fall to either side" (i.25).

He thus asserts justice in the human realm to be both the antithesis of Fortune and the appropriately human province of wit, of judgment based upon the rational evaluation of evidence.

"Sacrament," "ordele," and "blooddy fight" abrogate the necessity for judgment by providing a spurious certainty. In the absence of certainty, legal judgment becomes rhetorical, depending upon proof by ethos, pathos, and logos: indeed, "forensic" or law-court rhetoric had been accepted as one of three general classes of rhetoric since Aristotle's codification of the subject. Artegall's successful exploits in the sequence preceding his failure of wit against Radigund invoke this rhetorical quality of the forensic. He and Talus counter threats to public order arising from force, fraud, or theft and correct inequities in dealings among private parties. The narrative, like a record of courtroom proceedings, focuses on statements of claim and counter-claim or a bill of indictment germane to each case, and records the magistrate's decision together with any resulting disposition or punishment. The knight and his servitor of enforcement act as instruments of law, handling a varied docket of violations against an implied juridical code: to wrongfully seize a squire's woman as replacement for the one you have beheaded; to extort by threat tolls from travellers on the public ways and invest profitably the gains; to incite to anarchy; to violate the rules of ceremonial tournament; to impersonate another and claim what is due them; to steal a knight's horse; to abrogate by force your brother's dower rights.

Artegall's function in these cases intensifies their rhetorical character. Only with Amidas and Bracidas does he simply hear the evidence and render a decision; in the others his actions represent varying measures of advocacy.

6   REFUTATIO: THE GIANT WITH SCALES

It is in the central episode of this sequence, however, in a trial-by-combat of wit against the Giant with scales, that Spenser gives Artegall his most extensive and demanding advocatory role. Like Despaire, Busirane, Mammon, and Acrasia, the Giant is a propagandist voicing the refutatio to Spenser's inventio. Indeed, the Giant employs the same focal enthymeme as Spenser, one asserting dissolution in the natural and civil orders.[20] "Like as the sea (which plaine he shewed there) / Had worne the earth, so did the fire the aire, / So all the rest did others parts empaire. / And so were realmes and nations run awry" (ii.32). Since he "undertooke for to repaire" the "empaire[d]" ancient order and wields a counterfeit of Astraea's "righteous ballance" (i.11.9), the Giant represents himself in Artegall's role, and the ensuing debate engages rival champions of justice advocating rival conceptions of the virtue they champion. The Giant's initial strategy, in common with all Spenser's refutational propagandists until Mutabilitie, is one of pathos. His promise to "reduce vnto equality" all "things" by equalizing the weight of natural elements (ii.31) and by levelling social classes through an entropic dispersion of "all the wealth of rich men to the poore" (ii.38) repeats Mammon's utopian seductions and appeals to the appetitive motives of those who "hope by him great benefite to gaine, / And vncontrolled freedome to obtaine" (ii.33).[21] In response, Artegall's argument derives from the antithetical *inventio* which conceives the just order of nature, the state, and the soul to be a hierarchy not a plane, and his strategy is ethical not pathetic. Nature, he argues, by evoking scriptural ethos, is the subordinate creature of God, its separate elements given their relative weight and place "In goodly measure, by their Makers might" with each restrained to maintain its place in the order (ii.35). His opponent has the will and may have the power to re-order creation, but Artegall echoes God's response to Job's complaint against divine justice by asserting that the Giant lacks the knowledge (ii.34). When restraints and determinants imposed by omniscient will are withdrawn from the equation of creation, the product is chaos not cosmos, and the just rule of Providence becomes the arbitrary tyranny of Fortune: "All change is perillous, and all chaunce vnsound" (ii.36.7).[22] The just state and the just soul correspond to the hierarchical order of cosmos, where "Such heauenly iustice doth among them raine, / That euery one doe know their certaine bound" (ii.36.1–2). "Vncontrolled freedome," therefore, is an oxymoron: the Giant is enslaved by lack of knowledge to "surquedrie" and the appetite for power (ii.30) just as the "vulgar" who "flocke" to him are enslaved by the domination of appetite for gain over the restraining voice of skeptical reason articulated in Artegall's advocacy. "Licentious lust; / Which proudly did impugne her sentence iust" (V.iv.2.4–5), as the narrator asserts, is the enemy of justice as well as of all previous virtues.

In attempting rebuttal against that voice of skeptical restraint, the Giant is constrained to supplement pathos with proof by logos. The processes of tide and organic decay (ii.37), together with topographical ascendency of "mountaines hie" and "towring rocks" over "lowly plaine" and "deepest maine," become exempla of inequities in nature equivalent to and confirming the inequities of social hierarchy: "Tyrants that make men subiect to their law" and "Lordlings ... that commons ouer-aw" (ii.38). Artegall responds by asserting the indecorum of the Giant's exempla as proof of inequity, since tidal and organic processes are reciprocal (ii.39.4–41.2) and topographical differences, if they have any decorous relationship to social distinctions, more readily support than discredit gradation in the civic order: "The hills doe not the lowly dales disdaine; / The dales doe not the lofty hils enuy" (ii.41.3–4). Indeed, he argues, all the Giant's exempla prove Artegall's hierarchical inventio, since natural process and topography exemplify divinely ordained order in both cosmos and state:

> He maketh Kings to sit in soueranty;
> He maketh subiects to their powre obay;
> He pulleth downe, he setteth vp on hy;
> He giues to this, from that he takes away.
> For all we haue is his: what he list doe, he may.   (ii.41.5–9)

To turn your opponent's argument against him is the most potent form of refutation in debate, and Spenser gives his advocate a clear victory. Artegall uses to his advantage not only the Giant's exempla but also his emblem of justice, the scales. He forces the giant to prove, with his own instrument, that right and wrong cannot be weighed in balance: no quantity of wrong on one scale, even when supplemented with the Giant's "puissance strong" will balance right on the other (ii.46), and quantities of right cannot be weighed against each other since, being indivisible, neither right nor truth is quantifiable: "For truth is one, and right is euer one" (ii.48.6). The Giant's scales thus provide exempla to prove Artegall's enthymeme, an enthymeme which repeats and expands upon the import of his rejecting "Sacrament," "ordele," and "blooddy fight," all of which, like the Giant's scales, deny with their indecorous certainty the rhetorical nature of judgment.

> But in the mind the doome of right must bee;
> And so likewise of words, the which be spoken,
> The eare must be the ballance, to decree
> And iudge, whether with truth or falshood they agree.   (ii.47.6–9)

Here, the rhetorical genre of debate itself, as well as its content, amplify the rhetorical components of wit. Judgment is an act of mind interpreting the product of mind, words. To interpret justly, the judging mind must process knowledge not simply of law but of right and wrong, good and evil, truth and falsehood. These are the topoi to be applied by those who sit in judgment to the exempla of words given as testimony. From an interaction of topoi and exempla the judge must formulate by inference a decorous enthymeme, the "doome of right."

Only divine justice has no need of rhetoric. God is omniscient and omnipotent: in God all systems are closed, all things are certain. Spenser's stress on the rhetorical nature of Artegall's first exploits serves, like the preoccupation of those exploits with law and enforcement, to locate the knight structurally at the base of Ovid's degenerate spiral, estranged from the apex of ideal justice he courts. That estrangement is finally unbridgeable: man can never be God. Artegall, however, can acquire attributes predicated on divine justice by courting identity with the virtues taken on cumulatively by Britomart, since those virtues incorporate, from all previous books, topoi of right and wrong, good and evil, truth and falsehood. Essential to the rhetorical imitation of divine justice, such topoi realize an ideal in human virtue and as arbiters of judgment provide the optimum possibility that human justice might approach by mimesis the certainty inherent in divine wisdom. Artegall's argument against the Giant by appeal to the divine order of cosmos as the model for the just state and just soul anticipates the juridical topoi of Dame Nature on Arlo Hill and, like his other successful exploits, demonstrates his potential to court ideal justice by demonstrating both his rational understanding of its essential nature and his will to be its advocate.

7 PSYCHOMACHIA: ARTEGALL'S TOPOI

His subjection by Radigund, however, demonstrates contrarily that Artegall's self-governance by rational will is vulnerable to usurpation by his appetites, and this disorder mirrors its metalepsis in the civil disorders exemplified by the antagonists he takes on in his initial successes. Examples of Artegall's own intemperate passion are frequent in these episodes and ominously qualify the ethical persuasiveness of his success. At the sight of Sanglier's beheaded lady he "flam'd with zeale of vengeance inwardly" (i.14.7); against Pollente he becomes identical with the villain: "They each at other tyrannously flew; / Ne ought the water cooled their whot bloud, / But rather in them kindled choler new" (ii.13.2–4). He becomes "incenst" at Bragadoccio's insults and is restrained from violence only by the knight of temperance (iii.36). Thus Artegall takes on his own potential for injustice in the anti-exempla he takes on as opponents, and against this potential in his opponents he is ineffective. Therefore, even before his failure of self-governance against Radigund, Artegall stands collocated with his opponents at the degenerate base of Ovid's cone where laws and their enforcement impose from without the order once ideally maintained internally by the self-governance of all "during Saturnes ancient raigne" when "all loued vertue." Accordingly, in the central episode, he wins the debate against the Giant, but neither the Giant nor his adherents is persuaded by appeal to reason. Failing to restore rational order by wit, Artegall has recourse only to preserve order in the state by might: Talus "shoulder[s]" the Giant off his prominence into the sea (ii.49.8–9) and disperses the "lawlesse multitude" (ii.52.1) "mutining, to stirre vp ciuill faction, / For certaine losse of so great expectation" (ii.51.4–5).[23]

Hough finds "these brutal and summary methods" to be "faintly malodorous" as a means to "settle what is after all a real debate," and Alpers thinks Spenser's purpose is pathetic: "Spenser seems to expect us to relish the violence and fearfulness of Talus' power."[24] Talus acts, however, only after the debate is settled, and the judging spectator disciplined in rhetoric who recognizes Artegall's victory can hardly relish evidence of the failure of his advocacy in debate to obtain its purpose. The Giant dies "Like a ship, whom cruell tempest driues / Vpon a rock with horrible dismay" (iii.50.1–2), a commonplace echoing Britomart's love-sick complaint (III.iv.8–10) to evoke the ship as a metaphor of the soul piloted by passion rather than reason and driven toward destruction on the treacherous seas of Fortune.[25] Appropriately, the Giant is destroyed by the very chaos of passion he would create in order to manipulate and does in the event unleash through the "tumultuous rout" of his "lawlesse" followers.

The law's exaction may be decorous, but its decorum only highlights the absent resolution of psychomachia between intellect and appetite called for by Artegall's victory in debate, and reveals retrospectively an equivalent indecorum prevailing in each of Artegall's initial encounters. His legal wit and the power of law he commands serve to counter the public effects, not the metonymous "priuate" cause of injustice, the disorder of the mind engendering the words that are the subject of judgment. Artegall's success in these episodes demonstrates his potential to court justice and exemplifies the basic constituents of that virtue; his failure leaves him undistinguished from Talus and anticipates the subsequent demonstration through Radigund and Britomart of the higher attributes he lacks. In Artegall, as in his opponents, law is symptomatic of estrangement from the justice he courts.

6 Radigund, Britomart, and the Rhetoric of Psychomachia

Radigund is the common antagonist of Artegall and Britomart; an anti-exemplum, therefore, of justice, chastity, and their ideal marriage. Artegall's subjection to her diverts him from his mission. In the emotionless words of law delivered by Talus to Britomart, Artegall is vanquished "Not by that Tyrant, his intended foe; / But by a Tyrannesse," words whose brutal candour the highly emotional Britomart takes as euphemistic: "badly doest thou hide / Thy maisters shame, in harlots bondage tide" (vi.11). Despite their harshness, neither the legal nor the erotic version distorts Artegall's position: he is in violation of his duty to Gloriana, his service to Astraea, and his commitment to Britomart. All three have become coincident in Radigund, who thereby structurally displaces the goddess Iustice as ultimate term; before her Artegall assumes the posture of courtier pledged in fealty to her "law" and "lore" (iv.49.2–3).[1] His boast to Terpine echoes allusively Redcrosse's ominous call for vengeance against Despaire:

> I will not rest, till I her might doe trie,
> And venge the shame, that she on Knights doth show.
> Therefore, Sir Terpin from you lightly throw
> This squalid weede, the patterne of dispaire,
> And wend with me, the ye may see and know,
> How Fortune will your ruin'd name repaire.   (iv.34.3–8)

Artegall's naively confident boast underestimates the might he will "trie" and overestimates the ease with which "dispaire" may be "lightly" thrown aside. It not only identifies justice with the appetitive motive of vengeance but also evokes allusively Redcrosse's "rash ... doome" in confrontation with Despaire (I.ix.37), thereby intensifying the irony of Artegall's strictly eulogistic expectations of "Fortune" in defiance of both reason and his own experience. The consequent incontinence of his bargain with Radigund defies Guyon's counsel of temperance and enslaves Artegall to fortune as a causal prelude to his enslavement by the Amazon: he submits the issue of which law he will serve, Astraea's or Radigund's, to the mutable sovereignty of fortune in trial by combat, the parody of justice his own reason had weighed and rejected to mark his ascent from the animal to the human realm of action. In purporting to champion justice while motivated by his own passion for "greedy vengeance" (v.14.9), Artegall was already acting under the law and lore of Radigund; already in thrall to the dyslogistic attributes she exemplifies.

Radigund's rhetorical significance lies in the allusive range of dyslogistic topoi she demonstrates to be inherent in Spenser's inventio of justice, and the allusive echo in those topoi of cognate exempla from previous books. The duplicitous Clarin's assertion that Radigund "was not borne / Of Beares and Tygres, nor so saluage mynded" (v.40) confirms what it refutes, and locates Artegall structurally beneath the coincident starting points of his courtship in Books IV and V: a "saluage knight" among "wyld beasts" but subject to, not correcting, their "wrongful powre oppressing others of their kind" (i.7.8–9). Under Radigund's law and lore he has descended, in effect, to the base of an inverted hierarchy representing injustice, the demonic mirror-image to the virtue he courts, and it is Radigund, not Astraea and Britomart, who occupies that locus of courtship.

Radigund is thus analogically coincident with Busirane, and the narrative sequence projects that conjunction. By assuming his attributes through elocutional and dispositional parallels, Radigund contains Busirane, who is himself a metonymic attractor for the dyslogistic antagonists who precede him sequentially and so by logos lead to him consequentially. As the instrument of Artegall's condition, "lost" from his "selfe" and his "discretion" (1v.26), she, like Busirane, assumes allusively the ethos of Despaire, whose "squalid weede" Artegall ironically bid Terpine "from you lightly throw" (iv.34–5). Redcrosse succumbed to the spell of Despaire because his conscience, the very source of his potential redemption, would not let him deny his sins, and Artegall falls under the thrall of Radigund because his just nature, again the source of his potential redemption, will not let him deny the contract he has made. Like Despaire, too, Radigund is in thrall to her own nature: her unruly passions follow the "licentious libertie" of mutable fortune, moving like Artegall's from vengeful to erotic lust in a mutation she blames, like Terpine and Artegall, on a providence she labels "vniust" (v.29.7–9).

In a condition of domestic servitude, "a womans slaue" (v.23.5), Artegall becomes the object of erotic courtship by Radigund through the instrument of her appropriately faithless servant, Clarin, whose rhetorical strategies, "Armies of louely lookes and speeches wise," echo the rhetoric of Phaedria and Mammon: they seek to charm Artegall into identifying the bondage of marriage to Radigund with "freedom" from servitude under her (v.32.7–9). By advocating marriage as "maisterie," not mystery, and so rejecting the reciprocal dynamic of union between two equal complements who remain two while becoming one, Radigund functions as the female counterpart of Busirane and, "halfe like a man" (iv.36.8), becomes a dyslogistic parody of the hermaphroditic emblem of chaste love and ideal marriage.

Object of this advocacy and captive in the house of Radigund, Artegall parallels the roles of both Amoret and Britomart in the house of Busirane. Unlike Amoret, he earns his release before Britomart effects it by resisting the ordeal of fraudulent wit and arbitrary force (v.48–50; 56), and their re-union is a union of equal exemplars of chastity and concord, common adherents to an ideal of marriage each has proven individually in separate trials of advocacy endured in isolation.[2] Their renewed and extended estrangement during Artegall's enslavement, and their juxtaposed encounters with primary anti-exempla of precedent virtues embodied cumulatively in Radigund, recapitulate and recontextualize the elements of their courtship and provide the focus of rhetorical analysis in this chapter and the next.

2   BRITOMART AS A ELEMENT OF STRUCTURE

Britomart's importance to Book V has gained some recognition in allegorical interpretation by several commentators, notably Aptekar, Bieman, Dunseath, and Fletcher, who in varying degrees take account of her dispositio in the middle cantos, concentrating particularly on the vision in Isis's Church. While I concur in the centrality they afford Britomart's vision, I will argue in this chapter that these commentators and other of Spenser's best readers have been led by rhetorical inconsistencies into consistent mis-reading of the Isis-episode and hence of Britomart's demonstrative function; indeed, Britomart's vision offers a *locus classicus* for the interpretive consequences of fragmentation in rhetorical analysis. The vision warrants its central place because it constitutes a second instance in Book V of refutatio, engaging Britomart against a more dangerous opponent than Artegall's giant with scales: I contend that in Isis's Church Britomart, cotemporally and coincidentally with her co-protagonist in Radigund's dungeon, engages also and again the suasive force of Busirane. To make my case for this alternative reading of the vision, I must establish its context by grounding Britomart's function in Book V on its sequential continuity with her demonstrative functions in Books III and IV.

Reunion between Artegall and Britomart is consequent upon Britomart's defeating Radigund in battle (vii.24–34), an event Spenser delays through the two central cantos of Book V during which Britomart battles her own jealousy (vi.11–19) and defeats Dolon's attempt on her life (vi.20–40) before she experiences her vision in the temple of Isis (vii.1–23). Thus the structure of narrative sequence itself presents proof by logos that these episodes are necessary to both Britomart's victory and the attainment of Artegall's ends: they function less as a digressio on Artegall's courtship than its continuation, with Britomart as a surrogate, co-protagonist of justice whose erotic and transcendent motives complement and reciprocate Artegall's.

This sequential logos linking Britomart to Artegall projects a locus of analogy attracting details of elocutio. She is mistaken for Artegall by Dolon "chiefly" because Talus has become her guide and servitor (vi.34); she battles Dolon's sons "on that perillous Bridge / On which Pollente with Artegall did fight" (vi.36.6–7); she duplicates Artegall's posture on the eve of battle with Radigund (iv.46) by setting up her pavilion on the plain before Radegone with Talus on guard (vii.26). Other details of elocutio, however, forge identifications with Radigund as well as Artegall. The prosopographia depicting Britomart's mind before (vi.3–7) and after (11–15) Talus brings news of Artegall has particular resonance focused in an extended similtudo which compares her to "a wayward childe" who "kicks, and squals, and shriekes for fell despight" (vi.14). Here the unruly child joins the froward, disloyal servant, the knight in servitude, and the tyrannous woman among Spenser's commonplaces of disorder depicted in the domestic hierarchy of Radigund.

Of course, we forgive the recalcitrance of a child awakened from sleep by "fearfull dreames," and the depiction of Britomart's troubled, distrustful, ever-changing mind invites eulogistic pathos in

recognition of common human experience through its tone and commonplaces of comic love-lore. Britomart's childishness, however, carries structural implications of ethos which the pathetic tone
accentuates rather than mitigates. In its topoi of passionate mutability, the depiction echoes Britomart's love-sick state in Book III before
the outset of her mission to become champion of chastity and court
Artegall. The image of Artegall made her "sad, solemne, sowre, and
full of fancies fraile" (III.ii.27); it awakened her from sleep "with
dreames ... of dreadfull things" (III.ii.29) to be comforted in the arms
of her nurse, Glauce (III.ii.30). Her fear of self-identification with
Narcissus, expressed in the lament to Glauce (III.ii.44), she actually
realizes when she goes "to her chamber ... like a solitary cell"
(V.vi.11) and "[does] her self torment" (vi.13.4) with false images of
Artegall that mirror her own mind (V.vi.12). Her actions recall
Glauce's question "why make ye such Monster of your mind?"
(III.ii.40.2), just as her reversion to topoi of complaint (vi.12.1) evokes
again a formal exemplum of irrationality from Book III. Such allusions return Britomart structurally to the infancy of her courtship,
making her coincident with Artegall in his recidivistic subjection to
the "saluage" law of Radigund, and reinforce identification with
Radigund herself who, like the young Britomart, perceives "her fancies wound" (V.v.44) as a threat to the integrity and freedom of her
"warlike stowre" (cf. III.ii.5.3,6.3). The topos of child and adult thus
establishes an instrument of ethical proof through its inherent principle of decorum: actions and attitudes eulogistically appropriate to
a child become dyslogistically inappropriate in an adult.

Equally, the topos informs a transformational motif between binary
opposites that provides a flexible structure highly accommodating to
analogous polar pairs, and thereby generates the multiple parallelism
of allegoria. Any number of terms could be substituted without
absurdity for Britomart's child state, each implying an appropriate
adult state as its antithesis: naive, pre-feminine, irrational, faithless,
and infantile-regressive are among the possibilities, and the terms
chosen have tended to determine the allegorical interpretation of
these central exploits in Book V. For the rhetorical analyst, however,
it is the structural, not the psychological function of the child-adult
topos which commands attention. Through the devices of elocutio
making Artegall and Radigund coincident with Britomart at the child
pole of the topos, Britomart takes on the attributes of her coincident
exempla. Enthralled by intemperance to jealousy, a state symptomatic
of acquisitive not sacrificial motivation, she is the exemplar of chastity enslaved to its anti-type. Captivated as a frustrated courtier by
despair, back in the cave of Care with the jealous and deprived

Scudamour (IV.v)[3], she succumbs to the distorted pathos Busirane tried to exploit against her destined marriage with Artegall, the propaganda that she once resisted so heroically: "Oft did she blame her selfe, and often rew, / For yeelding to a straungers loue so light, / Whose life and manners straunge she neuer knew" (vi.12.5–7).

The culmination of these central episodes brings the polar inversion of the exemplifications and identifications with which they began. Britomart takes on Radigund as a mortal antagonist, estranging herself from the Amazon as she overcomes estrangement from Artegall. She thereby frees both Artegall and herself from identification in common thralldom to distinct metonyms of Despaire (Radigund and Busirane respectively), while re-establishing her identification with Artegall as an exemplary adherent to the ideal union of chastity and friendship, to marriage as mystery. Britomart's narrative exploits in these episodes preceding her encounter with Radigund provide a transformational dispositio between the poles. This dispositio demonstrates an inventio that melds Spenser's most intense concentration of generic topoi from psychomachia with those of heroica and fabula, as Britomart reiterates, through a reflexive struggle between her acquisitive and sacrificial volitions, both the conflict of Artegall with Radigund and her own courtship of chastity.

3   DOLON

Her struggle with jealousy in the first episode (vi.1–19) establishes the psychomachaic mode of the sequence. Having with "vnquiet fits / Her self there close afflicted long in vaine" (vi.15) she finally takes the step rationality might have dictated earlier and leaves her "solitary cell" (vi.11) to ascertain the facts of Artegall's capture from Talus (vi.17). Her response to Talus's report, however, is pathetic not rational, "soddaine stounds of wrath and grief attone" (vi.17.6), and, acting with a wordless immediacy of emotional response precluding reasoned decision, she undertakes a rescue mission dedicated to "fierce auengement of that womans pride" (vi.18), a motive no less acquisitive or more sacrificial than her jealousy. Echoing allusively her initial encounter with Marinell, when she also ventured "to seeke her knight," her jealousy and wrath here again are "Both coosen passions of distroubled spright" (III.iv.12), and she quests to take on Radigund in combat, having already taken on, like Artegall, the Amazon's attributes of despair and "greedy vengeance."

In Dolon she takes on and defeats a public exemplum of her private motive, acting both for herself and as surrogate for Artegall (vi.34). I can find no systematic analysis among commentators on this episode. Its placement, however, is significant: in the narrative projection of Spenser's argument, the Dolon incident leads to the incident at Isis's Church and is charged with elements of precedent and anticipation. Echoing Una and Redcrosse, who fail to penetrate the benign disguise of Archimago's rhetoric, both verbal and physical, and accept his hospitality for "timely rest ... now day is spent" (I.i.33),[4] Britomart and Talus fail to recognize behind Dolon's "curteous words" and "modest semblant" (vi.19–20) the threat represented by his "lawlesse" obsession for vengeance. Her "minde" like Dolon's is "whole possessed of one thought, / That gaue none other place" (vi.21.3–4) and she accepts his hospitality "Sith shady dampe had dimd the heauens reach" (vi.21.8). Spenser's allusion to the episode of Archimago identifies Britomart with Artegall as a parallel quester to Redcrosse and correlates with the decorum of psychomachia: Britomart, like Redcrosse, is victimized by false images of erotic betrayal symptomatic of the jealousy and vengeance that define Dolon's obsession. Thus her room in Dolon's house simply recreates the solitary cell in her own house as the scene of restless complaint (vi.26.1–4). Wakefulness and refusal to disarm "till she reuenge had wrought" (vi.23.7) parody her sacrificial motives for armed watchfulness in Busirane's house: they locate her paradoxically in the antithetical position of disarmed and careless sleep that allowed Amoret's capture by Lust and turned Malecasta's bed into a trap. Structurally, therefore, Spenser situates Britomart so as to identify lustful and vengeful appetites as concomitant threats which leave her vulnerable to analogous assaults: "All sodainely the bed, where she should lie, / By false trap was let adowne to fall / Into a lower roome" (vi.27.6–8).

The bed-trap is climactic, marking a diametrical shift in the demonstrative thrust of allusions in Spenser's elocutio. Dramatically, it alerts Britomart to Dolon's treachery; structurally, it moves her analogously from Malecasta's to Busirane's castle, from the child to the adult stage of her courtship in Book III. In "Perceiuing well the treason, which was ment" (vi.28.2), Britomart temporarily escapes the "one thought, / That gaue none other place," and she attains the wakeful state parodied in her previous "restlesse, recomfortlesse" watch. In effect, she recreates her posture in Busirane's castle: "Thus she all night wore out in watchfulnesse, / Ne suffred slothfull sleepe her eyelids to oppresse" (V.vi.34.8–9) deliberately echoes "Yet nould she d'off her weary armes, for feare / Of secret daunger, ne let sleepe oppresse / Her heauy eyes" (III.xi.55.5–7). Similarly, descriptive figures of Britomart's "restlesse" search for "ease" in "sundry chaunge" (vi.26) demonstrate her subjection under the mutable aegis of Fortune:

"she long had sought for ease / In euery place, and euery place thought best, / Yet found no place" (vi.7.1–3). These transform antithetically after the bed-trap. She "stirred not at all for doubt of more, / But kept her place with courage confident" (vi.28), a transformation demonstrating her partnership in the immutable volition of Providence: "But by Gods grace, and her good heedinesse, / She was preserued" (vi.34).[5] In the eulogistic context established by such details of elocutio, vengeance still appears as Britomart's motive: "wondrous wroth, and inly burning / To be auenged for so fowle a deede" (vi.31). The distinction in ethical context, however, anticipates the issue that is central to the trial of Duessa at Mercilla's court (V.ix) by asserting a distinction between just retribution and unjust vengeance. Britomart exemplifies the distinction in her shift of posture relative to Dolon from identification to antagonistic estrangement. Britomart is no longer "possessed"; awakened to the "right wary heede" of reason (vi.31), her perception, like her sphere of action, moves from darkness to light (vi.35.1–4).

Simultaneously, the narrator intervenes to enlighten the reader in a *causa* on Dolon's motivation (vi.32–4), while pointedly noting that Britomart does not share our privileged insight (vi.31.6–7). Dolon, in contrast to Britomart "that neuer euill ment in hart" (vi.31.9), feigns benevolence by "vestiment," "semblant" and "words" (vi.19.8–20.2) but acts from Radigund's motivation, "cankred hate," seeking "shame" to "all noble Knights" (vi.32–7). Unlike the Amazon, however, he shuns open force to act with "treason treacherous" and "guilty wile," dyslogistic inversions of wit, and his witlessness manifests itself not only in the impercipience of mistaken identity, taking Britomart for Artegall on the evidence of superficial appearance but also in his instinctive appetite, both pre-rational and childish, to avenge the death of his son killed during Artegall's battle with Pollente. This appetite negates particularly the human judgment which was Astraea's first principle of justice: "to weigh both right and wrong / In equall ballance with due recompence, / And equitie to measure out along, / According to the line of conscience" (i.7.1–4). Lacking the reader's privileged perspective, as in her confrontation with Busirane, Britomart finds the words of Dolon's indictment "strange," "Yet stayd she not for them" (vi.38). Again, repetition of a device asserts antithetical ethos: Britomart's dismissal of Dolon's false words here exemplifies awakened perception of "right and wrong / In equall balance" weighed as opposed to the impercipience of her "minde ... whole possessed" that "little lust ... ought to heare" of Dolon's deceptively "curteous words" or Talus's explanations (vi.21; 11). In this new state of awakened virtue, Britomart has no need of the narrator's explanations: Dolon's acts bespeak the agent, and Britomart demonstrates the rhetorical components of just wit by applying to his actions topoi not of law but of right and wrong, good and evil, truth and falsehood: topoi appropriate to the exempla of Dolon's guileful treachery. She also executes the resulting enthymeme of judgment herself. As the corporate surrogate of its dependent virtues, she assumes the championship of justice, taking on the functions of Artegall and of Talus, whose executive action she literally "over-rides" (vi.38.4–39.3). In this context, her wrath and its associated images of fire become elocutional signs of righteous zeal antithetical to the dark fires of vengeful jealousy.

The narrator's exposing of Dolon's motivation confirms the decorum of Britomart's judgment and serves, like Spenser's antithetical devices of elocutio, to distinguish between Dolon and Britomart as exempla of vengeance: the former is irrational, appetitive and acquisitive; the latter now rational but hardly sacrificial. Sequence argues consequence by logos: only after the episode in Isis's church and the battle with Radigund do such sacrificial motives emerge, leading to Britomart's resolved estrangement from Artegall and, subsequently, Mercilla's judgment on Duessa.

Since Britomart is first identified with, then estranged from, Dolon, their dramatic conflict alludes by allegoria to a psychomachia within Britomart. The narrative proves by sequential logos that she defeats Dolon's sons, the products of his corrupting nature, in battle only after, and by implication because, she overcomes the products of that corruption in herself.[6] Spenser focuses the significance of this dispositional sequence by setting its concluding battle at "that perillous Bridge, / On which Pollente with Artegall did fight" (vi.36.6–7). The identical setting juxtaposes comparatively Pollente against Dolon and Artegall against Britomart. Dolon is clearly a more subtle, dangerous opponent than Pollente, demanding, as the etymology of their names implies, wit before force to defeat: his appearance belies his nature, he assaults by guileful entrapment not forceful extortion and his bed-trap, unlike Pollente's bridge-trap (ii.12.5–7), operates in darkness against unawakened somnolence and false security. In his indirect strategy and misleading appearance, as well as in his motivation, Dolon projects an exemplum analogous to Radigund not Pollente. Britomart, in her victory on the bridge, demonstrates attributes of justice that both complement Artegall's in his victory over the Saracin and highlight those he lacks in his encounter with the Amazon; attributes therefore necessary to the reversal of his defeat at her hands.

4   ISIS'S CHURCH: THE DECORUM OF RECAPITULATION

Concurrently, Britomart effectively re-courts chastity, moving while in Dolon's house from a posture of careless distraction coincident with her sleeping-state in Malecasta's castle to one of armed awareness coincident with her position in Busirane's house on the eve of her witnessing the Masque of Cupid. Precedential decorum, therefore, determines that by crossing Dolon's bridge Britomart should immediately enter the Church of Isis, the topothesia of which evokes the eulogistic antithesis of Busirane's house,[7] and there experience a visionary dream, under the aegis of Isis (vii.12–16), that again advocates Busirane's illusionist propaganda against the destined marriage with Artegall (vii.22–3).

Spenser's depiction of Isis's "Idoll" (vii.6–8) is a prosopographia allusive of chastity and friendship as well as justice. The disposition of Isis with one foot "set vpon" a crocodile whose "wreathed taile" enfolds its own middle, "so meaning to suppresse both forged guile, / And open force" (vii.6.8–7.1), identifies the iconographic attributes of Isis with those asserted by Britomart in her suppression of Dolon. By the multiple comparisons of icon, Isis attracts through that identification the attributes of the idol of Venus (IV.x.40), itself a recapitulative exemplum of friendship, hermaphroditic emblem of ideal marriage, and anti-ultimate to Busirane's golden Cupid whose left foot suppresses the blinded and submissive dragon of Minerva, protector of chastity (III.xi.48). The allusive scope of Spenser's icon thus covers Britomart's entire career as a courtier, and his distributio of the three analogous idols, Cupid-Venus-Isis, projects through the logos of narrative sequence a grammar delineating their hierarchical order in his inventio of justice. Each accumulates exemplary resonance by juxtaposition with its predecessors in the narrative, and is perforce necessary to the exemplary import of its successors. Sequential priority argues hierarchical inferiority to and logical derivation from successors. As the last term in the sequence, Isis thus attains hierarchical precedence: she becomes an exemplum that recapitulates the interdependency of justice with her precedents, the previous virtues in this series. The same sequential logos also argues that Britomart's courtship of chastity and friendship, affirmed by recapitulation in the house of Dolon, represents stages of ascent in the ultimate courtship of justice. Spenser proves the argument dramatically by making entry into the temple of Isis immediately sequent to, and by implication consequent upon, Britomart's defeat of Dolon, whereupon the champion of chastity and co-champion of friendship appropriately assumes, "prostrate" and "humble," the posture of courtier to Isis.

Britomart's suppliant posture before the statue of Isis invites allusive comparison to the idolatry of Busirane's courtiers before the golden Cupid. Superficial similarities, however, only define a contrast of rhetorical significance. Britomart offers "silent prayers," but offers them ambiguously "Vnto her selfe" (vii.7.9). The ambiguity suggests an identity between Britomart and Isis that seems premature, since Britomart's mission of justice still requires for completion the defeat of Radigund, the release of and reunion with Artegall, and the reforming of Radigund's unjust civil order. That mission, however, is itself ambiguous in its motivation, responsive both to the injustice of Radigund and the suspected infidelity of Artegall; a mission therefore both transcendent and erotic. Britomart's avoidance of the bed-trick in Dolon's house and her victory on the bridge prove her capacity to defeat Radigund, but do not resolve the psychomachia with despair, her "melancholicke" doubts frustrating union in marriage with Artegall (vi.12–13). Before she can complete her mission as Artegall's co-champion of justice, those doubts must once again be confronted as they were in Book III, and the silent prayers addressed "vnto her selfe" are consistent with the mode of psychomachia. They evoke an appeal to the sovereignty of reason, the image and likeness of divinity, for resolution of the disputatious anarchy among her conflicting passions.

Isis is homologous with reason as a sovereign image of divine justice and thus an appropriate co-addressee with Britomart's "selfe" for silent prayers. The divinity of Isis is an invention of "the antique world" (vii.2.1) reflecting the rational discernment without benefit of revelation that "nought is on earth more sacred or diuine" than justice (vii.1–2). Her exemplification of this discerning *inventio*, not her pagan divinity, is the source of Isis's ethos. Accordingly, Spenser both reasserts the topos of correspondent orders from the Proem (V.pr.10) and incorporates within it Isis and the other pagan deities. They become, like reason in the soul and sovereign authority in the state, surrogates for Divine Justice, "rul[ing] by righteous lore / Of highest Ioue." The "lore" of "highest Ioue" stands at the polar antithesis to the lore and law of Radigund:

> Of highest Ioue, who doth true iustice deale
> To his inferiour Gods, and euermore
> Therewith containes his heuenly Common-weale:
> The skill whereof to Princes hearts he doth reueale!   (vii.1.5–9)

Britomart's prayer is rhetorically transcendent but not idolatrous: she courts not a pagan deity but the just order in her soul that Isis exemplifies, and her identity with Isis is only potential. Both this potential for courtship and the estrangement which occasions it compose the ambiguity of "silent prayers" offered "vnto her self".

Furthermore, the ambiguity inherent in Isis herself occasions a further, concomitant identification. In the inventio of pagan reason, "with fayned colours shading a true case" (vii.2.7), Isis becomes the deified exemplum of "That part of Iustice, which is Equity" (vii.3.4). This deification mythologizes the "true case" of her status as historical exemplum, the human consort of Osiris, "the iustest man aliue" (vii.2.9). The obvious analogy between Isis and Osiris on the one hand and Britomart and Artegall on the other involves again both identification and estrangement: the former signify an ideal which the latter court. Isis and Osiris have bridged the distinction between what is and what ought to be, achieving just sovereignty in the state and a harmonious union of complementary functions, of marriage without "maistrie." As ultimate terms they merge attributes of justice with those emblemized mythically by Venus and Adonis in the Garden of Adonis; they generate a hierarchical structure demanding of potential courtiers the complementary virtues of justice, chastity, and friendship as requirements for its ascent. Thus when Britomart prays "vnto her selfe" she courts both the "selfe" and the consort that "ought to be"; her estrangement from Artegall is coextensive with her estrangement from the ideal "selfe" embodied in Isis, and her prayer seeks their common resolution.

The answer to her prayers, the end of her courtship, Britomart envisions as the "amiable looke" and shaken wand of Isis' statue (vii.8.1–4) that, "as it were," animate the inanimate "Idoll." Allusively such tokens evoke the "amiable grace" of Venus's statue (IV.x.56) that encourages union in concord between Scudamour and Amoret, an ambiguous allusion since the estrangement stands unresolved on a matter of justice at the conclusion of IV.x. Britomart's vision also combines the white wand of sovereign authority with the magical wand of peace used by Cambina to resolve discord (IV.iii.42). The resulting complex exemplum figured in Isis asserts as topoi of justice the interdependency among three loci of concord (in the soul, in marriage, and in the state), and the common dependency of such concord on just rule. Britomart's prayers "unto her selfe" provide "priuate" proof for the assertion; "polliticke" proof comes in dramatic sequence through Britomart's subsequent, hence consequent, exploits releasing Artegall from Radigund and reforming the domestic disorder of her state.

5   DREAM-RHETORIC: BRITOMART AS BUSIRANE'S ADVOCATE

The dream vision that succeeds this waking vision fails to accord with the comfortable expectations Britomart perceives in the idol's encouraging gestures, which she interprets "as a token of good fortune" (vii.8.5). The dream leaves her "full of fearefull fright, / And doubtfully dismayd" (vii.16.8–9). It is less an answer to than an elaboration of her prayer, anatomizing through allegoria the discordant elements of her psychomachia. It also locates the specific motivation for courtship within a context reiterating the motivation and evolution of her general career as an erotic and transcendent courtier: "A wondrous vision, which did close implie / The course of all her fortune and posteritie" (vii.12.8–9). Thus her initial appearance in the dream recreates the ambiguities of role from her prayer. She is both transcendent courtier to Isis, "doing sacrifize" in the "linnen stole" of Isis' priests, and Isis herself "deckt with Mitre on her hed" (vii.13.1–3). "All sodainely" her priestly robe is "transfigured" to "scarlet red," and Isis's "Moone-like Mitre to a Crowne of gold": both details of elocutio exemplify the social apex of monarchy. "All sodainely" repeats the locution introducing Busirane's Masque of Cupid (III.xii.3) and Dolon's bed-trap (V.vi.27): it thereby imposes on Britomart's dream the structural and ethical significance of her ordeal in the houses of Busirane and Dolon, identifying it as a crucial retesting of her ethos.

Britomart's identification with the priests asserts the requirements for her courtship of Isis, requirements catalogued in the prosopographia of the priesthood Spenser presents as prelude to the dream (vii.9). The priests' acts of abstemious "sufferaunce" carry scriptural ethos by allusion (Col. 3.5), "proud rebellious flesh to mortify," and exemplify "stedfast chastity, / And continence of life" in accord with "the vow of their religion." In a mythical *causa* explaining their dietary discipline of abstinence from wine (vii.10.3–11.9), Spenser then identifies a synecdochal exemplum of disorder, the rebellion of the giant sons of Earth against the gods, with the psychic rebellion of appetite against reason: "the mindes of men with fury fraught ... Ne within reasons rule, her madding mood containe." The priests simultaneously counter the giants' rebelliousness and court Isis through exercise of holiness, chastity, and continence; these virtues thus become derivative attributes of Divine Justice, the ultimate term of cosmic order for which Isis functions as surrogate. Britomart's identification with the priests reiterates her role as the recapitulative exemplar of the virtues they inform, while configuring those virtues as stages of ascent leading to her courtship of justice.

Her transfiguration "all sodainely" from priest to monarch (vii.13.4–7) collapses Britomart's past and future courtship into a single moment of ascent; however, the ascent is purely social and lacks erotic or transcendent attributes. Her reaction, appropriately, is one of appetitive pathos: she "ioyed to behold / Her selfe, adorn'd with gems and iewels manifold" (vii.13.8–9). The end of courtship she envisions is merely acquisitive and distorts by suppression the ends mandated in Merlin's prophecy: she views as "felicity" her status of queen, but a queen, like Radigund, without consort or issue. She thus identifies herself with Isis only as a social ultimate, manifesting the attributes of neither domestic nor political concord. Psychic disorder, the source of this visionary distortion, appears immediately in the rebellious and seductive actions of the Crocodile (vii.15.6–16.6) heralded by tempest and flames, the elocutional images of cosmic and erotic chaos that coloured Busirane's tactics to equate the end of sacrificial courtship with subjection to acquisitive tyranny. Britomart's envisioned crocodile proves, again by pathos, the same enthymeme. From a posture of submissive subordination under the foot of Isis/Britomart, the Crocodile awakes "in horrible dismay" and "gaping greedily wide, [does] streight deuoure / Both flames and tempest" (15.5–6), appetitively internalizing their chaotic potential. His posture then changes from submission to rebellion, and the sequence implies a causal logos. "Swolne" like Orgoglio and the Earth-mother of rebel giants, "with pride of his owne peerelesse powre" (15.7), he courts appetitively to attain sovereign power by devouring Isis/Britomart, but is beaten back by Isis's rod, an instrument implicitly figuring equity but functioning simply as hierarchical power (15.9). So restrained by a "part of Iustice," the Crocodile again changes tactics and shifts his posture from rebellious social to suppliant erotic courtier: "Tho turning all his pride to humblesse meeke, / Him selfe before her feet he lowly threw, / And gan for grace and loue of her to seeke" (vii.16.1–3). Seduction succeeds where force failed; Britomart/Isis "soone enwombed grew" and bore a "Lion of great might" that "did all other beasts subdew" (16.6–8). In her vision Britomart thus gains consort and issue, but her consort is the instrument of chaos, his courtship appetitively motivated, and their issue is a bestial tyranny "of great might." The dream transfigures Artegall's eulogistic attributes (his courage before the forces of disorder, his posture of humble submission as the courtier of justice and Britomart, and his conquest of tyranny among the beasts) into dyslogistic exempla of incontinence and unchaste appetite issuing in the antithesis of justice.

Where Britomart stood unmoved by the pathetic appeal of Busirane's rhetoric, her "perplexity," "fearefull fright," and doubtful dismay testify to the suasive role of pathos in her response to this visionary parable. She interprets it as a reiteration of Busirane's argument, and this time is persuaded. Pathetic proof works to greatest effect when addressing the already-converted, and Britomart's "felicity" at reigning without consort or issue, as Spenser's rhyme suggests, is simply her "perplexity" in potential (vii.14.1, 9). It demonstrates Britomart's emotional predisposition to distrust Artegall's motives and so fear their fruitful union as a surrender of chastity to lust, a surrender reflected in the erotic pun on "doubtfully dismayd," and of sovereignty to tyranny in a betrayal, not a fulfilment, of the providential destiny envisioned by Merlin. Helmet "vnlaste" (vii.8.8) and "deeply drown'd" in "soft delight / Of sencelesse sleepe" (12.6–7), Britomart assumes a posture antithetical to her armed wakefulness in the houses of both Dolon and Busirane, a dramatic causa withdrawing awakened reason from battle and leaving the field to the mutable fortunes of passion. When passion rules unopposed, Britomart demonstrates its tyranny. She becomes advocate as well as audience of Busirane's case, using in proof his tactics of unjust distortion to make Artegall into a dyslogistic exemplum and Isis into a social absolute stripped of the complementary union with Osiris which defines her transcendent stature as the embodiment of "that part of Iustice, which is Equity."

Accordingly, Spenser associates the ascendency of the rational faction in her psychomachia with Britomart's wakened state, and exemplifies the voice of reason in the "greatest" and "grauest" of Isis' priests (18.5), who advocates a contradictory reading of the vision. He interprets the Crocodile as a eulogistic embodiment of Artegall identified with Osiris: "The righteous Knight, that is thy faithfull louer, / Like to Osyris in all iust endeuer" (22.4–5); he judges Isis and Britomart to be, by analogous association, common embodiments of equity in complementary union with their respective consorts (vii.22.6–9). The Crocodile's actions against tempest and flame thus become exempla of sacrificial, not acquisitive, motives in defence of Britomart and her "iust heritage" (23.1–4), acts of chaste courtship leading to union in equity not "maisterie" (23.5–6), and issuing in a son whose "Lion-like ... powre extreame" combines the forces of law and equity, not tyranny and lust.

Rhetorically, therefore, Britomart's experience in Isis's temple constitutes, like Artegall's confrontation with the Giant demagogue, a refutatio adapting generic topoi of the debate. Such topoi capture both the projection of contending factions constituting Britomart's psychomachia and the reiteration of Busirane's counter-advocacy against the case for chastity advocated in Book III. Since both sides in the debate use the same features of the vision itself as exempla, proof by logos is neutralized as a source of suasive advantage: victory goes, therefore, to the Priest of Isis who counters pathos with an ethos that is unassailable, since he shares, and in a sense epitomizes, the ethos of holiness, temperance, and chastity shared by all of Isis's priests and enhanced by his stature as "greatest" and "gravest" of her courtiers. His performance validates his reputation: he (unlike Dolon) discerns Britomart's identity through her "queint disguise" and demonstrates knowledge of her parentage and mission (vii.21) to establish that knowledgeable discernment characterizes his inter-pretation of the vision. Furthermore, his interpretation accords with the authoritative vision of Merlin that discerns providential will in history, and no ethos based on performance exceeds that of the prophet whose assertion history confirms. Britomart, like Spenser's audience, applies the criteria for victory in formal debate and recog-nizes that one case has been proven while the other has not. And unlike the Giant's riotous followers in the first refutatio of Book V, Britomart does acknowledge the voice of awakened reason as victor over the suasive distortions of her appetitive psyche (24.1–2).

Britomart's dream and the Priest's interpretation epitomize prob-lems of analytical inference that develop when readers fragment Spenser's rhetorical projection of his argument. For such readers the ethos of the Priest becomes absolute – indeed, so absolute that com-mentators on this dream almost without exception anticipate his authoritative interpretation and "pre-read" his eulogistic exegesis of the crocodile back into Britomart's dream-narrative, as if the dream all along meant what the Priest says it means, thereby pre-empting, indeed making invisible, Britomart's own interpretation. In effect, such readings attribute the dream to Spenser rather than Britomart. Rhetorically, however, the dream is a dispositio of Britomart's inven-tio: she is effectively the narrator, like Scudamour in IV.x, and the dream comes with, indeed is, her dyslogistic interpretation of Arte-gall as consort.[8]

The debate thus elaborates the psychomachaic elements of "trou-blous thought" expressed in Britomart's prayers "vnto her selfe" and answers their ambiguously directed petition for resolution of psychic discord.[9] The Priest's victory proffers what she petitioned of "her selfe," and in acceding to his suasion, Britomart takes on the ethos, as she takes on the rational perspective and structural function of the greatest and gravest of Isis' courtiers. She assimilates, perforce, his attributes of holiness, temperance, and chastity with his wisdom, and so reiterates the necessary components of transcendent justice, the "polliticke" virtue whose co-champion as surrogate to Artegall she has become through private psychomachia.[10]

6 BRITOMART / RADIGUND / PENELOPE

"Righteous" judgment requires not only such merging of might and wit (Pr.11) but also the subordination of the former to the latter, of law to justice, and the sequence of Britomart's exploits in Book V projects in narrative this fundamental topos of Spenser's inventio. The battle with Radigund inaugurates the final stage of his demonstration: it both tests and confirms the resolution of psychic discord Britomart gains under the aegis of Isis and her priest. Radigund embodies the anti-ultimate of Isis, the sterile social ultimate without consort or issue in Britomart's visionary distortion of both Merlin's prophecy and Isis's statue, and like Britomart in her dream, Radigund mimics Busirane's propaganda against chaste marriage, transfiguring Artegall literally, as Britomart did imagistically, into a dyslogistic inversion of exemplary knighthood. Thus Britomart's accusation against Radigund at the height of their battle, "Lewdly thou my loue deprauest" (vii.32), might be addressed to the image in her mirror. The "yron prison" wherein "her wretched loue was captiue layd" (vii.37) ambiguously defines both Britomart's heart and Radigund's dungeon where "her owne Loue" (38.1) lies captive: the capitalization of the latter "Loue" distinguishes a psychic motive for courtship from its object. Thus the heart-quake which awakens Britomart's powers of rational discrimination simultaneously breaks open Radigund's prison and reveals Artegall beneath the "disguize" of "womanishe attire" (37.7; 38.2), a physical manifestation of the psychic "dys-guise" which "deformed" (38.2) Artegall's ethos through the Busiranian distortions which Britomart re-advocated "vnto her selfe" in dream-vision.

> At sight thereof abasht with secrete shame,
> She turnd her head aside, as nothing glad,
> To haue beheld a spectacle so bad:
> And then too well beleeu'd, that which tofore
> Iealous suspect as true vntruely drad,
> Which vaine conceipt now nourishing no more,
> She sought with ruth to salue his sad misfortunes sore. (vii.38.3–9)

Her "secrete shame" anchors the complex ethical exemplum involved in the ambiguities of this reunion between Britomart and Artegall. Artegall's "womanishe" disguise is indeed a decorous elocutio ornamenting his "dys-grace," since his failure of wit results in the posture of subjection in servitude to Radigund that gives his costume its significance, a posture expressing graphically the structural inversion of his transcendent courtship from divine to demonic ultimate terms. He is the idolater, Radigund's "grace" is the dyslogistic parody of the end Artegall courts variously in Irena, Astraea, Gloriana, and Britomart. Britomart's passion for revenge recreates in private motive Artegall's failure of wit and clothes him in Radigund's false colours, while in public action she recreates his trial by combat with Radigund and succeeds in might where he failed. They function as complementary exempla, hence their "shame" is identical, but his is public, her's "secrete"; she is "abasht" and turns "her head aside" to demonstrate recognition ("at sight") of her secret self in his public shame. "Ruth" marks the point of recognition, pivoting between the then of estrangement, when she "too well believed" to be true the untrue "vaine conceipt" nourished by "iealous suspect," and the "now" of perceived identity penetrating the mere appearance of estrangement; between the then of appetitive and the now of sacrificial motives: "She sought with ruth to salue his sad misfortunes sore." As his surrogate, she reenacted his battle with Radigund and gained victory where he failed, but in so doing merely replicated the fairy-tale prowess of Artegall's initial exploits with Talus. And she, too, submitted this crucial test of justice to the fortune-bound, brutish ethos of trial-by-combat rejected by Artegall to signal his ascent from animal to human realms of action: "As when a Tygre and a Lionesse / Are met at spoyling of some hungry pray" (vii.30). "Chaunce" (32.2) not wit renders Radigund vulnerable to her "wrothfull" *Doppelgänger* who responds reflexively: Britomart "Stayd not, till she came to her selfe againe, / But in reuenge ... / She with one stroke both head and helmet cleft" (vii.34.2–6).

Beheading is a favoured method for dispatching major villains in Book V, a witty application, perhaps, of the Platonic causal analogy between public and private disorder confirming that tyrants suffer decapitation civically in consequence of their having lost their heads psychically.[11] As the House of Alma testifies, the head is the bodily equivalent of social and transcendent ultimates, "lifted high aboue this earthly masse," and "likest ... vnto that heauenly towre, / That God hath built for his owne blessed bowre" (II.ix.45; 47); in this "stately Turret" dwell the sage courtiers who counsel "faire Alma, how to gouerne well" (II.ix.48.9). By simply decapitating the head of Radigund's misgoverned state, Britomart ambiguously demonstrates the necessity for wit to temper might without herself exemplifying its possession. By virtue of might in conquest, she assumes Radigund's social eminence as sovereign, an assumption which merely extends to closure her identification with the Amazon: she gains schematic equivalence with the anti-Isis of her distorted vision in the church, not with the consort of Osiris. Thus the point of ascent in her public courtship of justice, corresponding to the moment of suasive identification with the wit of Isis's Priest, comes not with the beheading of Radigund but the subsequent, hence consequent, severing of identification with and assumption of sovereignty over Talus. His "reuenge" by slaughter of Radigund's subjects, being indiscriminate, is an act of Fortune, "Like to an hideous storme" (vii.35.9), not of Justice.

> And now by this the noble Conqueresse
> Her selfe came in, her glory to partake;
> Where though reuengefull vow she did professe,
> Yet when she saw the heapes, which he did make,
> Of slaughtred carkasses, her heart did quake
> For very ruth, which did it almost riue,
> That she his fury willed him to slake.   (vii.36.1–7)

"Ruth" frees Britomart from subjection to fortune and allows her to recognize a fellow subject in Artegall, and implicitly in Radigund who prevailed only "Whilest Fortune fauourd her successe in fight" (41.7).

The narrator compares Britomart's "great wonder and astonishment" at Artegall's physical metamorphosis to that of the "most chast Penelope" at her first sight of the returned Odysseus (vii.39). This allusive exemplum echoes the Proem to Book IV (IV.Pr.3) and is highly evocative rhetorically. The simile expresses Britomart's changed perception, the product of "wonder and astonishment": she discriminates within Artegall's anti-heroic appearance an exemplum of exceptional heroic ethos made vulnerable to the mutability of fortune by reliance on physical might alone against the enemies of justice: "Could so great courage stouped haue to ought? / Then farewell fleshly force; I see thy pride is nought" (40.8–9). Her sententia echoes the epiphonemic conclusion drawn by the narrator from the failures of Redcrosse against the "spirituall foes" of holiness (I.x.1). Both allusions attract redemptive attributes to Artegall's ethos, and simultaneously complete the redemptive untangling of Britomart's ethos from identity with Radigund, since she functionally replicates both Arthur in his rescue of Redcrosse from Orgoglio's dungeon and Penelope in her surrogate role for the absent Odysseus, defending just order at Ithaca and concord in marriage by maintaining the private virtues of chastity and temperance in herself.

Distinctions are as significant rhetorically as similarities in these juxtapositions. Penelope confronts a king disguised as a beggar; Britomart a knight disguised as a woman. Both disguises signify hierarchical inversion, but while Odysseus's loss of stature is voluntary and social, Artegall's is involuntary and transcendent, figuring in social topoi a loss of moral identity as the knight of justice and the dependent virtues which comprise justice. Because of this distinction, the allusive comparison implicitly favours Artegall ethically: his moral apocalypse after the mortal suppression of his vital identity under thrall to Radigund, his Calypso and his Circe, assimilates but surpasses as transcendent courtship the erotic and social apocalypse of Odysseus.

Another distinction within these coalescent exempla, however, introduces qualifications making Artegall's implicit advantage only potential. Like Odysseus he has proven his resurrected wit against a seductive Calypso-propaganda corrupting marriage from mystery to "maisterie"; unlike Odysseus he has not established just order in the state. Nor, unlike Penelope and Isis, has Britomart. By taking on and defeating Radigund's propaganda in a battle of wit, Artegall complements Britomart's victory by might and demonstrates narratively, as he takes on structurally, the attributes of temperance, chastity, and friendship exemplified by Britomart in both her knightly quest and its psychomachaic reiteration. Their individual struggles in isolation from each other thus issue in their identification as metonymic containers of the virtues demonstrated in previous books. The temporal priority of those virtues in the narrative asserts by sequential logos their deductive priority; they are dependent and necessarily prerequisite attributes of justice. As the figure of Ovid's cone argues, however, the dependency of these virtues consists precisely in their mere potentiality in the civil order; in their need of the virtue both additional and complementary, represented by Spenser's concept of justice, to effect their realization in the public realm. The fact that reunion and reconciliation between Artegall and Britomart no more represents an end to their role as courtiers than does recognition for Redcrosse on Contemplation's mountain reasserts through narrative sequence the principal topoi figured in Ovid's cone. Britomart and Artegall are merely potential exemplars of perfected Justice; neither has yet demonstrated realization in the civil order of the dependent attributes each has courted individually and both exemplify metonymously.

The fact that Britomart is the first to do so, demonstrating "true Iustice" by "changing all the forme of common weale" in Radegone (42.4), carries rhetorical significance conditioned by its obvious corollary that Artegall does so subsequently and independently. They do not act in concert, although Britomart tries to act as consort by forcing her newly-created magistrates to "sweare fealty to Artegall" (43.1–6). For Artegall, however, their reunion, unlike that of Odysseus and Penelope, inaugurates an involuntary sojourn, a hiatus imposed by the privations of his captivity under Radigund ("him to refresh"); effectively a continuation of that captivity and merely a interlude between separations. The apical point of union in marriage for Artegall and Britomart is coincident with justice as an ultimate term, and any resolution of erotic estrangement between them now would indecorously assert their combined resolution of the analogous transcendent estrangement from, hence their successful courtship of, justice. Since marriage is ideally a reciprocal dynamic of complementary equals, Britomart and Artegall must attain this resolution independently as a prior condition of union, and the fact that Britomart attains this transcendent status first, ascending from "Princess" (42.3) to "Goddesse" (42.8), demonstrates by sequential logos that her reform of Radegone is a prior necessity for the successful completion of Artegall's courtship of Justice. That mission, in turn, controls the resolution of her quest to fulfil both Merlin's vision and her own in Isis's church. "Equity" is a "part" of "Iustice" (vii.3.4): they are reciprocally dependent, and for Britomart to attain identity with the ultimate term figured mythically in Isis requires not only her own rejection of the rival, consortless social ultimate figured in Radigund but also Artegall's attaining the complementary stature figured in Isis's consort, Osiris "the iustest man alive, and truest" (vii.2.8–9).

7 Artegall, Mercilla, and Calidore: The *Ethos* of Fortune

1 ARTEGALL/OSIRIS/ARTHUR

By treating Artegall's ethos as a function of Britomart's, Spenser demonstrates the scope and summative significance of the virtue he exemplifies in its champion. To prove that "Iustice" is a metonymia of all previous virtues and fulfills them in the public realm, Artegall must complement and fulfill in that realm Britomart's accomplishments in its psychic and domestic analogues. Their separation in the narrative is thus a matter of decorum, a feature of dispositio contingent on Spenser's inventio of justice. Britomart subordinates possessive to sacrificial and ethical motives. She acts "wisely" (vii.44.3) in "seeing" that present physical estrangement from Artegall is a necessary condition of their destined marriage without "maisterie": "Seeing his honor, which she tendred chiefe, / Consisted much in that aduentures priefe" (44.4–5). However, the narrative focus in this passage on Britomart's psyche and its pathetic appeal "full sad and sorrowfull" (44.1) tends to eclipse the fact that Artegall also recognizes the call to "priefe" of "honor"; indeed, he recognizes it first and thereby both takes on Britomart's "wisedome" and anticipates her in "seeing" its application to a wider civic realm because that is his appropriate realm of action. In this mutual recognition of the ethical imperative to resume Artegall's quest they prove their potential for ideal marriage by functioning as reciprocal equals; they become complementary ethical exempla in the narrator's use of Artegall as a eulogistic antithesis to Samson, Hercules, and Antony who, possessed in "minde," abandon their civic mission for "beauties louely baite" (viii.1–3). This allusive topos is an attractor for the mythic parallel of Venus and Adonis in Malecasta's tapestry, and it gives Britomart status antithetical to that version of Venus as well as to Delilah, Iole, and Cleopatra. Her naive refusal to play Adonis to Malecasta's Venus in her first appearance stands in diametric contrast to the "wisedome" of her refusal to play Malecasta's Venus to Artegall in her last, a transformation demonstrating her hierarchical coincidence with the transfigured Venus in the Garden of Adonis, and reiterating, through their common identification in Britomart, the coincidence of that Venus with Isis.[1]

This strategic reiteration at the point of Artegall's separation from Britomart establishes the demonstrative function of Artegall's exploits in the final cantos. The merging of ultimate terms in Britomart positions her potentially in hierarchical equivalence with the female half of the emblematic ideal figured in Isis and Osiris, who have bridged the distinction between what is and what ought to be against the Ovidian vector of injustice: they have achieved just sovereignty in the state and concord in marriage without "maisterie." "In languor and vnrest" (viii.3.5) Britomart awaits analogous fulfilment of her potential through Artegall who must attain coincidence with Osiris. Her withdrawal from the narrative thus asserts Artegall's imperative in subsequent exploits to demonstrate what ought to be in his reciprocal, "male" realm of justice. It is the homology of these patterns that invites charges of historical indecorum from those who ignore the demands of structural decorum and so interpret the ethical idealization in these episodes as allegorical distortion of Elizabethan policy.[2] Rhetorically, however, the nature and function of topical exempla in the final cantos of Book V, including their allusive juxtaposition of what is in the now of current history at the base of the Ovidian spiral against the ideal of what ought to be, are consistent with both the topoi of justice they demonstrate and the development of Spenser's *dispositio* throughout.

The ethical censure occasioned by Spenser's strict adherence to the contingencies of decorum tends to implicate his creature as well, the "champion of true Iustice," since Artegall's attributes must complement, not replicate, attributes of justice associated with his feminine co-exemplars. Britomart together with Mercilla preempt such topoi of pathos as sorrow at parting, "ruth," and mercy to leave "sterne Artegall" (viii.3.1) functionally "ruth-less," with few resources of pathetic appeal until his final exploit when he duplicates Britomart's crucial acts of "ruth" by restraining Talus from the total slaughter of Grantorto's army (xii.8). As Hamilton puts it, "the virtue of justice has imposed limitations on the amount of sympathy the titular hero may generate."[3] For many readers Artegall's lack of pathos accordingly compromises his ethos, and if their response is technically indecorous it is hardly unreasonable. Spenser's narrator, after all, stands firmly with those who, despite what "Some Clarkes ... in their deuicefull art" (x.1) may debate philosophically, know what Una proved as advocate for Redcrosse against Despaire, that justice without mercy is not divine (x.i.5–9).

The immediate context for the narrator's assertion is the trial of Duessa at Mercilla's court where Artegall "for zeale of Iustice" stands "firme" in judgment against Duessa, opposing both Arthur's "fancies ruth" and Mercilla's "piteous ruth" (ix.49–50). Thus compounding the pathetic stress on Artegall's ethos is the re-appearance of Arthur coincidentally with Britomart's disappearance from the narrative action. Arthur joins Artegall in the final demonstration of justice, and his exploits, like Artegall's, represent what ought to be against allusive exempla from current events of what is. As in Book IV, Arthur replaces Britomart in exemplary function as Artegall's complement, and it is he, not Artegall, who assumes Britomart's ethos, leaving Artegall positioned as an exemplar of justice estranged from mercy, "the form taken by equity at the Court of Mercilla":[4] an estrangement projected dramatically in the belligerence of his first meeting with Arthur (viii.9).

Indeed, Arthur's first appearance in Book V is a complex attractor, eliding with those of Artegall and Britomart to argue the continuity of justice with precedent virtues. His entry, like theirs, is sequentially contiguous with the action of Book IV: it replicates in fundamentals his last appearance as a figure of justice in a context of concord, and effectively re-animates his frozen posture, decision unrendered, as both defender of Amoret and judge of Scudamour's case for her hand in marriage. Here he re-enters the action defending the oppressed Samient, whose name and actions mutually express her courtship of concord (viii.21), against the agents of Adicia whose name and actions identify "injustice" with "disdayning all accord" (22.3). Samient then occasions the conciliation of Arthur with Artegall in a scene replicating, in turn, Artegall's recognition encounter with Britomart in IV.vi:

> Tho when as Artegall did Arthure vew,
> So faire a creature, and so wondrous bold,
> He much admired both his heart and hew,
> And touched with intire affection, nigh him drew.   (V.viii.12.6–9)

Their battle preceding Samient's "enterdeale / Of finall peace and faire attonement" (21.7–8) occurs through failure of judgmental wit ["without discretion" (viii.9.2)]; it demonstrates equality of might in contrast to the reciprocity of wit and good will demonstrated in their union:

> So can they both them selues full eath perswade
> To faire accordaunce, and both faults to shade,
> Either embracing other louingly,
> And swearing faith to either on his blade,
> Neuer henceforth to nourish enmity,
> But either others cause to maintaine mutually.   (viii.14.4–9)

Thus their mutual courtship through Samient's agency, by persuasion without advantage (14.4), recapitulates the anatomy of justice and its dependent virtues of "faith" (7), love (6) and "accordaunce" (5).[5] Their exploits together against the Souldan, Adicia, and Malengin (viii.24–51; ix.4–19) in defence of Mercilla and the just order of "her happy state" (viii.18.1) extend this structure of allusive precedent to its focal point in the episode at Mercilla's court, establishing through dramatic sequence the issues of sovereignty at stake in the trial of Duessa.

2   THE SOULDAN/ADICIA/MALENGIN

Spenser depicts the Souldan through a Platonic topos as the creature of his own technology, merely a passenger on a war chariot powered by the "mal-engin" of horses driven by blind appetite for "flesh of men" (viii.28.7) which in the end he is unable to control (39–43).[6] Only the "charret wheeles" and "steedes" challenge Arthur directly (36), and even the "dart" that wounds him owes its efficacy to "some bad sprite" of "th'ayrie wyde" not the Souldan's skill (34.6–7). Yet the Souldan is a formidable opponent precisely because of the idolatrous, appetitive motives he unleashes (vii.19.6–9), motives echoing Busirane's Cupid and personified in Adicia. She "counsels him through confidence of might, / To breake all bonds of law, and rules of right" (20.4–5), and the Souldan expresses her motivation through the "unreined" power of his technology. Scything chariot wheels and "head-strong steeds" (viii.41.1) compose a dyslogistic elocutio, but they are elocutional equivalents of Talus and his flail, and the homology argues that only rational, sacrificial motivation divides the execution of justice from tyranny:

> Thus goe they both together to their geare,
> With like fierce minds, but meanings different:

For the proud Souldan with presumpteous cheare,

. . . .

Sought onely slaughter and avengement:
But the braue Prince for honour and for right,
Gainst tortious powre and lawlesse regiment,
In the behalfe of wronged weake did fight.   (V.viii.30)

The same thin line between eulogistic and dyslogistic motivation occurs literally in the exemplum of Malfont (ix.25–6), drawn through the "Bon" in "Bonfont" to substitute "Mal," and figuratively in the distinction between simile and metaphor dividing Arthur from Adicia. Arthur raves "like to a Lyon wood" (viii.35.5) while Adicia "transformed was" into a Tiger (viii.49.6–9), shedding human stature like a disguise after falling victim to Artegall's assumed guise as an agent of injustice (46.6). A string of similes prior to the transformation defines her dissembled essence in the lexis of radical unreason. Her similitude to "raging Ino," "fell Medea," and the "madding mother" of Bacchus (viii.47) implicates her in the domestic disorder consequent on Radigund's psychic misrule and, together with "as a mad bytch" (49.1) and the ludicrous "like an enraged cow" (46.1), asserts through epitheta the same enthymeme demonstrated by plot-sequence when she goes from thwarted suicide through transformation and transposition in a regression to the state of primal injustice where Artegall began his courtship: "Not fit mongst men, that doe with reason mell, / But mongst wyld beasts and saluage woods to dwell" (ix.1.4–5).

As exempla of injustice the Souldan and Adicia thus resonate with narrative precedents and homologous patterns, and this episode surely functions as something more than an enabling allegorical gloss on the external, topical exemplum of the Spanish Armada. Arthur's need to evoke grace implicates his antagonists here with the unholy Orgoglio and Duessa – their behaviour is wholly intemperate: the Souldan shares the unchaste idolatry of Busirane's court and Adicia replicates the metamorphic radicalism of Proteus, Malbecco, and the Ovidian caricatures in Busirane's etchings while "disdayning all accord." In concert they form a recapitulative exemplum demonstrating that injustice at its primal core subsumes the antitheses of all previous virtues and that the locus of such primal injustice, the "mal-font" of its "mal-engin," lies in the dynamic metalepsis of private and politic appetites.

Aptekar is perhaps not entirely accurate in characterizing this encounter as the first time Arthur has resort to stratagem over simple force:[7] his action against Corflambo's keep involved similar artifice

(IV.ix.4). Nevertheless, Arthur's "thinking best" to "counterfet disguise" (V.viii.25.1) is sufficiently anomalous to accentuate the special ethos of wit at this point in Spenser's demonstration of his *inventio*. "More in his causes truth [Arthur] trusted then in might" (viii.30.9), and at the crises of battle he chooses first prudent strategy (32.1–3) then Grace (37.6–9) over rash physical prowess, thereby successfully courting transcendent Justice: "by heauens high decree, / Iustice that day of wrong her selfe had wroken" (viii.44.6–7).

Both the limitations and dangers of wit reside in the exemplum of Malengin, "So smooth of tongue, and subtile in his tale" (ix.5.6). His prosopographia and the topothesia of his "hollow caue" (ix.10–11) attach topoi allusive of Archimago and Despaire to "wylie wit" (5.1) and his protean regression from man to snake (17.1–19.1) is itself an act of calculated wit not the "franticke passion" of Adicia which it subsumes and surpasses.[8] Here the line between champion and villain is again one of motive. Malengin does not "out-wit" Arthur and Artegall: he falls into their trap but escapes through adroitness that neither "armed knight" could "thinke to follow" (ix.15.8–9). To take on Malengin they must not follow his "leaping" and "dauncing," since to match his "lightness" they would need to shed their armour and thereby "dys-grace" their knighthood. The advantage they hold over Malengin lies in the power Artegall exercises through Talus: the villain is no less sure-footed than Talus but his "yron hooke" (11.2) is no match for Artegall's "yron man" (16.1) with his "yron flayle" wielded with "so huge might and maine" (19.2–3).

However we may interpret these villains allegorically, it is clear that as exempla of injustice they are virtually doublets, each recapitulating anti-exempla of previous virtues. Although neither Arthur nor Artegall is sufficient to counter this injustice without the aid of grace and law respectively, this insufficiency does not diminish their ethos. On the contrary, it functions rhetorically like that of Redcrosse as a component of ethos, discrediting topoi of fairy tale and offering proof that "wondrous wit" must not only recognize the need for grace and law but also resist adopting the law and lore of injustice. Such a resistance inverts the failure of wit that enthralled Artegall to Radigund and thereby advances his courtship of ethical equivalence with Britomart insofar as he duplicates the conditions that enabled her to effect his freedom. The logos of sequence proves that the attributes of wit demonstrated in these exploits are logically prior to those demonstrated in the subsequent structural junction of Arthur and Artegall with Mercilla, forming a tribunal to sit in judgment on Duessa (ix.34–50). Mercilla's court is a locus of justice precisely because her deliberations include both Arthur and Artegall, both grace and law. The issue raised by the trial of Duessa concerns the conditions under which mercy is decorous with justice: for Spenser and his readers it is not Duessa but her judges who undergo the rhetorically significant trial.

3 DUESSA'S TRIAL: THE DECORUM OF REPUTATION AND PERFORMANCE

The prosopographia of Mercilla and the topothesia of her castle, through their common and repeated allusion to Lucifera's "house of Pride," produce a concerted antiphrasis to generate ethos: they use similarities to accentuate differences. The superlative mode expressing Mercilla's setting and appearance is not hyperbole: there is no indecorum between the social (ix.21,27) and transcendent (28–9) elements composing the elocutio of her stature; indeed, rather than aspiring like Lucifera in narcissistic amazement to be "higher than the highest" she is voluntarily accorded attributes of divine power by "high Joue" (ix.31–2). These ceded attributes, however, that "doe by his diuine permission, / Vpon the thrones of mortall Princes tend" (32.1–2), reiterate from Spenser's Proem (V.Pr.10) the derivative nature of all secular power to dispense justice. Despite her stature as an object of courtship, Mercilla is thus herself a transcendent courtier, and her structural function, like that of the Souldan and Adicia, surely involves more than a topical referent enabling transparent flattery of Elizabeth. The elocutio of glory in Spenser's description defining Mercilla as an ultimate term simply elaborates the elocutio and inventio of praise in Samient's superlatives (20.6–9). Her appearance gives credence to Samient's words; the eye confirms the ear (21.1–2), but both are sources of ethos by reputation and, like Artegall, Mercilla must justify reputation with performance.

The ethical necessity for decorum between reputation and performance, however, involves the corollary of reciprocal effect: reputation must be congruent with performance. Hence, by the reciprocities inherent in decorum itself, to discredit the former is to compromise the latter, and the rhetorical dynamic of Spenser's epic becomes increasingly focused on this issue in the concluding cantos of Book V as well as Book VI and the Mutabilitie Cantos. Envie, Detraction, and the Blatant Beast are dyslogistic anti-exempla equally of justice and courtesy, and, like their spiritual sister Sclaunder, of concord: each violates a principle of decorum common to all three virtues. Together they subvert Artegall's courtship and occasion Calidore's; their rhetorical significance in both functions is contingent upon the precedents established in Duessa's trial. Allegoria stresses the particular dependency of Mercilla's court on this decorum between reputation and performance in the just execution of law: Spenser makes Awe (ix.22) the first requirement in preserving the integrity of Mercilla's court as a place of justice. Order "commaunding peace" (23.8) is the second, and together they make possible Mercilla's ethical performance: "Dealing iust iudgements, that mot not be broken / For any brybes, or threates of any to be wroken" (24.8–9). Accordingly, Awe and Order "lead to" their dyslogistic antagonist under constraint, the admonitory, and unforgettable, figure of Malfont "whose tongue was for his trespasse vyle / Nayld to a post, adiudged so by law" (25.2–3) precisely because his "bold speaches" and "lewd poems" violate the necessary decorum that makes reputation the just reflection of ethical performance: "he falsely did reuyle, / And foule blaspheme that Queene for forged guyle" (25.4–5).

Malfont, in short, joins the giant demagogue with scales, Radigund, and Britomart's psychomachaic Busirane as yet another figure of refutatio in Book V, one whose very efficacy as counter-advocate depends upon his being mute until the Blatant Beast's "blasphemous perversion of eloquence"[9] gives him voice, "blatting" in a "thousand tongues" (VI.xii.27–8). Few can experience Spenser's elocutio of the grotesque in Malfont's prosopographia without an empathetic shiver and a consequent sense of ethical ambiguity generated by its juxtaposition, virtually oxymoronic, of physical pathos with negative ethos. This rare effect is intensified here by evoking the ultimate eulogistic exemplum of physical pathos in an icon "grotesquely, obliquely, and incompletely mimetic of the crucifixion."[10] Whatever autobiographical motives might dictate the apparent indecorum between ethos and pathos in the figure of a poet condemned for libels uttered against a queen's juridical reputation, Spenser's structural motive is surely to demonstrate through the provocative exemplum of Malfont the issue of intense focus in canto ix: the problem of commensurate decorum in reconciling pathos with ethos, mercy with justice, which engages Mercilla, Arthur, and Artegall in the trial of Duessa. For Spenser's readers the pathos of Malfont places the ethos of his judges on trial. Since we can harbour no doubts about the guilt of Duessa, we have no reason to doubt Malfont's guilt "adiudged so by law." Spenser has neutralized culpability as a factor in this episode, and proof against his mute testimony that the law which "adiudged" Malfont and ordered his pathos-inducing punishment warrants its reputation for justice thus depends upon evidence in Duessa's trial that pathetic proof receives equitable, or decorous, weight in the proceedings: that our sensibilities were anticipated and given full consideration. Crime and punishment motivate the exemplum of

Mercilla's court only as symptomatic issues of sovereignty: under scrutiny in Duessa's trial is the "thin line" of restraints and determinants that distinguishes just exercise of the power to punish from its tyrannous exercise exemplified in the villainies of Book V.

And indeed, Duessa's case rests entirely upon pathos. Her appearance, "that wretched semblant," arouses "the peoples great compassion" (ix.38) and acts as exemplum for her advocates (Pittie, Regard of womanhead, Daunger from "high alliance vnto forren powre," Nobilitie of birth, and Griefe). They plead not Duessa's innocence but the indecorum of treating her as a object of punishment rather than "great ruth" (ix.45). In contrast, her prosecutors, led by Zele, present a case founded entirely on ethos, their abstract names "proving" the truth of their accusations (ix.43–4). "Iustice" is the last of these in sequence and so by implication their consequence (after Kingdomes care, Authority, law of Nations, Religion, and the Communs); its functioning simply as an element of prosecution, however, rather than one transcendently coevil with Mercilla argues that such a restricted role is consistent with a notion of justice confined narrowly to "breach of lawes" (44.9) and refuted in the ironic succession of success in Artegall's early exploits. It exemplifies only one subordinate component of Spenser's inventio and joins Artegall in graphic positioning at the base of a triad he forms with Arthur under Mercilla. His posture toward Duessa is directly aligned with the stance of Zele, Iustice, and her other prosecutors: "But Artegall with constant firme intent, / For zeale of Iustice was against her bent" (49.4–5). At the other base-extremity of the triad under Mercilla, Arthur aligns himself with the stance of Duessa's defence: "[he] woxe inclined much vnto her part," and "for great ruth his courage gan relent" (46.3; 6). One knight is persuaded by ethos, the other by pathos, to diametrically opposed judgments, a polarity bridged only when Zele, seeing that Arthur favours the defence, "augment[s]" his "fervour" with proof by logos. He calls Ate, Murder, Sedition, Incontinence of lyfe, Adulterie, and Impietie to present direct evidence and sworn testimony (47.7–48.9). None can rely on ethos or appeal to pity: they act rather as exempla demonstrating consequences in the public realm of Duessa's will to disorder, "her wilfull fall" (x.4.7).

Thus, although Duessa stands trial ostensibly for the sort of villainy common in Book V, for wilfully subverting rightful rule by conspiring to "depryue / Mercilla of her crowne" (ix.40–1), her prosecution in both forms, ethos and logos, treats this violation of social courtship as only one consequence of unjust motivations manifested equally in corruptions of erotic and transcendent courtship. She epitomizes Spenser's inventio of justice by epitomizing in her crimes against the state all previous private and public villainies: the "injustice" for which she stands indicted is a cluster of structural components including crimes against holiness, temperance, chastity, and concord. Indeed, here at Mercilla's court Duessa emerges from the pack of villains prowling the first five books of Spenser's epic to become his ultimate synecdochal anti-exemplum of both courtship and justice. He demonstrates through this one dyslogistic figure, as with her eulogistic counterpart Britomart, the interdependence of all previous quests for virtue with the courtship of justice.

The resonance Spenser accords Duessa as a corporate metonymia of injustice stresses the rhetorical significance of her trial, and contests the restrictiveness of readings that implicate her only in an allegoria on Mary Stuart.[11] Through her as surrogate all the enemies of justice not only stand accused, they also participate in a forensic process of advocacy and evidence, of wit and judgment, rather than the fortune-charged procedures of "blooddy fight," "Sacrament," and "ordele" rejected *pro forma* by Artegall to mark his emergence from animal to human realms of justice (V.i.25) but practiced *pro re nata* by all the champions of justice in their exploits prior to the episode at Mercilla's court: "law," Fletcher notes, "is the progeny of trial."[12] What Artegall preached, Mercilla practices; what Artegall courts, Mercilla is. Hence the estrangement of both Artegall and Arthur, "those two strange knights" (ix.34.2), from Mercilla is stressed by repetition (ix.21.9, 24.2, 35.6, 36.2, 37.5.), and the appearance of a commitment to trial by might in their "armour bright as day" initially threatens to disrupt the just order of her court (24.2–5). In sequence, hence in consequence, both knights assume identical postures as her courtiers, "bowing low before her Maiestie" to make "myld obeysance" (34.3–4) and "homage" (35.6). Mercilla's responsive posture, "inclyning her withal" through "chearefull countenance" and "more myld aspect" (34.8,35.9) to "bate somewhat of that Maiestie and awe" (35.7), echoes the "laugh" of the juridical Venus when Arthur and Britomart "hear" Scudamour's "case" for union with Amoret (IV.x.56) and the "amiable looke" bestowed by Isis' statue on Britomart (V.vii.8). Furthermore, in their decorum of reciprocity these gestures of courtier and courted produce another locus of symmetrical persuasion without advantage that characterizes the ultimate term of both chastity and concord in the ideal of marriage without "maisterie." Such fusion of allusive topoi conflates Mercilla's court with the Garden of Adonis, Venus's temple and Isis's church: it takes on their accumulated eulogistic attributes and becomes their topographical synecdoche and surrogate locus.[13] Here, as in the structural inventio of Contemplation's mountain in Book I, but exploiting allusions internal to the epic rather than external to biblical and classical sources, topography demonstrates typology: common topoi, the places of inventio, identify in the dispositio a common-place underlying manifest local differences. Mercilla perforce assumes the allusive resonance of her court, becoming a recapitulative structural exemplum of Venus and Isis and hence assuming, by the logos of sequential priority, hierarchical precedence over the exempla whom she succeeds and incorporates.

In becoming Mercilla's courtiers, Artegall and Arthur thus replicate Britomart's courtship of Isis. When Mercilla invites them to ascend "vp vnto her stately throne" (37.6) the "straunge knights" bridge social and transcendent estrangement to attain not only status over the entire court, equalling Britomart in her identification with Isis's chief priest, but also temporary functional identity with Mercilla herself in the tribunal she forms to judge Duessa's case: "she placed th'one on th'one, / The other on the other side, and neare them none" (37.8–9). Yet this tribunal, however egalitarian it may appear, is actually an hierarchical triad with Mercilla at the apex, a structure distinguishing the subordinated power to judge guilt and innocence, which she delegates, from the sovereign power to punish or pardon which she retains absolutely. Viewed as a logical structure, the triad thus positions Artegall and Arthur as derivative aspects of Mercilla, a configuration readily supporting psychomachaic interpretation of Duessa's trial. The division between and eventual reconciliation of Arthur's "great ruth" and Artegall's "zeale of Iustice" projects through dramatic exempla the inner struggle between the "piteous ruth" of Mercilla's "priuate morall" person and the "iust vengeance" demanded of her "polliticke" person.

While Mercilla subsumes the qualities of both knights, however, there is no resolution of "ruth" and "zeale" within her psyche corresponding to that between Arthur and Artegall. Arthur is persuaded to "repent" his "fancies ruth" and shift his perspective into identity with that of Artegall; "ruth" is eliminated as a factor and, in effect, the base of the triad collapses to the point occupied by Artegall. He contains Arthur metonymically, and indeed so contains "them all" who "loudly call / Vnto Mercilla myld for Iustice gainst the thrall" (49.8–9), yet stands isolated in estrangement from Mercilla as the opening "but" of the next stanza stresses:

> But she, whose Princely breast was touched nere
> With piteous ruth of her so wretched plight,
> Though plaine she saw by all, that she did heare,
> That she of death was guiltie found by right,

> Yet would not let iust vengeance on her light:
> But rather let in stead thereof to fall
> Few perling drops from her faire lampes of light;
> The which she couering with her purple pall
> Would haue the passion hid, and vp arose withall.   (ix.50)

Clearly Artegall has attained identity only with Mercilla's public person. His abrupt polar isolation from her at the very moment when the ethos of his perspective seems triumphantly affirmed by Arthur stresses through peripeteia Spenser's distinction between the concepts of justice demonstrated in the two exempla. From Mercilla, the exemplum who incorporates and transcends all antecedent icons of secular justice and embodies the supreme ethos of that ultimate position, Spenser estranges not only Artegall but "all" who identify "Iustice" only with "iust vengenance" and consider Mercy to be a conflicting alternative to Justice rather than an essential component. Mercilla, "that herein doest all earthly Princes pas" (x.3.2), occupies the social apex structurally coincident with the ultimate term of transcendent justice, precisely because her actions acknowledge that she derives her authority to punish from the Source of Mercy.

By implication it is her capacity for "piteous ruth" that makes her fit to exact "just vengeance." Nothing earthly restrains the power of the sovereign except the sovereign's self-restraint. Justice in the state depends, in Spenser's inventio as in Plato's, upon just order in the soul of the Prince, and the sacrificial motive of mercy in the "Princely breast" is the locus of that "thin line" preserving the body of the state from the tyranny of princely cupiditas.[14] Artegall's being destined to found a dynasty of princes makes this crux of just sovereignty particularly acute and explains Spenser's peripetaic stress on the knight's isolation from Mercilla's private person, an estrangement defining the attribute he must take on in order to complete both his erotic courtship of Britomart, whose "ruth" freed him from self-willed tyranny, and his coincident courtship of transcendent Justice.

4   ARTEGALL'S COURTSHIP AND THE TOPOI OF "PEACE"

Mercilla invites Artegall and Arthur to share her judicial authority from rhetorical motives, courting both their education in, and her reputation for, justice: "that those knights likewise mote vnderstand, / And witnesse forth aright in forrain land" (ix.37.4–5). She is the third and last of Artegall's teachers on the nature of justice, after Astraea and Isis through Britomart, and to redeem his ethos the knight's action against Grantorto on behalf of Burbon and Irena must "witnesse forth" his understanding of their lessons. By taking on Grantorto and overcoming him, Artegall overcomes the failure of wit that enthralled him to Radigund; he thus ascends beyond the point in his courtship of justice that he occupied on the eve of battle with the Amazon. Indeed, the logos of narrative sequence argues that he is able to free Irena from the thralldom in which his failure of wit placed her, a thralldom that duplicates his own even in such details as "squalid garments" and "doleful spright" (xii.12.2–3), because he has freed himself from the thralldom in which he placed himself to Radigund's law and lore. Accordingly, upon freeing Irena he becomes coincident with Mercilla and Britomart at the apex of civil hierarchy, assuming their function as the locus of justice in the state:

> His studie was true Iustice how to deale,
> And day and night employ'd his busie paine
> How to reforme that ragged common-weale.
> And that same yron man which could reueale
> All hidden crimes, through all that realme he sent,
> To search out those, that vsd to rob and steale,
> Or did rebell against lawfull gouernment;
> On whom he did inflict most grieuous punishment.   (xii.26.2–9)

His position of "polliticke" sovereignty is analogous to the sovereignty of reason over appetite and of justice over law: his motive, like that of Mercilla and of Britomart at Radegone, is "reforme" not vengeance. The "yron man" now serves as an agent of reason, searching and selective, exacting "grievous punishment" only as a decorous means subservient to the ends of "true Iustice."

In function and hierarchical status Artegall thus achieves structural identity with the ultimate terms of justice, including ethical equality with Britomart. His courtships – erotic, social, and transcendent – like those of Redcrosse, converge on the coincident point of fairy-tale closure with his victory over the Giant and the rescue of the Princess. Yet his ethos at the end of this fabulaic mission is no more that of a fairy-tale hero than was Redcrosse's. Insofar as Artegall demonstrates only physical prowess, good intentions, dependence on supernatural weapons and magical helpers – all the topoi of daydream questers – he is discredited as a courtier of justice: such attributes prove necessary but not sufficient to define a synecdochal exemplum of the just hero. Indeed, it is really against the enemies of psychic order that Artegall, like Britomart, fights his most crucial battles: the success or failure of his mission to establish the public virtue of justice turns on his prior attainment of the private virtues. Narrative priority figures structural and logical priority; for Artegall, as for Britomart and Mercilla, psychomachia is the prior, hence necessary condition of the battle for public order. Moral hierarchy itself presumes rational order, and justice depends, as the dramatic exempla of Book V repeatedly demonstrate, not on mechanical enforcement of law but on the rational, human act of judgment, an act in which the law's letter is merely one source of topoi in a rhetorical process demanding the discernment to recognize the principles of decorum relating a specific case to general principles which include those championed by Redcrosse, Guyon, and Britomart. Like equity, law is a part of justice in Spenser's inventio, as are grace and mercy: the subject of justice in Spenser's inventio both demands and accommodates a merging of their topoi with those of the private virtues.

That accommodation in the civil order defines the condition of "peace," whose ends sovereignty ideally serves through justice, as the etymology of Irena's name and Artegall's actions assert (xii.25.1–4). The concept of "peace" had long-established transcendent as well as social and erotic resonance in Humanist tradition during the Renaissance, derived from Petrarch's adaptation, particularly in *Il Canzoniere*, of Augustinian topoi. In Spenser's rhetorical structure, "Peace" is the state of absolute reciprocity, of ideal decorum, between "polliticke" and "priuate" motives. At the apex of Spenser's Ovidian spiral "Peace vniuersall rayn'd mongst men and beasts" because "all loued vertue" and "Iustice sate high ador'd with solemne feasts" (V.Pr.9). Thus "peace" expresses in the civil order a state of resolved estrangement between ruler and ruled, sovereign and courtier, in a reciprocal dynamic free of "maistrie".[15]

Within the dynamics of Ovid's cone, however, such moments of resolution are transient preludes to dissolution, as the disjunction between the chaotic spiral opening Book V and the harmonious coda to Book IV synecdochally demonstrates. The "mal-engine" of this dissolution emerges in Book V as the spinning wheel of Fortuna, but its "mal-font" is irrational appetite, the "Sacred hunger" and "impotent desire of men to raine" specified in the epiphonemic assertion of Spenser's principal enthymeme (V.xii.1) and demonstrated ultimately and dramatically in the advocacy of its principal exemplar, Mutabilitie. Artegall's trial by combat with Grantorto, since it is decided by wit rather than chance or might (xii.18–22), becomes a eulogistic counter-exemplum to the fortune-charged combat with other villains, particularly with the synecdochal Radigund. Here the strategies of antiphrasis serve to meld accredited principles of forensic decorum exemplified in the just procedure at Mercilla's court with previously discredited topoi of chivalric tournament – the polar contrast in ethos again determined by and accentuating the distinction between rational and irrational motivation.

Yet the final canto of Book V repeats the disjunction of its Proem. An elocutio of natural rebirth heralds Artegall's arrival to release Irena from Grantorto's thrall, revitalizing her "as a tender rose ... that with vntimely drought nigh withered was" responds to "few drops of raine" (xii.13): the trope echoes those of natural resolution ending Book IV with Florimell's emergence from captivity to revitalize the dying Marinell "as a withered weed through cruel winters tine" responds to spring (IV.xii.34). Since Irena functions metonymously as Artegall's enthralled psyche, the seasonal analogy asserts here, as it does in Book IV and the Proem to Book V (Pr.9.), the congruence of psychic, social, and natural orders: By resolving his disordered reason Artegall brings to resolution Irena's disordered kingdom and the "vntimely" cycle of nature. Simultaneously he bridges estrangement from all objects of courtship: Astraea, Gloriana, and Britomart. Within two stanza's, however, resolution transmutes to dissolution.

> But ere he could reforme it thoroughly,
> He through occasion called was away,
> To Faerie Court, that of necessity
> His course of Iustice he was forst to stay,
> And Talus to reuoke from the right way,
> In which he was that Realme for to redresse.
> But enuies cloud still dimmeth vertues ray.   (V.xii.27.1–7)

As the metaphor of occluded sunlight counters and displaces the elocutio of natural regeneration associated with Irena's release, so "occasion" and "necessity" displace Artegall hierarchically, aborting his power to function as a locus of peace and generative source of justice; thwarting both his will and his wit. Even the enlightened mariner cannot hold "his course of Iustice" (xii.18), and Gloriana's Faerie Court itself is compromised.[16]

"Occasion," the proximate cause of Artegall's frustration and "root of all wrath and despight" (II.iv.10.9), appears first as an anti-exemplum of temperance but anticipates in her prosopographia (II.iv.4) both the enemy of concord, Sclaunder (IV.viii.23–4), and the dyslogistic trinity whom Artegall takes on immediately sequent to his forced abandonment of just reform in Irena's realm: Enuie (V.xii.29–32), Detraction (33–6), and their Blatant Beast (37). "Mortall fone" (37.3) to Artegall and enemies to both private and "polliticke" virtues (35.8–9), Enuie, Detraction, and the Beast suddenly resuscitate in its final stanzas the apparently dead and defeated villainy of Book V, assuming in a demonic version of the regeneration trope associated with Marinell and Irena the corporate function of all anti-exempla to justice. Accordingly, they identify themselves with Grantorto as the source of Irena's enthrallment and they act from the discredited motive of vengeance against Artegall "for freeing from their snares Irena thrall" (37.5).

5   ARTEGALL/CALIDORE: A PROBLEMATIC OF TRANSITIO

Unlike Grantorto and the villains he epitomizes, however, the Blatant Beast and the principals it serves act to undermine justice not by usurping the locus of sovereignty to abuse its power but by discrediting indecorously the reputation of those who wield power justly: they displace the attributes of injustice from ruler to ruled. Artegall gains ethos by ignoring, Calidore by engaging, this villainy: "where ye ended haue," says Calidore, "now I begin" (VI.i.6.1). This characteristic of Spenser's *transitio* (the narrative *distributio* bridging Books V and VI) creates a problematic, a complex of questions, for the analyst of rhetorical structure. The Beast functions in Book V as the rejuvenated epitome of injustice, and evokes, at the apparent conclusion of his mission, the locus among "wyld beasts" where the knight of justice began. Why does it require a new book, a new mission, a new champion to take on this villain?

A fragmentary replica of this question has been latent from the outset of this essay. If Spenser's *inventio* of justice is a *metonymia* for topoi of all virtues, "priuate" and "polliticke," why does this hierarchical priority not project into sequential conclusion? "Why," it must be asked, "does the *The Faerie Queene* end with the book of Courtesy, not of Justice?" So formulated, the question in its simplifications and assumptions becomes itself a problematic, requiring I think three related but distinguishable lines of response. One is obvious: the epic "ends" with neither book, indeed with no "Book" at all but with two "un-booked" cantos dealing with the trial of Mutabilitie on Arlo Hill followed by two "un-cantoed" stanzas composing a prayer, and I will address directly the issues of contiguity and sequence they entail in my next chapter. This line of response untangles topoi of structural culmination and sequential closure from the question of why "Courtesy" should follow "Iustice" and displaces those issues temporarily to another locus. Implicated in both these responses, however, but occluded by their focus on sequence, is a third provoked by the under-structure of poetic formalism itself – the arbitrary contingencies of artifice: books, cantos, stanzas and their metrical scaffold. Designated "schemes of words" in rhetorical anatomies, these, like all elements of elocutio, are constrained by decorum to serve, not dictate, the dispositio of subject and inventio. Arbitrarily applied, such arbitrary contingencies would mimic the indecorum of fortune and make Spenser complicit with Malfont in its agenda, inscribing Talus-like the iron letter as absolute. I broach this line of response here in part because with the Book of Courtesy this covert implication of the artist in the dynamics of Spenser's argument becomes overt on Mount Acidale, and in part because the question provoking it occasions retrospective notice that Spenser's transitio to Book VI is consistent with, not a departure from, its precedents: no book exhausts within its formal limits the dispositio of its nominal subject. That Artegall's mission cannot achieve closure argues the inadequacy of Book V to invest Spenser's inventio of its nominal subject, but every book displays the same inadequacy. The meaning of justice is contingent upon the precedent virtues it accommodates and this contingency is reciprocal; Book V took account of the sequence of precedential legendary accounts and in turn accounted for them. It is my contention that the dispositio of justice does not end, any more than it begins with exemplification in Artegall: sequentially, and by logos consequently, Book VI and the trial of Mutabilitie take account of and account for Book V.

I would therefore recode the problem of why the Blatant Beast requires a new book, champion, and mission into a question with more analytical potential: "With what inventio of Justice and of Courtesy is this transitio in Spenser's dispositio decorous?" A shared anti-exemplum, especially one so major as the Blatant Beast, demonstrates a manifold inventio, here merging topoi of justice, and through justice topoi of the prior virtues it assumes, with those of courtesy. Enuie, Detraction, and their Beast, as anti-exempla of justice and agents of fortune, recapitulate with particular stress the causal link between injustice and disordered reason, expressing a source of tyranny immune to the correctives of reformed statutes or procedures, and outside the power of the magistrate to control no matter how "wondrous" his wit or "magnificke" his might. They inscribe limits to any possible accommodation of private virtue in the civil order – of possible action, as it were, against the chaotic vector of Ovidian decline. Indeed, as Spenser demonstrates through the logos of narrative sequence, their tyranny perversely arises from the very success of the magistrate in courting just order both within himself and within the state. The higher he rises toward identification with the ultimate term of justice, the more likely he is to "occasion" the injustice that "turne[s] to ill the thing, that well was ment" (V.xii.34.5), a locution identifying injustice by allusive echo with the perverse motives of all Lucifera's counsellors epitomized in Enuie's moral indecorum: "So euery good to bad he doth abuse" (I.iv.32.5), and by anticipation with Mutabilitie who "wrong of right and bad of good did make" (VII.vi.6.3). Only within himself can Artegall counter these agents of Fortuna and disorder by maintaining the integrity of "priuate peace" against their provocations, refusing to yield to the discredited, fortune-driven justice of vengeance (xii.42.3–4), and restraining Talus (43.3–5): in effect, he is a successful courtier only of the private virtues interdependent with justice and consequentially of Britomart who embodies them. His public mission, however, to reverse the dynamic of Ovid's cone by re-establishing a "polliticke" order incorporating in the public realm all private virtues, cannot finally succeed in a world governed by the irrational flux and moral indecorum of fortune. Justice is predicated upon, or linked "prophetically," in Fletcher's sense, to "peace vniuersall": "Book V recounts the liberation of Irena but does not predict, though it does prophesy or 'speak out for,' a final peace."[17] Unaided, Artegall cannot establish a social locus structurally analogous to the transcendent locus of "peace vniuersall" where "Iustice sat high ador'd" and "all loued vertue."

The correlative locus and source of "peace" in the social model is, of course, its apex, the seat of sovereignty, occupied as ideal fabulous exemplum by the court of Gloriana (VI.i.1) and as ideal historical exemplum by the court of Elizabeth (VI.Pr.7). Artegall, however, is "forst to stay" his "course of Iustice" because he is recalled to "Faerie Court," and the cause in turn of his recall is "enuies cloud [that] still dimmeth vertues rays" (V.xii.27.7): Spenser's causal sequence implicitly locates the source of blight on Artegall's mission in Gloriana's court – in the very place that should sustain it and nurture all the composite virtues it strives to express in the social order. Among Gloriana's courtiers lurks at least one of Lucifera's counsellors. Even Gloriana, therefore, whose stature as ultimate term makes her structurally coincident with transcendent "Iustice" herself, can only provide through just sovereignty, like Artegall and Mercilla, a social ultimate worthy of service: she cannot impose on her Faerie Court the love of virtue that would motivate such courtship. Spenser's conclusion to Book V is thus consistent with principles argued through the entire dispositio of Britomart and Artegall: love cannot be impelled or commanded, "maisterie" precludes the ideal "marriage" of private virtues with public order, and the limit of Artegall's power to attain their accommodation by governing with "true iustice" occurs in consequence at precisely the point where a complementary and reciprocal commitment from the governed fails to occur.

Elizabeth's court, being the idealized historical exemplum, combines just this attribute of reciprocity in the topos of "welling" generation, attracting precedent tropes central to the ideals of marriage and natural cycle associated with the ultimate terms of chastity and friendship in Books III and IV:

> Then pardon me, most dreaded Soueraine,
> That from your selfe I doe this vertue bring,
> And to your selfe doe it returne againe:
> So from the Ocean all riuers spring,
> And tribute backe repay as to their King.
> Right so from you all goodly vertues well
> Into the rest, which round about you ring,
> Faire Lords and Ladies, which about you dwell,
> And doe adorne your Court, where courtesies excell.   (VI.Pr.7)

"Courtesy" is the term Spenser appropriates to label this ideal of social courtship and locus of "all goodly vertues," and his dispositio at the juncture of Books V and VI introducing it as the necessary complement of justice signals clearly that "courtesy" in Spenser's inventio represents a concept more densely allusive and resonant than common usage of the term would encompass. Calidore's mission demonstrates this inventio, and upon its successful prosecution depends the successful resolution of Artegall's curtailed mission to establish a civil order accommodating and expressing "all goodly vertues," private and "polliticke," comprised in Spenser's inventio of justice. "Courtesy," together with its champion, thereby assume at the outset the ethos of expectation attached to Artegall at the outset of his mission, an ethos enhanced by the proof in Artegall's frustration that a mission *civilitatis causa* to counter the historical degeneration established through Ovidian topoi in the Proem to Book V is not only important but also exceedingly difficult, perhaps impossible.

In an homologous variant of Calidore's role, Spenser concomitantly begins the Proem to Book VI with a rhetorically crucial presentation of himself in a sudden posture of overburdened quester, reasserting his role as courtier to the Muses in a fresh invocation asking renewed inspiration. Through this abruptly illuminated stance of a suppliant courting the summit of Parnassus, weary from "tedious trauell" through "strange waies where neuer foote did vse" (VI.Pr.1–2), he identifies his role as poet with Calidore's taking up the burden of Artegall's mission: "To tread an endlesse trace, withouten guyde, /

Or good direction, how to enter in, / Or how to issue forth in waies
vntryde, / In perils strange, in labours long and wide" (VI.i.6.2–5).
Courtesy gains transcendent ethos in this identification from equivalency with the Muses as an object of courtship, and the hierarchical
coincidence implied by this equivalency anticipates the topothesia of
Mount Acidale (VI.x.5ff). Accordingly, Spenser invokes guidance
from the "sacred imps that on Parnasso dwell" whose ethos depends,
as it does with the exemplars of justice, upon the attributes of wit
evidenced in their custody of "learnings threasures" which reveal
"the sacred noursery / Of vertue" represented through allusive
elocutio as a secret "siluer bower" planted "by the Gods" with
"heauenly seedes of bounty soueraine" (VI.Pr.1–3). Spenser's elocutional detail here evokes precedents in both the Garden of Adonis,
with its synecdochal exemplum of fruitful marriage without "maisterie," and its dyslogistic anti-types in the Bower of Bliss and the fallen
garden infested with "wicked seede of vice" at the base of Ovid's
cone (V.i.1–2) where Artegall joins Bacchus and Hercules among
those "of the vertuous race" who must periodically act with "heroicke heat" to cut back the "fruitfull rancknes" (V.i.1.6–9). The garden
trope situates courtesy among the fairest flowers of virtue (VI.Pr.4.1–
2) with the growth-habit of a spreading climber, a geometrically conic
habit like the Ovidian spiral of degeneration but antithetical in its
moral vector: "Which though it on a lowly stalke doe bowre, / Yet
brancheth forth in braue nobilitie, / And spreds itself through all
ciuilitie" (VI.Pr.4.3–5).

   Since it is the apex of this spreading presence "through all ciuilitie,"
the "lowly stalke" from which courtesy climbs and spreads is paradoxically coincident with the "highest" point in the analogous hierarchical model of the state. From the court, apex of the state and
centre of power, "spreads" influence for good or ill "through all
ciuilitie" from apex to base and centre to margin. Like Artegall, we
are "recalled" to that point at the beginning of Book VI, to "Faery
Court" among Gloriana's courtiers where this virtue upon which
depends the realization of all other virtues in the civil order ought
to find its "ground" and establish its "roote." Indeed, the ethical
imperative for the colligation of "court" and "courtesy" is argued
explicitly, with economy, through the narrator's introductory folk-
etymology:

> Of Court it seemes, men Courtesie doe call,
> For that it there most vseth to abound:
> And well beseemeth that in Princes hall
> That vertue should be plentifully found,

Which of all goodly manners is the ground,
And roote of ciuill conuersation.
Right so in Faery court it did redound,
Where courteous Knights and Ladies most did won
Of all on earth, and made a matchlesse paragon.   (VI.i.1)

6   "COURTESY": TOPOI AND SYNTAX

Spenser's inventio of courtesy thus attracts topoi of ideal courtship
(or "courtier-ship") common among Erasmian humanists, represented most influentially perhaps by the referent that is the source of
Kenneth Burke's theory: Castiglione's version of a "matchlesse par-
gon" in his account of the courtiers in Frederico's court at Urbino.
More's namesake also evokes its topoi during his sometimes rancor-
ous debate with the anti-Erasmian Hythloday in Book I of *Utopia*. By
eliminating princes and courtiers along with private property, Hythloday's ideal social structure radically alters presuppositions, derived
substantially from Neoplatonic tradition, that underlie *The Education
of A Christian Prince* [*Institutio principis Christiani* (1516)], Erasmus's
preeminently authoritative source of topoi on political theory which
demands of the humanist courtier a sacrificial motivation to act for
the general good by educating his sovereign to virtuous action. Aes-
thetically, of course, decorum could hardly allow Spenser to construct
a topothesia like More's that eliminated both princes and courtiers
from an epic founded on generic topoi of chivalric romance, even if
he were so inclined politically. His dispositio of "Courtesie," however, contains strategies arguing principles that Hytholoday would
find congenial. Richard Neuse, in a persuasive and challenging essay,
reconstructs Spenser's enthymeme for Book VI as an interrogatio:
"Can a poet whose ideals are summed up in the term 'chivalry'
validly reflect and give shape to the modern courtier and polity?"
Although we explore this question from different points of departure,
Neuse and I clearly converge in proposing that for Spenser the "legend of ... Courtesie," like Hythloday's Utopian fabula for More,
provides a "testing ground" for "political hypotheses."[18] Castiglione,
fashioning his ideal courtier after the Erasmian pattern, first adduces
over three books the acquisitively motivated strategies by which
attributes of inherited rank, appearance, and acquired skills function
suasively to court princely favour, then argues in Book IV that such
favour be used to promote the general good rather than personal
aggrandizement, thereby transmuting acquisitive motives to sacrificial and social ends to transcendent.[19] Spenser is perhaps more
explicit than his humanist analogues in emphasizing that the general

good requires such ends and motives reciprocally of the prince as well as the courtier, but his dispositio argues an Erasmian case in making justice, the art of the ruler, and courtesy, the art of the courtier, necessary complements.

That dispositio, however, obeys an internal decorum more compelling than conformity to any external authority. *The Faerie Queene* goes much further than any humanist source to anatomize the components of an ideal polis into private as well as "polliticke" virtues, and Courtesy is not only the virtue contiguous with and complementary to Justice but also the conclusion of a series, the final virtue to be championed in Spenser's epic. Both aspects of structural placement argue its crucial status. Not quite a "priuate" or entirely a "polliticke" virtue, courtesy is a complex hybrid: a virtue required of "all," hence of "each"; seated "deepe within the mynd" (Pr.5.8), yet catalyst for the public effectiveness of all other components in Spenser's anatomy of the good society. Its sequential disposition, therefore, making it the necessary complement of justice and hence essential to all Gloriana's champions if their missions are to issue in service to the ends of a general social good, is consistent with the dynamics of courtship in Spenser's entire rhetorical structure. "Courtesy" has from the outset been symbiotic with Holiness, Temperance, Chastity, Concord, and Justice because every virtue is an object of courtship and every champion a courtier requiring, perforce, "the art of the courtier" to complete their mission. Thus I would intensify Cheney's characterization of Spenser's courtesy "as a virtue of sufficient magnitude to warrant comparison with the five already treated in his poem" by arguing that "accommodation" and "incorporation" rather than simply "comparison" are involved. Nevertheless, I agree with Cheney's incisive statement of the "double burden" Spenser assumes: "first, of giving that virtue a significance beyond its conventional implications regarding courtly behaviour, and secondl1y, of relating these conventional implications to that larger significance."[20] Rhetorically, every book of *The Faerie Queene* anticipates the demonstration of "Courtesie"; each thereby keeps decorum with a Castiglionian *narratio*[21] for the epic expressed in Spenser's letter to Raleigh: "The generall end therefore of all the booke is to fashion a gentleman or noble person in vertuous and gentle discipline."

That "end" is rhetorically complex since the "noble person" he aims to "fashion" is ambiguously both the exempla he creates to demonstrate his conception and the "person" he would "fashion" from his audience were his demonstration persuasive. "Gentle" and "noble" carry both social and transcendent values. Since Spenser addresses an audience at Elizabeth's court drawn from the class already possessed of the former values, his "end" is to persuade it to embrace the latter. He courts through his art a suasive union of minds with that audience on the virtues that compose the subject of his epic, seeking thereby to fashion a "person" who embodies not only position on the social hierarchy sufficiently close to the centre of power to "spread" influence generally through the civil order but also the virtuous discipline to influence that order for good – to act socially for transcendent ends. Spenser himself, in short, is an Erasmian courtier "educating" in virtue those who court power through a Christian prince, and the identification of his artistic "quest" with Calidore's mission for courtesy is therefore decorous with that end, as is the elocutio of weariness stressing that he has been pursuing this mission, "the waies through which my weary steps I guyde" (VI.Pr.1.1), since he first joined "A Gentle Knight ... pricking on the plaine" (I.i.1.1).[22]

PART FOUR

"(Who Knowes Not Arlo-Hill?)": A Grammar of Closure

8 Mount Acidale, Arlo Hill, and the *Ethos* of Pastoral

1 CALIDORE'S ETHOS

The "person" Spenser "fashioned" as the "end" of his advocacy would equally satisfy Castiglione's ideal and grace the Elizabethan "Court where courtesies excell." Such a courtier would complete the "marriage" of courtesy with justice by providing a complementary, reciprocal exemplar to the sovereign Elizabeth, Spenser's idealized historical exemplum, his "patterne" of "Princely curtesie" (VI.Pr.6.1–4). Although the strategies of praise generating this historical idealization of the Tudor court closely parallel those of Book V, they occasion among commentators little of the critical dismay aroused by Spenser's projecting Elizabeth in that book as a "patterne" of justice, perhaps because the justice of Elizabeth and her court is more easily contested on historical grounds than their possession of what the court would understand by "courtesy," or perhaps because Spenser's role as advocate rather than apologist is here more evident.[1] The transitio from Artegall to Calidore argues that for Spenser there could be no courtesy without justice, and the rhetorical effect of encomium is again heavily influenced here by its juxtaposition against a brief but provocative re-invocation of the Ovidian context of history. Courtesy in the "present age doe[s] plenteous seeme," but "being matcht with plaine Antiquitie" reveals itself to the insightful as "fayned showes ... nought but forgerie," the mere appearance of reality (VI.Pr.4.6–5.9).

Immediately subsequent to this reminder that the Elizabethan court exists at the base of Ovid's cone, Spenser abruptly attributes to it eulogistic topoi of courtesy decorous with its being at the apex, "from low to high vplifted:"

> But where shall I in all Antiquity
> So faire a patterne finde, where may be seene
> The goodly praise of Princely curtesie,
> As in your selfe, O soueraine Lady Queene.
> In whose pure minde, as in a mirrour sheene,
> It showes, and with her brightnesse doth inflame
> The eyes of all, which thereon fixed beene;
> But meriteth indeede an higher name:
> Yet so from low to high vplifted is your name.   (VI.Pr.6)

Spenser's use of the interrogative rather than assertive mode in this encomium aptly reinforces the ironic effect of oxymoronic reversal pivoting on its opening qualifier "but," and both devices of irony are congruent with his abutting what is against what ought to be by praising Elizabeth and her courtiers for being what they would become should his Erasmian courtship prove persuasive. Furthermore, his topoi of praise epitomize the significance of courtesy in the civil consummation of previous virtues: an idealized Elizabeth embodies the ultimate term of courtesy both because she is the source of "all goodly virtues" in the state and because that source lies in the "pure minde" upon which the efficacy of those virtues for the general good depends. By juxtaposing "antique" and "stonie" Ovidian ages, therefore, he coalesces their equivalent polarities (reality and illusion, ideal and actual, what is and what ought to be) to form again in Elizabeth and her court, for courtesy as for justice, a powerfully evocative synecdochal emblem of the poles Calidore must negotiate in the narrative dispositio and the issues at stake in his quest to reconcile the ends of courtesy with those of justice.[2]

In his initial appearance, however, Calidore is indecorous with the intense background of anticipatory ethos developed in the Proem, and the narrative begins appropriately by reflecting this disjunction: it recreates from the Proem an oxymoronic distinction between what is and what ought to be. Calidore's prosopographia (VI.i.2–3) locates him, like the idealized Elizabeth, at the apex of courtesy; there is "none more courteous Knight" at Gloriana's court, itself identified in the narrator's encomium as "a matchlesse paragon" of courtesy (i.1.9). The superlative mode, however, seems naively and ominously inconsistent with the evident "dys-courtesy" at Gloriana's court which aborts Artegall's mission, and with the ambiguous ethos of Calidore's attributes, natural and acquired (i.2), which read like a summary catalogue of the topoi recommended by Castiglione's interlocutors as ideally suasive in their worldly appeal for those of appetitive motives who court identity with the powerful, "and with the greatest purchas[e] greatest grace:"

> Ne was there Knight, ne was there Lady found
> In Faery court, but him did deare embrace,
> For his faire vsage and conditions sound,
> The which in all mens liking gayned place,
> And with the greatest purchast greatest grace:
> Which he could wisely vse, and well apply
> To please the best, and th'euill to embase.
> For he loathed leasing, and base flattery,
> And loued simple truth and stedfast honesty.   (VI.i.3)

Spenser's lexical tropes in this stanza intensify the ethical ambiguity of such topoi. In the pivotal fifth line, "purchast" brings commercial implications to its trans-acting role between repetitions of "greatest" that function like antiphrasis to juxtapose social and transcendent connotations of the same word while participating in a *paroemion* linking both occurrences to "grace." In concert these elocutional devices blur distinctions between ultimate terms of social and transcendent hierarchies, implicitly making "greatest grace" a benefice within the gift of secular not divine power, rendered in exchange for such currency as "gentlenesse" by birth, "comely guize," "gracious speach," and prowess in "batteilous affray" (i.2.3–9).[3] Furthermore, since attributes of congruent ultimate terms are interchangeable, "grace" can, and frequently does, function rhetorically to express the desired end of erotic as well as social and transcendent courtship. As its pivotal word, "grace" occurs in the configuration of this stanza at a point of transition equivalent to the juncture of Books Three and Four in Castiglione's structure, where the social preferment gained on the strength of such qualities becomes not simply a worldly end in itself but the means to a higher moral end, sacrificial rather than acquisitive, rational rather than appetitive. The ambiguous "could" rather than "did" in line 6 and a pointed replacement of "the greatest" with "the best" as moral antithesis to "th'euill" in line 7 anticipate Calidore's failure to make this transition, a failure of wit "wisely [to] vse and well apply" his advantages. For if the ideal of courtesy is to act socially for transcendent ends, then to accept social, or erotic "grace" as substitute for the transcendent ultimate would parody that ideal in a failure of rational, moral discernment. Calidore so fails when he abandons his quest for the Blatant Beast to court erotically Pastorella, whom he equates with Colin's Graces on Mount Acidale, and to court socially a "misdeemed" ideal from fairy tale projected onto Meliboe's kingdom, "Fearlesse of foes, or fortunes wrackfull yre" (ix.27.7). Spenser's narrative dispositio thus argues an inventio of courtesy including not only the moral discernment to judge decorously among orders of grace but also a discernment fundamentally more aesthetic than political of the decorum relating fairy tale to social reality.

"In the triall of true curtesie," however, it is not until his ascent of Mount Acidale to encounter Colin Clout and *his* "Graces" that Calidore will take on dramatically this structural collocation of moral, social, and aesthetic topoi. Prior to that ascent, in keeping with the summative function of "Courtesie," Calidore as its champion in "legend" epitomizes the evolution of all previous champions from fairy tale to epic ethos. Indeed, the eulogistic catalogue comprising Calidore's introductory prosopographia makes the public attributes of courtesy, more than those of any other virtue, simply cognate with the topoi of heroism from fairy tale (courage, cleverness, presence of mind, generosity, willingness to listen to good advice, and common decency). Castiglione has his interlocutors (anticipating a legion of imitators) exploit this close correspondence by recommending the timeless pathetic appeal of such topoi to appetitive social courtiers in need of a suasive exordium. Calidore's "legend" is accordingly replete with commonplaces of fabula. Committed to "simple truth and stedfast honesty," he embarks upon a perilous quest "to tread an endlesse trace, withouten guyde" in pursuit of a monster, the Blatant Beast. He defeats in battle the villain Crudor, and by good example reforms his defeated enemy. He rescues two maidens in distress, Serena from the Blatant Beast and Pastorella first from a tiger and then from the hideout of a band of brigands. His reward is betrothal to Pastorella who, it transpires, is not the simple shepherdess she appears but the long-lost daughter of a nobleman.

Calidore thus presents problems of transmutation from fairy tale to epic heroism, and they appropriately combine aspects of those problems raised by his immediate predecessors. Like Britomart and Artegall he seems to begin his quest already possessed of the virtue he courts, a virtue exemplified in his case by attributes wholly circumscribed, like Britomart's invincibility and Artegall's Talus-backed prowess, within the simplistic ethos of fairy tale. Again in Book VI Spenser uses this ethos strategically first to invite our pathetic identification with its exemplar and then to undermine the basis of that

identification in a rhetorical strategy courting, like the aporia provoked by Socrates in Plato's dialogues, a re-examination of our presuppositions. Inadequacies in their exemplars demonstrate the
inadequacies of attributes, however attractive and admirable, to represent the virtue as Spenser conceives it. Just as the chivalric qualities
of Redcrosse prove inadequate to represent holiness, of celibacy and
virginity to represent chastity, of law enforcement to represent justice,
so the qualities attributed to Calidore and demonstrated through the
cantos leading to Mount Acidale prove necessary but not sufficient
to represent courtesy. "Only later," as Tonkin puts it, "does [Calidore]
discover a new set of standards outside the chivalric framework, and
this set of standards turns out ultimately to be the true courtesy."[4] It
is this "ultimate" discovery that Spenser's rhetorical strategies induce
his audience to share.

Spenser's structural method for Book VI resembles Book III in its
use of multiple heroes (Bruin and Calepine as well as Calidore and
the pandemic Arthur), and Book IV in the functional importance it
affords digressio, particularly those involving Bruin and the Hermit.
Narrated by his childless wife, Mathilde, Bruin's story in canto iv
reduces complex issues of good, evil, fortune, and heroism to their
simplest elements. Through them Spenser evokes a world decorous
with Bruin's defeat of Cormoraunt: conditional, uncertain, and subject to the changes of time. Indeed, "fortune," "fate," "chance," and
their variants occur so frequently in Book VI that they form its most
significant feature of elocutio: here they exceed the rate of occurrence
in the other five books by a ratio of 2:1.[5] Cormoraunt abides as a
brooding menace and the aging Bruin has no heir to sustain his
conditional victory. The "cruell fate" of childlessness afflicting both
Bruin and the peace of his quiet state thus characterizes synecdochally the larger, fortune-afflicted world through which Calidore
moves. Implicitly, Spenser evokes the specific case of England lacking
security of royal succession as an historical exemplum of such afflic-
tion, and the episode surely advocates, however obliquely, that
Elizabeth recognize her lack of an heir as a "polliticke" issue of justice
and courtesy as well as chastity. More generally, the structural correspondence between Bruin's world and Calidore's reiterates the conceptual antipathy to fortune which links justice to courtesy and
argues a functional equivalency between Calidore and Bruin's child,
with the knight of Courtesy questing to fulfill in the macrocosm the
child's providential role in the microcosm.

Accordingly Bruin and his foundling in this digressio anticipate by
synecdoche the heroes and helpers, as the Bear and Cormoraunt
anticipate the villains, whom Calidore takes on in the dispositio of

his courtship. The foundling's antithesis is Pastorella, who cannot save the quiet pastoral state from destruction and precipitates the death of her protector Meliboe. Meliboe is Bruin without Bruin's child, and the doomed shepherd's words, like the child, confute Matilde's lamentation on "cruell fate" in a strong echo from Boethius: "In vaine ... doe men / The heauens of their fortunes faulte accuse, / ... Sith each unto himselfe his life may fortunize" (ix.29,30), a doctrine re-echoed in the Hermit's prescription of self-control as the cure for the physically untreatable bite of the Blatant Beast (vi.7,14).

As a source of topoi on the subject of fortune, Boethius' *Consolation of Philosophy* is perhaps the most authoritative available to Spenser. Although Boethius uses strategies of discursive rather than narrative dispositio, his perplexity, or Platonic aporia, when faced with the moral indecorum of goodness suffering and evil prospering in a world reputedly ruled by providential benevolence serves to generate a transcendent courtship of justice through dialogue with Lady Philosophy and exemplifies an inventio consistent with Spenser's. Lady Philosophy's argument and Calidore's narrative can be persuasive in accounting for the moral discrepancy between virtue and reward only if they first acknowledge through convincingly recognizable exempla that the discrepancy exists, or at least appears to exist. However, insofar as its topoi of heroism and its simple ethos prove invariably that good is rewarded and evil punished, fairy tale denies the primary rhetorical condition of Boethian perplexity. In the synecdochal digressio of Bruin, therefore, by first evoking this ethos and then undermining it Spenser necessarily creates a sense of the human condition akin to that of Boethius.

Calidore's early exploits fail to address this perplexity. When Briana upbraids him for his violence in cleaving Maleffort's head and slaying the Porter (i.1.25), Calidore's reply makes clear the simplistic nature of his ethos: "Bloud is no blemish; for it is no blame / To punish those, that doe deserue the same." Here speaks the voice of Talus and the "saluage" Artegall in commonplaces of primitive justice oxymoronically inadequate as exempla of the sententia forming Calidore's summative epiphonema: "No greater shame to man than inhumanitie" (i.26). Similarly, the enthymeme elaborated in Calidore's string of sententiae (i.41) finds no demonstration in this exploit. Virtue conquers all, and the encounter ends with commonplaces of concord: a celebration and the hero's reward. "And after all, vnto Sir Calidore / She freely gave that Castle for his paine, / And her selfe bound to him for euermore; / So wondrously now chaung'd, from that she was afore" (i.46). Wondrous indeed is the change: the wonder of fairy tale, echoing allusively the "wonder" and "maruaile" of "so mortall foes so friendly to agree" in the "sudden change" wrought by Cambina's magic (IV.iii.49). Here no agent of magic appears: only the effect of such agency in the sudden transmutation of absolutes from discord to concord creating an exemplum of pathos without ethos. The victory of good over evil is too sudden, too easy, and too final for a world in which "All flesh is frayle, and full of ficklenesse, / Subiect to fortunes chance" (i.41.7–8). Thus indecorum between word and deed in Calidore's first encounter recapitulates functionally the opening exploits of Redcrosse, Guyon, Britomart, and Artegall: it defines the estrangement between Spenser's exemplary courtier and the virtue he courts. Against Crudor and Blandina, Calidore demonstrates the will and power to achieve courtesy but not the understanding: his knowledge of the principles underlying his quest, professed so glibly in catalogued sententiae, is theoretical and untested. Spenser brings Calidore to his episode of instruction in the fortune-ravaged world of Meliboe.

In a second digressio anticipating that episode, the Hermit attracts the ambiguities of analogy: he is both a surrogate for Spenser as a collateral source of instruction and his counter-advocate in an unusual form of refutatio. He seems an Erasmian "paragone" of the courtier: "through long experience of his dayes / Which had in many fortunes tossed beene" he has gained "great insight" into "the minds of men" (vi.3) and so learned to counter the Blatant Beast:

> Abstaine from pleasure, and restraine your will,
> Subdue desire, and bridle loose delight,
> Use scanted diet, and forbeare your fill,
> Shun secresie, and talke in open sight.   (vi.14)

By constructing an asyndetonic passage from balanced polysyndetonic lines, Spenser imitates the idiom of incantation and ritual practice. This elocutional pattern inflects his common topos expressing spiritual problems through a metaphora of "frail" or wounded flesh to impose on prudential wisdom an aura of the curative talisman of magic and evoke the generic topos from fairy tale of a "magical helper." Spenser's "magical" elocutio, however, merely accentuates the anti-magical inventio of the Hermit's enthymemes. His sententiae are allusive of Guyon's Palmer, and his effectiveness as a helper derives not from magic but the "sage counsell" of experience (vi.3). Furthermore, his assertion that "in your selfe your onely helpe doth lie" (vi.7.1) makes explicit an enthymeme already demonstrated in the exploits of Britomart and Artegall.

Despite this ethical reinforcement of the Hermit's "sage counsell," Spenser pointedly limits his creature's ethos as an exemplar of courtesy by creating a disjunction between elocutio and distributio. The echo of Guyon's Palmer in his words and of Redcrosse's Contemplation in both the Hermit's "dooinges" and the topothesia of his hermitage (I.xi.46; VI.v.34–5) again accentuate crucial difference against a ground of similarity. In contradistinction to such figures of highest ethos, he does not meet, influence, or instruct the central heroic exemplum of his book, the principal courtier of Courtesy. Like the nominal heroes of Book IV, the Hermit remains isolated in a digressio, a structural marginalization decorous with his own motives and actions. As one of Gloriana's courtiers (vi.4.1–5; v.37) his response to "the worlds vnquiet waies" was simply to withdraw from the court: "He tooke him selfe vnto his Hermitage, / In which he liu'd alone, like carelesse bird in cage" (vi.4.8–9). "Timely age" (4.6) justifies the Hermit's retreat; he is "a-courteous" rather than "dyscourteous," with a formal relationship to Calidore closely resembling that of Belphoebe to Britomart in Book III. Spenser, like Milton, propounds a humanist balance of the active and contemplative life and withholds praise from the Hermit's "fugitive and cloistered virtue." The Hermit seeks acquisitively a personal peace, "alone like carelesse bird in cage," choosing not to court sacrificially (as Artegall and Calidore must) the ultimate term of reestablished "Peace universall" when "all loued virtue." Accordingly, he can cure the bite of the Blatant Beast only in those who "follow in his path" to the isolated Hermitage; who digress, in fact, from the path to courtesy. Indeed, he recapitulates the dilemma figured in Ovid's cone since the virtues of holiness, temperance, chastity, and friendship he evinces privately in his careless cage have no public effect, availing nothing against the Beast's "poisonous gall" pouring forth "to infest" the whole civil order with the chaotic moral indecorum of fortune: "all, both good and bad, both most and least" (vi.12). Against such indiscriminate attack, the Hermit's "sage counsell" to avoid the occasion for envy and detraction appears at best a tenuous defence: Artegall's experience pre-emptively denies it logos, and the contemplative ethos the Hermit advocates is indecorous with Calidore's mission to engage the Blatant Beast itself, the source of general infection not its symptoms. Thus when Calidore courts functional identity with the Hermit by seeking his own "careless cage" among Meliboe's shepherds, he substitutes a derivative term for the ultimate he is pledged to court, and his attempted withdrawal demonstrates a moral truancy carrying pathetic appeal incompatible with the ethos of both justice and courtesy, and, indeed, of epic heroism. The Hermit's "digressive" status asserts the indecorum of "magical helpers" against the villainy embodied in the Blatant Beast.

2 MOUNT ACIDALE

By abandoning his quest to dally with Meliboe and court Pastorella, Calidore merely confirms the ethos evidenced by his early exploits: far from being "paragon" at the apex of Courtesy, he remains structurally at the base where he began, estranged from the ultimate term he still must court. "The greatest mistake that can be made about [Book VI]," argues C.S. Lewis, "is to suppose that Calidore's long delay among the shepherds is a pastoral truancy of Spenser's from his moral intention. On the contrary, the shepherds' country and Mount Acidale in the midst of it are the core of the book, and the key to Spenser's whole conception of Courtesy."[6] Lewis's metaphors of "core" and "key" nicely characterize the structural significance of Mount Acidale. As an advocate for the defence, however, he seems to have the wrong client: it is not Spenser but his creature who must answer to charges of moral truancy, and Spenser's narrator begins Canto x by unequivocally making a case for the prosecution against Calidore's dereliction (x.1.1–6). Calidore has replaced Gloriana's "high beheast" demanding transcendent and sacrificial motivation with "another quest," erotic and appetitive, "the guerdon of his loue to gaine" (x.2). By default Calidore replicates the enforced curtailment of Artegall's mission: like the Hermit, he accepts a "happy peace" of pastoral "perfect pleasures" (x.3) as substitute for the Ovidian "peace vniversall" of "Iustice high ador'd" where "all loued vertue." With his "hungry eye" on Pastorella he ingratiatingly courts her father through glib *sententiae* that invoke again the *elocutio* of Fortuna's moral *indecorum*, repeating without any advancement of understanding the rhetorical strategy he used to reform Briana and Crudor:

> Yet to occasion meanes, to worke his mind,
> And to insinuate his harts desire,
> He thus replyde; Now surely syre, I find,
> That all the worlds gay showes, which we admire,
> Be but vaine shadowes to this safe retyre
> Of life, which here in lowlinesse ye lead,
> Fearelesse of foes, or fortunes wrackfull yre,
> Which tosseth states, and vnder foot doth tread
> The mightie ones, affrayd of euery chaunges dread.   (ix.27)

In the context of Bruin's paradigmatic *exemplum* and its subsequent elaborations, Calidore's platitudinous expectations of this pastoral "quiet state ... Fearelesse of foes, or fortunes wrackfull yre," create an intense structural oxymoron. It occasions the tone of Chaucerian irony in Spenser's narrative interjection: "Ne certes mote he greatly blamed be" (x.3), and demonstrates that the "painted show" and "false blisse" which "entrap vnwary fooles" pose as much risk in Meliboe's pastoral world as in Gloriana's (or indeed Lucifera's and Malacasta's) courtly "world of beauties rare" (x.3,4): their real habitation is the irrational psyche compelled by distortions of the "hungry eye" (ix.26.7).

Structurally, both pastoral and courtly worlds coalesce at the summit of Mount Acidale, locus of not only the "iolly shepheard" Colin Clout but also the court of Venus whose "handmaides," the Graces, dance to Colin's pipe and embody "all the complements of curtesie," especially the topoi of social courtship "which skill men call Ciuility" (x.23). Acidale's summit thus replicates in demonstrative function the Mount of Contemplation and the "stately Mount" centering the Garden of Adonis as Spenser's topographical analogue to an ultimate term, here the ultimate term of courtesy. Furthermore, its topothesia (x.5–9) reinforces such functional echoes with elocutional ones, combining the superlative mode with paradisiac and Ovidian topoi that together replicate allusively, or "attract," the attributes of Parnassus in Contemplation's mountain (I.x.54), Belphoebe's "saluage" retreat "with mountaines round about enuironed" (III.v.39–40), and the temple of Spenser's "Hermaphroditic" Venus (IV.x.21–5) evoked when Britomart and Arthur judge Scudamour's case for Amoret. At its centre, "in the midst ... placed parauaunt" (x.15.7), stands Colin's object of courtship, Rosalind, the country lass "aduaunst to be another Grace" (x.16.9), whose "parauaunt" posture relative to the other Graces, the "handmaides" of Venus "which on her depend" (x.21.6), gives Rosalind hierarchical coincidence with Venus. This tableau enriches particularly the functional analogy between Acidale's summit and the "stately Mount" of Venus in the Garden of Adonis, "Right in the middest of that Paradise" (III.vi.43), and thereby links Mount Acidale allusively with the topographical metonymia conflating Mercilla's court, the Garden of Adonis, Venus's temple, and Isis's Church. Such a cluster of allusive exempla evoking holiness, chastity, concord, and justice argues that Mount Acidale is itself a structural synecdoche "parauaunt" to its predecessors; it takes on the topographical analogues of virtues that precede it sequentially and thus depend upon it structurally and derive from it logically; Acidale subsumes their attributes as courtesy assumes the virtues themselves. It seems consistent therefore that one likely etymological derivation for "acidale" should suggest "prominent summit" [Gr. *Akis* + *Delos*] to make

"Mount Acidale" an apt doublet effectively rendering "Mount of Mounts."

Decorum precludes Calidore's attaining this resonant summit by right of quest. He happens upon it by chance, like Calepine upon Bruin's child, demonstrating his ethos as an agent of fortune not courtesy: "He chaunst to come, far from all peoples troad, / Vnto a place, whose pleasaunce did appere / To passe all others, on the earth which were" (VI.x.5.3–5). The remoteness of this place from "all peoples troad" accentuates Calidore's estrangement from the "Ciuility" his mission ostensibly serves just as his voyeuristic isolation, "Beholding all, yet of them vnespyde" (x.11.5), accentuates estrangement from the dancing "Graces," source of "all the complements of curtesie" he ostensibly courts, and whose disappearance at his appearance he attributes with unintended ironic prescience to "my ill fortune" (x.20.7). Calidore's "wonder" at the "straunge sight" (x.17) sows the seeds of Boethean perplexity and Socratic aporia, but initially involves a suspension not an engagement of wit: "And standing long astonished in spright, / And rapt with pleasaunce, [he] wist not what to weene" (x.17.3–9). He fails to recognize any distinction between Meliboe's world and the "Faerie" world of Colin Clout where Fortuna has no dominion; where the Graces dance to the poet's tune, the season is always summer (x.6), and the brook is surrounded by "Nymphes and Faeries" to keep away "all noysome thinges," a protection notably absent from Bruin's world as well as Meliboe's. "His greedy fancy fed" and "sences rauished" by Colin's "words" and the "pleasures rare" of the place, Calidore "had no will away to fare, / But wisht, that with that shepheard he mote dwelling share" (x.30). The specifier "that shepheard" in its ironic ambiguity accentuates Calidore's lack of discrimination between the two worlds, and anchors with decorum Spenser's replication here of his elocutio characterizing Calidore's perceptions, distorted through "greedy eare" and "hungry eye," of Meliboe's "speach" and Meliboe's daughter. They become the "double ravishment" motivating Calidore's desire to adopt "that shepheards" pastoral life: "That twixt his pleasing tongue, and her faire hew, / He lost himselfe, and like one halfe entraunced grew" (ix.26). The entrancing sight of Pastorella anticipates exactly the response to Calidore's first sight of Colin and his Graces; it too robs him of motivation "Although his quest were farre afore him gon" (ix.12). The logos of narrative sequence argues that this state of entrancement and "lost" identity as quester leads causally to Calidore's chance finding of Mount Acidale: he simply strays onto Acidale as if it were merely a geographical extension of the pastoral setting. Being on Acidale and being "lost" from "himselfe" are identical states for Calidore.

Does he "find himselfe" in Colin Clout? Colin certainly exemplifies eulogistic topoi which Calidore lacks: the shepherd is not a chance-intruder on Acidale but seems native to the place, and the Graces from whom derive "all the complements of curtesie" do not vanish at the sight of him as they do from Calidore (x.18) but dance to his tune. While such antithetical topoi of ethos argue an estrangement between them, knight and shepherd in their postures as erotic court-iers are virtually identical. Pastorella and Rosalind are both "countrey lasses" and each is "aduaunst" by her erotic courtier to transcendent status as the ultimate object of courtship. The rhetorical structure of relationship between Calidore and Colin is therefore complex, min-gling ethical estrangement with functional analogy.

3   ANTI-REFUTATIO:
COLIN CLOUT'S CONE

The primary focus of this analogy is Spenser's prosopographia of Colin's fourth Grace dancing "in the midst ... placed parauaunt" on Mount Acidale, surrounded by the other three Graces and "an hun-dred naked maidens lilly white" (x.11–15). In visual pattern it repli-cates both the emblematic depiction of Queen Elizabeth in the Proem (Pr.7.6–9) and Calidore's first sight of Pastorella, dancing on a "little hillocke ... higher then all the rest" encircled by "a girland, goodly graced, / Of louely lasses" (ix.8). Again, details of elocutio elide contiguously with these analogies of posture and pattern. Colin's encomium on Rosalind begins with a dubitatio that asserts what it doubts, "what creature mote she bee, / Whether a creature, or a goddesse graced / With heauenly gifts from heuen first enraced?" (x.25), and becomes quite explicit in attributing transcendent and social topoi to an ultimate term of erotic courtship. In both "beauty-full array" and "vertue" she exceeds "the rest of all her race" to the same degree that the morning and evening stars of Venus "All other lesser lights in light excell[s]" (x.26). Her ascendency in physical and moral "graces" produces hierarchical consequences: "the Graces ... have for more honor ... graced her so much to be another Grace" (x.26). The decorum of merit and reward is stressed not only by the *ploce* on "grace" in these lines but also by extension to a second stanza through assertive conduplicatio ("to be another Grace. / Another Grace she well deserues to be") and the reiteration of detail which makes Rosalind's case for social ascendency by identifying her deserved social "degree" with transcendent and social ultimates, "diuine" and "soueraine":

> Another Grace she well deserues to be,
> In whom so many Graces gathered are,
> Excelling much the meane of her degree;
> Diuine resemblaunce, beauty soueraine rare,
> Firme Chastity, that spight ne blemish dare;
> All which she with such courtesie doth grace,
> That all her peres cannot with her compare,
> But quite are dimmed, when she is in place.
> She made me oft to pipe and now to pipe apace.   (x.27)

Colin's topoi of praise here, even at times his exact wording, echo the encomium on Pastorella, "some miracle of heauenly hew ... descended in that earthly vew" (ix.8), representing Calidore's first perception of her as a "soueraine goddesse" (ix.9.7) in the vision precipitating his lost identity (ix.9.1–7; 11.1–5).

This structural analogy, however, again creates the effect of antiphrasis, accenting differences against a ground of similarities. In common Colin and Calidore treat their beloved "countrey lasses" as exempla of hierarchical indecorum, radically "out of place" in their lowly pastoral degree. Both evoke by implication principles of decorum inherent in "that part of Iustice which is Equity" to argue that such paragons of beauty in both body and soul have their "proper place" at the centre not the margin, the apex not the base, the court not the country (ix.11). Necessarily implicit too in both advocacies is the reciprocal principle of ethical decorum requiring the court in turn to be a "matchlesse paragon" fit for such "graces" of Courtesy: "And well beseemeth that in Princes hall / That vertue should be plentifully found" (i.1). Since it is home to Colin's Graces, Acidale takes on the ethos of "Princes hall" as it ought to be, but Calidore fails to recognize in Acidale this ultimate term. The failure of rational discrimination that mistakes Meliboe's world for Colin's also identifies Meliboe's daughter with Colin's Rosalind. Calidore's unexamined ideal locus of courtesy remains the court: in contradistinction to Colin he elevates his erotic object of courtship merely to the status of a social, not a transcendent ultimate: "in his mind her worthy deemed, / To be a Princes Paragone esteemed" (ix.11.4–5).

Colin's interpretation, of course, contradicts Calidore's misperception. The vision that dances to Colin's pipe and dissolves upon Calidore's intrusion proves that Acidale's summit has absorbed the attributes of courtesy and become its transcendent locus, structurally coincident perforce with the courts of Gloriana and Elizabeth, just as Rosalind, "In whom so many Graces gathered are," transcends those

Graces metonymously, "gather[ing] in" their attributes to become structurally coincident with Gloriana and Elizabeth themselves. Equally, as the paragon of "Firme Chastity that spight ne blemish dare" she is coincident with the ideal exempla represented by Belphoebe and Britomart. Finally, hence by logos consequentially, she appropriates the function of the Muses as the source of Colin's inspiration: "She made me often pipe and now to pipe apace." Structurally Rosalind represents to Colin what the idealized Elizabeth represents to Spenser: "dreaded Soueraine" and well-spring of "all goodly virtues" depicted in the Proem surrounded by the "ring" of "Lords and Ladies" that "adorne" her "court where courtesies excell" (Pr.7).

Indeed, Colin makes an apology to Gloriana for the hierarchical implications of his encomium to Rosalind. He combines incrementum, ("great glory ... Great Gloriana, greatest Maiesty") with the metaphoric paronomasia "Sunne of the world" to assert social and transcendent norms, re-establishing his posture as Gloriana's courtier by presenting Rosalind as her "poore handmayd" and his praise of Rosalind as an act of social courtship to Gloriana: "Pardon thy shepheard, mongst so many layes, / As he hath sung of thee in all his dayes, / To make one minime of thy poore handmayd, / And vnderneath thy feete to place her prayse" (x.28.4–7). Whatever its relative size, his "minime" performs one vital rhetorical function of the microcosmic: it establishes a synecdoche, indeed an ultimate term, and the rhetorical effect of Colin's apology is simply to reinforce the argument of his "minime" by stressing in an elocutio of superlatives the structural identity of Rosalind with, not her subordination to, Gloriana and the other exempla of transcendent virtue.

Minimes are short musical notes, and Hamilton suggests Spenser uses the term literally, since "in his present song of some 4000 stanzas, the two given [Colin's fourth grace] amount to no more than a note."[7] Certainly for the analyst of rhetorical structure, Colin's two-stanza "minime" provides one highly resonant "key-note" to the entire dispositio of his creator insofar as the fourth grace is not only a metonymic locus of ingathered ultimate terms but also, by virtue of her "parauaunt" station, a catalyst between static and dynamic states in the tableau of Graces. Her function is therefore crucial to the significance of that tableau as a structural exemplum. In his depiction, Spenser reverses the traditional pictorial convention of the three graces, represented preeminently in Botticelli's "Primavera."[8] His elocutional strategy, however, preserves their static pose as if the reader were viewing a picture: "two of them still froward seem'd to bee, / But one still towards shew'd her selfe afore; / That good should from vs goe, then come in greater store" (x.24.7–9). Spenser thereby preserves a pictorial composition that is not only static but also triadic and conical. Moreover, without this "freeze-frame" tactic the triadic matrix would remain invisible within his initial depiction of the Graces seen through Calidore's voyeuristic hungry eye as an essentially circular dynamic of dance (x.12). In short, Colin's explication of the vision reveals what Calidore's distracted hungry eye did not notice. The reversal of pictorial convention gives particular stress to conic form: it inverts apex and base to present only a single figure facing us and so focuses lines of convergence from base to apex. Along those lines, ideally, "good" should "goe" motivated sacrificially "from vs" to the apex and return "in greater store" to "vs" at the base and thence return again, an allusive trope of reciprocity echoing the "welling" generation attributed to Elizabeth and her court (Pr.7). A reciprocal dynamic thus melds with a static triad frozen and accentuated within the circular movement of lesser graces to recapitulate structurally on Mount Acidale the now-familiar topoi first broached in the Garden of Adonis to limn the ideal of "court-ing" and "marriage" as gerundials of complementary reciprocity without advantage. Keeping decorum with its setting, therefore, the tableau of Graces, like the summative summit of Acidale, incorporates topoi central to the dispositio of chastity, friendship, and justice, and to the resolution of "peace universall" from the mutual commitment of ruler and ruled in a complementary dynamic of justice and courtesy.

Colin's fourth Grace, in turn, gathers in these topoi. Considered graphically, her introduction "in the middest and parauaunt" changes perspective on this triad-within-a-circle, revealing its two-dimensional pattern to be the cross section of a three-dimensional cone. The reciprocal vectors of motivation to "good" within the conic section thus resolve geometrically onto this single transcendent point at the conic apex occupied by Colin's beloved: it becomes an Archimedean point of reference that makes dance from random movement, provides a source of order and muse of art, occupies the common locus of beauty and good – a "still point of the turning world." Colin's "cone," in short, at the summit and centre of Mount Acidale, generates the antithetical paradigm to Ovid's cone. Indeed, Spenser's entire epic dispositio amplifies Sidney's case for the defence of poetry, demonstrating that insofar as the poet can better the suasive power of historical exempla to advocate virtuous action, by presenting what ought to be in opposition to what is, his art replicates the movement of justice and courtesy against the chaotic vector of Ovidian degeneration.

4 THE HEROIC POET AND
THE INDICTED AUDIENCE

There can be little point in iterating further this catalogue of allusive topoi: such exempla demonstrate cumulatively the sequential significance and rhetorical function of Mount Acidale and Colin Clout. Acidale's summit is clearly summative, and Colin's "cone" a synecdoche, adumbrating in pastoral topoi the structure and "generall end" of Spenser's epic dispositio: Colin's vision and his interpretation of it aim suasively "to fashion" Calidore "in uertuous and gentle discipline." Colin is the antithetical paradigm to all prior figures of refutatio: he makes Spenser's case for courtesy. In this sense at least Colin is identical with his creator, a homologue of Spenser "in lowly Shepheards weeds" before his "enforst" Virgilian gradatio from "Oaten reeds" to "trumpets sterne" (I.Pr.1). The homologous point in Colin's career corresponding structurally to his creator's "enforst" crux occurs at the moment when the pastoral vision vanishes with Calidore's intrusion and Colin responds dramatically by breaking his bagpipe (x.18.5). The very drama of its elocutio marks this enigmatic moment as a significant dispositional exemplum, urgently inviting our speculation on the implied enthymeme for which the exemplum functions in proof. Such speculation, decorously if dauntingly, traces lines of analytical inference as complex as the moment itself is enigmatic, lines leading eventually to further enigmas in "The Cantos of Mutabilitie."

That the vision on which Colin's case for courtesy depends should vanish when the nominal Knight of Courtesy intrudes argues an obvious point of ethos through sequential logos: it asserts with dramatic force how much Calidore stands in need of Colin's suasion. Equally the "wonder" (x.17.1) preceding and instigating this sequence also demonstrates by logos that the vision functions as a stimulus to aporia, provoking Calidore's resolve "to know" (x.17.8). In his gloss to this line, Hamilton notes that "the sight of beauty which drives man to 'know' provides the poem's central myth, Arthur's quest of the Faerie Queene." Britomart, of course, demonstrates the same dynamic in her response to the vision of Artegall in Merlin's mirror, and in turn anticipates schematically, in the central tableau of Book IV, the role of Colin's vision as stimulus to understanding: her "divine" beauty causes Artegall "of his wonder [to make] religion" and Scudamour to "worship her as some celestiall vision" (IV.vi.22–4).

Erotic stimulus as the source of transcendent courtship disposes an inventio resonant with authoritative precedents, primarily Plato's

Symposium, Castiglione's humanist redaction of Plato's topoi in Bembo's peroratio to *The Book of The Courtier*, and Sidney's inventio for *The Defence of Poetry*. Indeed, Sidney's inventio, like Spenser's for *The Faerie Queene*, attributes to poetry the suasive "end" Castiglione assigns to the Erasmian courtier; Sidney's courtier-poet Astrophel attributes it erotically to Stella: "So while thy beauty draws the heart to love / As fast thy virtue bends that love to good: / 'But ah,' Desire still cries, 'give me some food.'"[9] Desire's appetitive cry distorts Calidore's perception of Pastorella, Meliboe's kingdom, and Colin's Graces as severely as it does Astrophel's judgment of Stella. Calidore misperceives and misjudges the pastoral vision, apprehending it only as a species of fabula, escapist and wish-fulfilling. In exemplary proof of this misapprehension, the Graces vanish when Calidore attempts to comprehend them without benefit of Colin's explication. Colin's action in breaking his pipe thus argues an implicit enthymeme asserting the inadequacy of his pastoral vision to make a suasive case for courtesy to an intruder from the court, one who naively equates "courtesy" with "courtliness" and presents an ethical perception circumscribed by chivalric and courtly topoi. Both vanished Graces and broken pipe demonstrate by logos an indecorum among the poet's subject, his generic topoi, and his audience. Spenser's metonymic identification with Colin Clout, a figure allusively resonant because imported to Mount Acidale from *The Shepheardes Calender*, argues collaterally that Spenser's own pastoral vision in the *Calender* was analogously inadequate to make the case for courtesy to a courtly audience, occasioning his "enforst" change to epic.[10]

As exempla of ethos, however, the vanishing Graces and the broken pipe to which they danced on Acidale identify Calidore's inability to comprehend the pastoral vision and the significance of Acidale with his lack of courtesy. Indecorum, in short, redounds here to the discredit of the audience not the rhetor, and particularly not his pastoral vision. Acidale's graces embody "the skill men call Ciuility" and demonstrate in the topos of dance their concord and harmony with the shepherd-poet's pipe: no indecorum exists between the inventio of courtesy and a pastoral dispositio. Spenser's "enforst" change to epic therefore indicts the courtesy of an audience which, like Colin's, can recognize the inventio of courtesy only in topoi of a genre whose preeminent literary ethos flatters their social ethos. His implied courtly audience demonstrates a sense of decorum without ethical discernment that identifies power with virtue and perceives anything remote from the preoccupations of the court as a species of fabula. Perhaps it is a particular reminder to Elizabeth's court that Ireland is not a fairy tale. The "beauty" of the pastoral vision cannot draw the mind to good if it evokes escapist fantasy rather than engagement through aporia.[11]

In this very estrangement from the pastoral vision, therefore, Spenser's audience, like Colin's Calidore, demonstrates the antithesis of courtesy. The private virtues will never find public expression in the civil order of a good society so long as the centre and "roote" of civil order, the court, equates the social status quo with the transcendent ideal that must be courted. To bring justice and its infolded, "in-gathered" virtues to realization in the state demands the realization (both cognitive and effective) of courtesy in the court. Invidia corrupts Gloriana's court, and invidia, or more generally the moral indecorum of fortune it focuses, becomes in the last two stanzas of Book VI the enemy-in-common of the poet and his champions of justice and courtesy.[12] Spenser's introducing (Pr.1–2; i.6) and closing (xii.1–2) Book VI by identifying the poetic courtship of his audience with Calidore's courtship of courtesy is therefore doubly evocative, befitting both the "generall end of all the booke" and the particular "end" of its culminating "legend." He assumes the generic burdens, so to speak, of *heroica* to "demonstrate" courtesy (simultaneously explicating and exemplifying it) in response to the same imperative, *civilitatis causa*, which commits Calidore to assume from Artegall the burden of heroic quest that defines his epic ethos: the courtship of justice demands it.

5   MUTABILITIE AND THE COURT ON ARLO HILL

It is this same rhetorical imperative, surely, that mandates and justifies Spenser's concluding the dispositio of his epic in "The Two Cantos of Mutabilitie" with a species of "envoy" as judicial "appeale," appropriately larded with topoi from fabula, notably Ovidian myth, and set at the transcendent court of Dame Nature "vpon the highest hights / of Arlo-hill" whence Mutabilitie ascends courting justice. To the same court for the same purpose, "For triall of their Titles and best Rights" come "all, both heauenly Powers, and earthly wights" (VII.vi.36) including, perforce, the poet and his readers. To be a courtier of justice is the universal condition on Arlo Hill.

Here, then, is the "attractor of attractors," and here Spenser situates coterminally the court of courts and the ultimate term of ultimate terms: "But to the highest him, that is behight / Father of Gods and men by equall might; / To weet, the God of Nature, I appeale" (VII.vi.35.3–6). Here fortune with all its accumulated attributes as the antitype of justice and courtesy, and hence antitype of all the prior virtues they assume, undergoes rhetorical metamorphosis to become through prosopopeia, like Venus and Diana in Book III, an element of dispositio: Mutabilitie "takes on" the topoi of fortune and gives the mute abstraction a voice.

Indeed this "voice" functions in strictest accord with the rhetorical motive of justice, since Mutabilitie here serves not only structurally as an ultimate term and corporate exemplar for all Spenser's agents of "dys-order" but also dramatically as their advocate. Child of Earth and Chaos, synecdoche of moral indecorum, she oxymoronically adopts before Dame Nature the "suppliant" decorum of stance and topoi proclaiming herself a social and transcendent courtier of justice:

> To thee O greatest goddesse, onely great,
> An humble suppliant loe, I lowely fly
> Seeking for Right, which I of thee entreat;
> Who Right to all dost deal indifferently,
> Damning all Wrong and tortious Iniurie,
> Which any of thy creatures doe to other
> (Oppressing them with power, vnequally).
> Sith of them all thou art the equall mother,
> And knittest each to each, as brother vnto brother.   (VII.vii.14)

Mutabilitie's oratorical posture obviously creates an aporiatic complex of discontinuities, an organizing locus of disorganization, for it is not only as a courtier of justice that she displays qualities of ethos reserved by precedent for Spenser's eulogistic exempla: her youth, beauty, and mission of social ascent against entrenched and dangerous powers also appropriate familiar topoi of fairy tale heroism used by Spenser as strategies of exordium to invite pathetic identification with knight-champions of each virtue. Allusively she claims identity with Una and Irena as a victim of rightful sovereignty wrongfully usurped "by Conquest of ... soveraine might" (vi.33.5). Her beauty converts Jove's "greatest wrath" to "grace" (vi.31), replicating Britomart's effect on Artegall and Scudamour (IV.vi) and prompting Jove's attempt to convert her social courtship to erotic and its end from sovereignty to subjection (vi.34.1–5). Her resistance to arbitrary Olympian authority and threatening erotic subjection evoke the plight of Florimell in bondage to Proteus (III.viii) and recall not only the mortal victims of lawless power depicted in Busirane's Ovidian distortions but also the captive targets of this propaganda, Amoret and Britomart (III.xi).

Judged simply on the grounds of such allusive resonance, Mutabilitie attracts exempla whose corporate ethos is perfectly indecorous with the ethos of both fortune in previous books and Mutabilitie herself in the prosopographia introducing the envoy with an account (VII.vi.1–6) of her origin and "bad dooinges" (vi.4.9). By her "dooinges" Mutabilitie appropriates the function of Duessa as corporate icon for anti-exempla of justice and all its dependent virtues (V.ix). Mutabilitie is the summative apotheosis of Duessa, symmetric with Dame Nature who, as locus of resolved contraries (vii.13.2–4), is the summative apotheosis of Una. Like Duessa, Mutabilitie invests lapsarian will (V.x.4; VII.vi.5) and her topoi recapitulate Spenser's identification of this perverse motivation with Lucifera's synecdochal counsellor Enuy, who "wrong of right, and bad of good did make," and the "euer-whirling wheele" of Fortune (vi.1) that drives the degenerate Ovidian spiral:

> Ne she the lawes of Nature onely brake,
> But eke of Iustice, and of Policie;
> And wrong of right, and bad of good did make,
> And death for life exchanged foolishlie:
> Since which, all liuing wights haue learn'd to die,
> And all this world is woxen daily worse.   (vi.6.1–6).

Reputation and performance are ethically incommensurate: the figure who courts justice with such formal decorum is clearly the quintessential exemplum of injustice, and hence of radical indecorum – "great Chaos child" (vi.26.6).

If her ethos composes incongruous topoi, so too does the logos of her trial. Its conduct does not accord with Fortune's mode of "Sacrament," "ordele," or "blooddy fight" rejected by Artegall because "ill perhaps mote fall to either side" (V.i.25); rather it follows the counter-exemplary procedures of argument, testimony, and judgment characterizing Duessa's trial at Mercilla's court.[13] Together with its conduct, the very fact of the trial and of Mutabilitie's submitting to any juridical authority obviate her case: both introduce, a priori, exempla to prove the enthymeme expressed by Dame Nature as a judgment "rigthly wayd" on the pageant of witness (vii.17–46) Mutabilitie calls to prove the antithetical enthymeme:

> I well consider all that ye haue sayd,
> And find that all things stedfastnes doe hate
> And changed be: yet being rightly wayd
> They are not changed from their first estate;
> But by their change their being doe dilate:
> And turning to themselues at length againe,
> Doe worke their owne perfection so by fate:

Then ouer them Change doth not rule and raigne;
But they raigne ouer change, and doe their states maintaine.   (VII.vii.58)

Mutabilitie, in her prosopographic dichotomies of ethos and pathos, contains, as it were, the seeds of her own moral antithesis, anticipating the burden of Dame Nature's judgment.

6   DAME NATURE

Dame Nature not only complements Mutabilitie's function as a summative metonymia but also embodies the very motivational tap roots of rhetoric. The perception of both nature and the supernatural as estranged orders-of-being generates the mystery inciting strategies of transcendent courtship. Nature often shares ethos with scripture in Christian rhetoric as the dispositio of God's inventio, and Spenser identifies nature's "garment" with the aporiatic revelation of Christ's transfiguration (vii.7). In secular as well as religious rhetoric, the appeal to natural order or natural law has a long (and continuing) history of suasive effectiveness when an enthymeme requires exempla accepted by an audience as both transcending and appropriating topoi specific to any particular time, place, and custom. In logical paradigms, Nature so considered corresponds functionally with either the abstract end of induction from the universe of empirical particulars or the abstract principle from which such particulars may be deduced. In the corresponding biological model appropriate to mythic cosmology and fabula nature is, like Venus in the Garden of Adonis, progenetrix: "great Grandmother of all creatures bred;" "equall mother / [who] knittest each to each, as brother vnto brother" (vii.13.1; 14.8–9). Thus nature stands uniformly in rhetorical, logical, biological, and mythic analogues at the apex of a common schematic. Accordingly, when it functions in persuasion as the model of order and law, the natural order stands in relation to all particular, artificial social orders constituting the base of its triad identically with the relation of Platonic Form to imitation, cause to effect, ideal to actual, Muse to artistic expression, or justice to law. Such analogues to the order of nature have manifested themselves diversely throughout this analysis of Spenser's dispositio, and the position of Dame Nature as both focus of sequential resolution and hierarchical ultimate of courtship epitomizes Spenser's principles of narrative decorum. She is a reiterative attractor, configuring Spenser's dispositio to "in-gather" all prior, cognate triadic moments and conflate them.

Her dramatic functions project an apt complement to this formal priority. The abstracted distance of nature from all particular civic orders or legal codes provides attributes of universality and disinterestedness that make its prosopopeia in Dame Nature specifically decorous as Spenser's ultimate dramatic exemplum of both sovereignty and justice, his magistrate of magistrates. The logos of narrative priority gives Dame Nature and her court ultimate priority of place, epitomizing previous loci of conflation, Colin's fourth Grace on Acidale and Mercilla's court, together with the infolded exemplars of justice they recapitulate. Thus Dame Nature functions in metonymic identity with "the highest him ... the God of Nature" and so occupies the ultimate position of ascendency, "greatest goddesse only great" and "soueraigne goddesse" (vii.14.1, 16.1); she realizes in a dramatic exemplum the oft-repeated topos asserting a divine source of all secular authority to rule. Accordingly she transcends and reinvests all objects of deputed authority, not only Mercilla (V.ix.31–2) but also Isis/Osiris (V.vii.1) and Gloriana/Elizabeth (V.pr.10) whose topoi of praise become hers by right of successive priority: "Dread Souerayne Goddesse, that doest highest sit / In seat of iudgement, in th'Almighties stead" (V.pr.11). Furthermore, as the female synonym for "the highest him," Dame Nature echoes the hermaphroditic trope to infold its precedents, Britomart and the juridical Venus: "Whether she man or woman inly were, / That could not any creature well descry" (vii.5.5–6). "Father of Gods and men by equall might" and variously "great Grandmother" and "equall mother" of "all creatures," Dame Nature also inhabits the procreative locus occupied by Venus and Adonis at the summit of the Garden of Adonis and incorporated by Colin's fourth Grace at the summit of Mount Acidale; she assumes their status as ultimate exemplar of the reciprocal mystery of ideal marriage.

Indeed, her topoi define a locus of dynamic reciprocity where other fundamental contraries of the male/female class resolve estrangement in mystery: "euer young yet full of eld, / Still moouing, yet vnmoued from her sted; / Vnseene of any, yet of all beheld" (vii.13.2–4). To accommodate and resolve contraries by transcending and containing both extremes without eliminating either defines the rhetorical ideal of "persuasion without advantage" that models Spenser's ideal of marriage as mystery. Dame Nature demonstrates that an ideally just polis incorporates this ideal and its topoi of "mystery" insofar as it too must accommodate contraries: resolve estrangement between individuals without loss of individual integrity, achieve identification in "the many" without loss of identity as "the one."[14] Hence Dame Nature emblematically recapitulates the argument projected in Spenser's narrative sequence that the ideals of marriage and social concord come before, and by logical analogy are predicates derivative from, the ideal of just polity.

Such qualities of elocutio give Dame Nature functional equivalency with "Iustice high ador'd" at the apex and still-point of Ovidian history and so at long last, here on Arlo Hill, re-establish the coincident locus of "Peace vniversall ... mongst man and beasts." The Blatant Beast, by escaping "his yron chaine" through "wicked fate" or "fault of men" (VI.xii.38), demonstrates the failure of Calidore, like Artegall whose mission he assumed, to achieve that re-establishment. The "Cantos of Mutabilitie" make it clear that the common failure of Artegall and Calidore in their common mission to overcome the moral indecorum of fortune through heroic action was inevitable if Spenser's dispositio of justice were not to confound epic ethos with the pathos of fairy tale. In Spenser's inventio, as in Plato's, "wicked fate" is not an alternative but a metonymia for "fault of men," and the failure of heroic action to achieve absolute victory over the antidecorum of fortune in the lapsarian, sublunar world proves by narrative logos an implicit enthymeme made explicit in Mutabilitie's prosopographia (vi.5,6) and the exempla she presents in proof of her case (vii.17–46). In such a world the courtship of justice can find no closure: the world's ultimate term is Mutabilitie – it is governed, because it is defined, by an paradoxical simulacrum of organization without precedent or syntax, its only decorum a radical indecorum. The court on Arlo Hill resolves this limitation on closure by providing an object of courtship with the ethos of a scriptural exemplum, incorporating by transcendence both the ideal historical exemplum of Elizabeth's court and its ideal fabulous counterpart in Gloriana's. Moreover it also gathers in its dyslogistic anti-ideal: the court on Arlo Hill is absolute; even Mutabilitie must come there as a courtier.

9 Envoy and *Peroratio*: Spenser on Arlo Hill

1 THE PROBLEM OF CLOSURE

Dame Nature and Arlo Hill transcend the formerly summative structural position of Colin's fourth Grace and Mount Acidale by incorporating and amplifying their function. Qualities summative or ultimate in Book VI become abruptly recontextualized in the two-canto adjunct that follows, standing revealed in "Book VII" as contributive and subordinate attributes of a higher and sequentially successive ultimate term. Of course Mount Acidale in its turn was also recapitulative: the process of incorporation and amplification by successive metonymic and synecdochal exempla of their prior analogues gives allusive resonance and pattern to Spenser's entire dispositio. Indeed, it gives functional definition to the term "structure" as an attribute of his rhetorical practice in *The Faerie Queene* and is hardly an innovation of the "Mutabilitie Cantos." On the contrary, what makes these cantos appear innovative, and to some readers disjunctive, is not the extension of this process but its termination. The vantage point from Arlo Hill is not simply a step higher than that of Mount Acidale, and the perspective a degree more comprehensive. Between Acidale and the "highest hights / of Arlo Hill" we "jump over" (as it were) all the anticipated peaks epitomizing all the "priuate morall" and "polliticke" virtues projected in the letter to Raleigh but "missing" from the narrative, and effect a discontinuous, sudden arrival at the terminal point of ascent, the highest, least obstructed prospect possible on the entire landscape of Spenser's

Faeryland. Such discontinuities and thwarted anticipations generate aporia, and readers have attempted to resolve their resulting perplexities by one form of variation or another on the strategy of Matthew Lownes, the first publisher of the "Cantos," who simply denied any problem of discontinuity by choosing an effective label: the "Two Cantos of Mutabilitie" become a "parcel of some following Booke … Vnder the Legend of Constancie." Those readers who follow Lownes categorize the Cantos as a "core" or "fragment" of an uncompleted Book VII. A dissenting majority use other labels such as "coda," "epilogue," "culmination," and "detached retrospective,"[1] recognizing discontinuity but arguing on grounds of allegorical interpretation that it represents decorous closure, not the accidental truncation occasioned by the mutable chance of Spenser's own mortality: "the *Cantos* are usually regarded now as an independent philosophical and cosmological poem that relates time to eternity, change to permanence, and mortality to God's providential scheme."[2] Spenser's inventio clearly accommodates such binaries as attributes of Dame Nature, locus of resolution for all polarities, and they are implicit in her judgment of Mutabilitie's case. Indeed, the weight of evidence adduced from analysis of Spenser's rhetorical structure supports those who argue on allegorical grounds for decorous closure: insofar as the subject of justice is concerned, the "Mutabilitie Cantos" bring its inventio to a demonstrative completion.

I have used "envoy" as yet another alternative generic label for the "Cantos of Mutabilitie," this one suggested by the suddenness as well as the universal scope of Spenser's shift in perspective on Arlo Hill and derived from the analogous rhetorical function of Chaucer's sudden shift to his own version of "detached retrospective commentary"[3] in the "Envoi" for *Troilus And Criseyde* (ll.1807–25) where Troilus passes posthumous judgment on his own failure of public duty for private ends and his subjection to the fortunes of lust midst the fortunes of war. Plato's "Myth of Er" concluding his *Republic* provides another functional analogy (but without a usable label) in its disjunctive generic shift from discursive to fabulaic dispositio that universalizes Socrates' perspective on justice. Even more decorous perhaps with Spenser's structure of courtship, but equally unlabeled, is the abrupt shift from social to transcendent perspectives and consequent qualification of appetitive motives with sacrificial ones effected by Castiglione's introduction, between Book III and IV of *The Book of the Courtier*, of renowned courtiers who have died and Machiavelli's sudden acknowledgment of Fortune in the final two chapters of *The Prince* to open suddenly the closed calculus of power he has constructed relentlessly for the twenty-five preceding chapters. There are insufficient data to establish influence on Spenser's "Cantos of Mutabilitie" from any or all of these models. My point is simply that precedents of high ethos and sufficient number exist to constitute a topos of closure particularly congruent with the rhetorical constituents of the "Cantos": their inventio of sovereignty and justice, their dispositional dynamic of courtship, and their combination of functions from two accepted figures for ending an oration, iteratio[4] and digressio. All characterize the rhetorical mode of the "Mutabilitie Cantos" relative to the six books that precede them. I can find no term in rhetorical handbooks to designate any such topos, but borrowing "envoy" from the distinguished exemplum represented in Chaucer, "pure well head of Poesie" (VII.vii.9.4), seems apt.

The envoy as a rhetorical form, by using apparent disjunction to accentuate actual coherence, replicates some characteristics of an oxymoron, and with any oxymoron the question "what does it mean?" concedes necessary priority to "where does it come from?" Meaning depends upon retracing the provenance from antithetical categories of terms that collide incompatibly in the novel context of oxymoron. Envoys invite a similar response. Through a sudden shift in narrative perspective to look down and back on the preceding sequence, Spenser, like Chaucer and the other cited exemplars, creates aporiatic perplexity that characteristically demands retrospection and reconsideration to resolve.[5] His strategy thereby fosters recognition that an ostensibly digressive innovation is actually composed of elements always latent in the work but now brought to unanticipated prominence by their unfamiliar configuration within the envoy.

2   "CONSTANCIE," FAUNUS AND DIANA

The analysis of rhetorical structure in this essay constitutes one such retrospective, and clearly it is my thesis that Spenser's structure as it develops throughout the epic is decorous with, or anticipates, not only the sudden "unanticipated" topical prominence given the collocation of justice, rightful sovereignty, and fortune in the Mutabilitie Cantos but also the associated topographical prominence, literal and structural, of Arlo Hill and its Ovidian myth. Indeed, it is the burden of the last chapter that the summative functions of Arlo Hill and Dame Nature are anticipated respectively by Mount Acidale and Colin's fourth Grace: in short, the elements of structural completion were already inherent in Book VI. There is no precipitate jump over missing virtues to a conclusion. Nor is there any necessity on the evidence of Spenser's rhetorical structure to assume an incomplete Book VII, on "constancie" or any other subject. Lownes' notion of a fragmentary "Book VII" to account for the "Mutabilitie Cantos" evidently rests on two assumptions: that "constancie," rather than justice and courtesy, represents the virtue for which Mutabilitie serves as villainous anti-exemplum and that Spenser's *divisio* announced in the letter to Raleigh is identical with the *divisio* of his actual work. He concludes that Spenser still had either six or eighteen books to go, that the "Cantos" were a fragment of one of these, and that its subject must have been "constancie." Without confirming Lownes's attribution of the "Cantos" to a putative Book VII, Hamilton's authoritative edition evidently shares the second of his assumptions. "That Constancy should be the subject of a book seems inevitable," Hamilton argues, "it is implied in the virtue of each hero."[6]

The fact that constancy is "implied" in the virtue of each hero, however, would not explain the prominence afforded by its further demonstration at the dispositional point of summation. On the evidence of rhetorical structure it appears that by the time he began work on Books IV through VII, possibly earlier, Spenser had superimposed strategies of cumulative integration on the horizontal, episodic, seriatim catalogue of discretely demonstrated virtues proposed in the letter to Raleigh. Such changes argue a shift of rhetorical motive, and the specific direction of change suggests a clarification of Spenser's "end" from demonstrating two-dozen discrete virtues that "fashion" an individual "gentleman or noble person in vertuous and gentle discipline" to demonstrating the infolded "grammar" of virtues that "fashion[s]" a polity of just order. It lies beyond the possibilities of proof to decide whether this shift represents a strategic adjustment dictated by the familiar recognition that art is long but life is short, or by the kind of recognition that comes from the actual labour of composition, the discovery of artistic direction which often comes only after the journey is well under way. Perhaps a combination of such "priuate" factors together with "politicke" contingencies of Elizabethan history provide the most likely source.

Whatever the provenance of change, in Spenser's rhetorical structure as it is, not as projected in the letter, justice and its complement courtesy emerge through Books IV, V, and VI as antitheses to fortune and hence to its prosopopeia in Mutabilitie. All component virtues, "politicke" and "priuate," are cumulatively represented by justice and courtesy. This representation includes constancy, because it is inherent in the component virtues of faith, temperance, love, and friendship, and is so represented from its first citation in the narrator's first epiphonema, featuring the knight of Holiness as an exemplum of "rash misweening" and its outcome, "inconstancie in loue" (I.iv.1). As much a private as a public virtue, therefore, "constancie"

represents on its own merits a significant attribute of both justice and
courtesy, as the inconstancy demonstrated in Artegall's willful subjection to Radigund, Britomart's psychomachia in Isis's Church and
Calidore's dereliction among the shepherds proves by logos.

Constancy, however, is merely one component of justice, not its
equivalent. "Constancy" implies a decorum both sequential and self-
reflective, with past determining future; its prime exemplar is perhaps Talus whose constancy is absolute; it precludes arbitrary law at
the magistrate's whim but lacks the power of equity to make the
application of law decorous with contextual circumstance rather than
mere conformity to the letter of prior analogues. If Dame Nature
demonstrated "constancie" by simply allowing precedent to determine consequent, Mutabilitie would win her case (VII.vii.58), as
would Despaire. Instead, Dame Nature makes her ruling on principles of justice by which the decorum of providential will transcends
both experience and the imperatives of temporal sequence.

On grounds of rhetorical structure, therefore, I conclude that a
summative book of Constancie would be redundant to Spenser's
argument and would, in any case, represent an indecorous context
for the "Cantos of Mutabilitie." Their appropriate context is the six
books which precede them, and the effect of the "Cantos" is to
demonstrate explicitly that constancy, in addition to the qualities
normally attributed to it and already demonstrated in previous
books, is explicitly a significant component of divine justice. Equally,
they demonstrate that "Constancie" as a human virtue, public or
private, is merely a cognate reflection, temporal, linear, and necessarily rhetorical, of the absolute, logical "consistency" represented by
the principles of providential will governing the order of nature and
derivative causally from the ultimate term of ultimate terms, the
"God of Nature." Framed within this structure, the apparent, visible
inconstancy of all exempla, natural, social, and psychic, adduced as
supporting evidence by Mutabilitie, actually demonstrate, if "rightly
wayd," the product of absolute logical consistency, the derivative
"end" of deduction, and hence compose graphically the base of a
hierarchical triad linked by the dilation of cause and effect to its apex,
as essence dilates to accidents and reality to appearances: "They are
not changed from their first estate; / But by their change their being
do dilate" (vii.58.4–5).[7]

That no discontinuity of inventio exists between the "Mutabilitie
Cantos" and the demonstration of justice and courtesy developed
through Book VI is evidenced in Spenser's dispositional stress on the
contiguity of Arlo Hill and Mount Acidale; indeed some allusive
topoi suggest their coincidence. His question in parenthesis "(Who

knows not Arlo-hill?)" (vi.36.6) immediately precedes an explication of Arlo Hill in mythic digressio (vi.37–55). The view induced from "the highest hights / Of Arlo-hill" is necessarily retrospective, and Spenser's interrogatio provokes ambiguity congruent with retrospection and the summative function of the "Cantos." "(Who knows not Arlo-hill?)" is Janus-like: it both anticipates the mythic digressio which ostensibly answers it and asserts that the answer is already known – that the digressio succeeding the question merely recapitulates what precedes it and to have read the preceding six books is to know Arlo Hill. Spenser's immediate referent for knowledge of Arlo is clearly the immediately preceding Mount Acidale. The three lines subsequent to the parenthetical question (36.7–9), by allusion to *Colin Clout's Come Home Again* (104–5), identify the shepherd-poet with "old father Mole" and "Arlo-hill" with its "highest head," thereby locating Mount Acidale, Colin's "home" in *The Faerie Queene*, in the same range with Arlo Hill if not at the same co-ordinates.

On Arlo Hill, therefore, in a retrospective digressio composed of topoi from Ovidian fabula merged with those of heroica in a context of pastoralia, Spenser recapitulates the vital elements from his demonstration of justice summarized on Mount Acidale. From that summative summit he not only imports Colin Clout but also functionally replicates Venus and her encircling graces with Diana and "all her Nymphes enranged on a rowe" (vi.39). Similarly, the voyeuristic Faunus (vi.46) replicates in dys-courtesy both Calidore and implicitly Spenser's putative courtly audience who, rendered imperceptive by escapist fantasy, like the "foolish Faune … wouldest needs [their] owne conceit areed." Faith, temperance, chastity, and concord fall victim to Faunus' passion, and in recapitulation of Spenser's inventio of sequential interdependence among virtues, his violation of courtesy becomes an issue of justice, with Diana, like Venus in Book IV, assuming a juridical role as magistrate.

As a figure of justice, however, Diana develops ambiguous ethos. She cites the principle that punishment must be decorous with the crime (vi.51), a topos essential in Spenser's inventio to distinguish justice antithetically from fortune, but Spenser distances his audience from Diana's perception and subverts her judgment. His extended similtudo constituting Faunus's crime as an annoying disturbance of domestic economy (vi.48–9) defuses any strong dyslogistic pathos, and so infuses his punishment with indecorous hyperbole. Diana's motives become irrationally appetitive, her judgment an act of "vengefull mind," "more angry then the rest" (51.1), and her exercise of power a demonstration of "magnificke might" without "wondrous wit." Thus her sentencing Molanna to death by stoning (vi.53.3–4) and her laying a "heavy haplesse curse" on Arlo Hill (vi.55) demonstrate an absolutism more evocative of Talus than any exemplum of equity or mercy, and (as with her ward Belphoebe in Book III) certainly an absolutism more appropriate to the ultimate term of virginity than to justice and chastity or any other component virtues of *civilitas*.

Such qualification of ethos intensifies the summative resonance of Spenser's digressio on Arlo Hill. He makes Diana an exemplum of judgment without mercy, the "old dispensation" of Divine Judgment, but the strategies of ambiguous ethos juxtapose simultaneously topoi of the "new dispensation" she fails to demonstrate. It is Faunus who exercises mercy and redeems the virtues he has violated, keeping faith with Molanna and uniting her with "her beloued Fanchin" in a figure evoking one exemplary emblem of concord, the just marriage of Thames and Medway (IV.xi.8–53). In contrast, Diana's "command'ment" specifying the method of Molanna's punishment, that she be "whelm'd with stones," uses a detail of elocutio to create the same juxtaposition of dispensations by evoking reciprocally Christ's call (John 8:7) for empathetic identity with the condemned from those who would "first cast a stone at her." In their echo of Christ's scriptural topos, Belphoebe's words to Timias create the same disjunction with the "commandment" of her mythic paradigm Diana: "We mortall wights, whose liues and fortunes bee / To commun accidents still open layd, / Are bound with commun bond of frailtee" (III.v.36). Calidore's words, too, resonate in this context, their meaning fully realized only in the disastrous aftermath of his own "frailtee":

> In vaine he seeketh others to suppresse,
> Who hath not learned him selfe first to subdew.
> All flesh is frayle, and full of ficklenesse,
> Subject to fortunes chance, still chaunging new;
> What haps to day to me, to morrow may to you.   (VI.1.41)

Ultimately, this scriptural echo and the import of Diana's ethical ambiguity lead by allusive precedent back through Spenser's everchanging dispositio to Una's words of salvation from Despaire for the "fraile, feeble, fleshly" Redcrosse: "In heauenly mercies hast thou not a part? ... Where iustice growes, there grows eke greater grace" (I.ix.53), and to the Mount of Contemplation whose topothesia demonstrates Una's enthymeme by subsuming the mountain-loci of Law and Mercy, thereby reconciling the two dispensations.

Thus Arlo Hill, Spenser's last natural analogue of hierarchical structure, reiterates the function of his first and paradigm of all such analogues, the Mount of Contemplation. At the summit of Arlo Hill, Dame Nature reconciles the two dispensations of Divine Judgment in herself: she is synonymous with "the God of Nature" and incorporates in her prosopographia robes of juridical authority identified by similtudo with the transfigured Christ on Mount Thabor (VII.vii.7).[8] The ambiguity of Diana's ethos as exemplar of the old dispensation in her function as judge of Faunus argues the structural and ethical stature of Dame Nature, who assumes Diana's function and transcends her as she does Diana's sister Venus and Venus's Graces from Mount Acidale. Ethos corresponds here with sequential logos: Diana's priority anticipating Dame Nature in the order of narrative projects her hierarchical subordination to the ultimate term of justice. By allegoria this sequence attracts the analogous sequence of providential history, where too the Dispensation of Law is transcended in temporal sequence by the Dispensation of Mercy revealed through Christ to be a subordinate component of Divine Judgment.

3   ARTEGALL / CALIDORE / SPENSER

On Arlo Hill, moreover, Spenser collocates himself with Dame Nature. His presence is implicit in the presence of Colin Clout, his metonymia at the summit of Mount Acidale, and, equally, with particular resonance, in Spenser's atypically clumsy transition to the digressio explicating Arlo Hill. It first raises then deliberately flouts the assumption of indecorum ("ill fitting") in mingling topoi of pastoralia with heroica (vi.37). This strategy draws signal attention to his reiteration within the context of Arlo Hill of the issues exemplified in Colin's broken pipe and the Graces' vanishing when Calidore reveals himself. Hamilton notes that Spenser here "imitates Calidore who left wars and knights to live 'in hils, in woods, in dales' (VI.x.3.6),"[9] but the imitation functions rhetorically as antiphrasis. The purpose of Spenser's digression is precisely the opposite of Calidore's dereliction: he seeks to engage, not avoid, issues of justice and courtesy in a pastoral setting.[10] Court and country merge on Arlo Hill; Dame Nature, by transcending them, accommodates the ideal exemplars of justice and courtesy and through them takes on all the virtues they incorporate as courtiers. Thus "all" who "loue virtue" become her courtiers, and a pastoral setting becomes the ultimate locus of courtship, just as, by the same principle of decorum, a digressio explicating Arlo Hill in pastoralia becomes the locus of summation for Spenser's entire dispositio in heroica, *The Faerie Queene* itself. An assertion of indecorum between pastoralia and heroica thus lingers into the "Cantos of Mutabilitie" from the episode on Mount Acidale where it exemplified "dys-courtesy," mere court-liness within Gloriana's court masquerading as courtesy. On Arlo Hill the assertion is accentuated by repetition and finally refuted. Spenser's narrator raises the issue of indecorum only to ignore it and thereby make strategically the same refutation that the transcendent status of Arlo Hill makes structurally. It is not, therefore, as a mimetic analogue of Calidore escaping from the burdens of quest that Spenser appears on Arlo Hill. Rather he re-appears as the metonymic Colin Clout from Acidale, establishing his presence on Arlo Hill as poet-quester at the "end" of his poetic courtship and so evoking again by allusion the identification of that quest with Calidore's for courtesy. Spenser closes Book VI as he opens it with this identification, and his relation to Calidore in "Book VII" corresponds to that of Calidore with Artegall in Book VI: Spenser has assumed their burdens of quest – he is Calidore's surrogate not his *Doppelgänger*.

Calidore's ethos as epic hero depends upon his possessing human weakness: infallibility, like invincibility, belongs to the heroic topoi of fairy tale. His love for Pastorella and his desire for a stable, simple community providing escape from the hardships of quest and the uncertainty of the mutable world echo those of Redcrosse on Con-templation's Mountain (I.x.63) and express weakness we would be quick to recognize and forgive in ourselves. However, the structural rhetoric of Book VI reiterates that of Book I in locating these under-standable desires among the commonplaces of fairy tale. Colin's pastoral vision and his interpretation of it on Mount Acidale failed in their suasive "end" to "fashion" Calidore "in uertuous and gentle discipline" because Calidore lacked the ethical and aesthetic discern-ment to recognize courtesy in any guise but the courtly and chivalric one that his experience conditioned him to expect. Determined by these precedents of unexamined experience, Calidore thus exempli-fies in anticipation Mutabilitie's claim to sovereignty, and the narra-tive sequence of Book VI argues by logos a specific *ominatio*[11] that the "Cantos of Mutabilitie" generalize. After, and by sequential logos, because Colin's art fails to provoke illuminating aporia Calidore comes to apprehend the meaning of his quest through the conse-quences of his dereliction, through an aporia of catastrophic chance and change represented dramatically in the Brigants' destruction of Meliboe's pastoral society and emblematically in the agent of For-tuna's moral indecorum, the Blatant Beast, who "rends without regard of person or of time" (VI.xii.40.9). As an aporiatic spur to transcendent courtship, the beauty of Spenser's art will fail, like its synecdochal reflection in the pastoral beauty of Pastorella, Acidale, and Colin's vision, if his courtly audience, like Calidore, misconceives and hence misperceives his art as escapist fantasy. By incorporating fabulaic topoi of fairy tale and romance as elements of logos in order subsequently to discredit their ethos, his rhetorical strategies from the outset anticipate and move to counter not only such aesthetic misperception but also the social disorder treated as their consequence in the "Mutabilitie Cantos." Since Colin Clout and Calidore figure metonymically Spenser and his audience, the analogy argues a concomitant threat to just order in Spenser's society consequent upon any failure of his suasive end, and so implies an enthymeme making art the alternative to civil chaos as the source of illumination on the meaning and value of a good society. If the aporia of art fails, the aporia of catastrophic change "succeeds."[12]

Rhetorically, therefore, Spenser's envoy argues an enthymeme in which art and justice are effectively cognate attractors, reciprocally generative of each other. Arlo Hill, where no indecorum exists between art and nature (vi.8, 10), assumes the attributes of Parnassus from Mount Acidale, as Dame Nature assumes its Graces, and so completes the replication of Contemplation's Mountain by conflating the locus of the Muses with those of Law and Mercy joined in Dame Nature. Spenser's use of natural analogues for hierarchical structures thus comes full circle: the digressio on Arlo Hill summarizes specifically the evidence of Spenser's narrative dispositio generally that his inventio treats the orders of divine justice and providential history as homologues of natural order. Each forms graphically a conic hierarchy of causal generation; each dilates from a single source, from apices coincident in the same ultimate term occupied dramatically by "Dame Nature."

Spenser's narrative history converges on the same point. The ultimate term of justice occupied by Dame Nature is the sequential end of his narrative. By structural analogy she is also coincident with the source of that narrative: she thus invests topoi of justice identical with those of Spenser's inventio, topoi anatomized in the dispositio of his epic. Her "sergeant," like Mercilla's, is Order; he is her only immediate subordinate, and his appearance contiguously before her entry demonstrates Dame Nature's "first" logical predicate through this simple priority of narrative sequence: he establishes universal social order on Arlo Hill among gods and "all other creatures" (vii.4). Dame Nature is not the ultimate term of any single virtue but the principle of principles according to which all virtues essential to the just society collate into an ordered hierarchy: she corresponds to the principles of decorum determining the cumulative, interdependent grammar of virtues developed in Spenser's dispositio. The end of Spenser's narrative history corresponds to its suasive end: both are embodied in the ultimate object of courtship occupied by Dame Nature. Spenser has been courting that end from the outset of his narration: courting simultaneously, through his art, both the just order emblemized in Dame Nature and his audience's identification with its principles. Each episode in the narrative demonstration of *The Faerie Queene* is at once dramatically a step towards this end, logically a derivative attribute of it, and rhetorically an element of dispositio effecting its demonstration.

Spenser's homologous patterns, therefore, preclude his using "Book VII" to demonstrate any specific virtue: its subject is dictated by its summative function and it can, perforce, have no champion to embody its subject except one who is coincident with the principle of all virtues embodied in Dame Nature. She invests dramatically the transcendent object of courtship for this book in particular and the epic in general. "Of Constancie" appears to be a fragment with only a villain and neither champion nor legend because Spenser comes to Arlo Hill having assumed fully the function of questing courtier. He is surrogate and synecdoche for all champions of all virtues component in justice: they are his eulogistic exempla and compose his ethical proof. The legend of "Book VII" has been told in Books I through VI.

4   MUTABILITIE AND THE SUMMATION OF REFUTATIO

Spenser's presence at the "appeale" of Mutabilitie thus embodies ironically, on Arlo's "equall Hill," the sort of dual juridical function which she found indecorous at Jove's court, where judge and counter-claimant were one: "But thee, O Ioue, no equall Iudge I deeme ... That in thine own behalfe maist partiall seeme" (vi.35.1–3). Coincident with Dame Nature as locus of identical topoi of justice, Spenser is present on Arlo Hill in the posture of Mutabilitie's judge, while as summative courtier to Dame Nature he functions implicitly as Mutabilitie's counter-advocate. He does not speak at her "appeale" because he has already spoken: Books I through VI compose his cumulative case for moral decorum in analogous private, "politicke," and universal orders. Thus Mutabilitie's "appeale" functions rhetorically as a final and summative example of refutatio against Spenser's advocacy, and the atypical, two-canto dispositio of Book VII is wholly consistent with this structural function; the "envoy" need only provide a venue and vehicle for the corporate exemplar and advocate of "dys-order" to make her case.

The topothesia of her venue on Arlo Hill presents the absolute congruence of art and nature that characterizes Dame Nature's impromptu pavilion (vii.9–10), and so evokes an elocutional trope antithetical to the commonplace of nature-corrupted-by-art in dyslogistic settings associated particularly with such prior counter-advocates as Despaire, Acrasia, Malecasta, and Busirane. This elocutional inversion accentuates the estrangement between Mutabilitie and Dame Nature. Mutabilitie is radically indecorous with this redeemed/uncorrupted setting: the "end" of her rhetorical art is not to contest directly the cognate discourses of art and justice but to deconstruct their common mimetic ground of validation, the very order of nature itself. Such estrangement generates the motive for courtship and defines its vector; Dame Nature is the alienated identity Mutabilitie courts: she would be herself the ultimate term of ultimate terms. The case Mutabilitie argues precludes her accepting transcendent subordination to Dame Nature any more than she could accept erotic and social subordination to Jove. As an advocate in refutatio, her beauty and other topoi of fabula evoke allusively the pathos of Acrasia and Malecasta, but her dispositio is most evocative of Busirane, as her inventio is most evocative of Despaire. Like all such counter-advocates, her subject is Spenser's: "an humble suppliant," she seeks "Right" by defining legitimate sovereignty.

Unlike her predecessors, however, she stresses proof by logos, not pathos: indeed, her insistence on the primacy of logos over ethos is a strategy to discredit Jove's claim to be the unseen cause of visible change (vii.49.1–5). Such a restriction would also discredit the ethos of Spenser's art (II.Pr.1–4) and, in anticipation, the persuasiveness of any decision Dame Nature might render based on an authority outside the evidence Mutabilitie adduces, all of which is visible and concrete. The earth and "her tenants ... man and beasts" (vii.19), like the four elements, "the ground-work ... of all the world, and of all liuing wights" (vii.25), provide Aristotle's "available and appropriate" exempla to prove her enthymeme of sovereignty: "in them all raignes Mutabilitie" (vii.26.1). Even the generation of new life from "decay and mortal crime" she treats as exemplary only of simple change without direction or other purpose, denying implicitly any natural analogue to spiritual salvation and the providential dispensation of mercy: "So turne they still about, and change in restlesse wise" (vii.18). Like Busirane's Masque of Cupid, her pageant of seasons, months, day and night, hours, life and death (vii.28–36) uses processional form to re-state the enthymeme and its causal implications in the successive dispositio of narrative and history. This expansion of her witness to include the whole natural order universalizes her proof, as does the ingenious copia and dense elocutio of cultural allusion Spenser lavishes on the figures of icon and allegoria composing her pageant.

The very evocative power of these figures, however, effectively denies the enthymeme Mutabilitie asserts they prove: no decorum could exist to evoke affective meaning from a nexus such as that of October with a "dreadfull Scorpion" and Orion's suffering "Dianaes doom vniust" (vii.39) if cultural history were exemplary only of random flux. Spenser's elocutio undercuts by indecorum his creature's inventio. Indeed, Hawkins argues that her dispositio is also disconnected from its inventio: that the mere invariability of their cyclical nature undermines the validity of seasons and years as proof of change and so confutes Mutabilitie's case. Thus he sees Mutabilitie as "the victim of a vast dramatic irony," but excuses the victimization on the grounds that "Spenser is a poet, not a philosopher: he gives us his essential realities in images, not arguments."[13] Image and argument, however, are commensurate: decorum requires it. As poet Spenser is also rhetor and his images are, precisely, elements of argument. So is Mutabilitie. She exists to make Spenser's case, and as she courts suasive identity with Dame Nature, Spenser simultaneously courts suasive identity with his audience. It is we who are the real judges at the court on Arlo Hill. If Dame Nature speaks for Spenser, then we must be persuaded that she also speaks for us. Dramatic irony certainly courts identity between playwright and audience: they share knowledge the character on stage lacks. If, however, Spenser creates ironic distance from Mutabilitie in such a way that we see her as victim, he persuades us not that Mutabilitie is wrong and Dame Nature right but that Spenser can make the case for providential order only by misrepresenting the counter-argument.

His case for psychic and civic order rests ultimately on their both being analogous to the absolute order of providential will expressed in nature and history: Dame Nature thus epitomizes Spenser's case in her decision (vii.58–9). Change itself projects a Divine inventio, just as Mutabilitie's being allowed to present her case for disorder within the orders of due process and rhetorical dispositio, using "appeale" as refutatio, argues that disorder is simply a mode of decorum. Absent decorum, Mutabilitie would have no voice or venue: the very fact that she makes her case where she does and the way she does provides an exemplum disputing her case. This built-in irony of Mutabilitie's appearance is both dramatic irony and built-in because it is also built in to Spenser's dispositio as the necessary consequence of his decision to impose prosopopeia on the anarchic and bring this anarch on stage in the role of advocate to make an ordered case in an ordered context for disorder. Simply by giving her an audience Spenser necessarily relates that audience to her ironically. Mutabilitie, therefore, is not a victim of Spenser's inability or disinclination to sustain philosophic discourse: Mutabilitie is rather a decorous exemplum in rhetorical discourse of a philosophical paradox.

Paradox, like oxymoron and envoy, functions rhetorically not to distance an audience through irony but to engage them through perplexity, and the problem of rhetorical analysis here involves issues of commensurate expectation and a discrimination among audiences. Surely the largest portion of Spenser's contemporaries required no manipulation on Spenser's part to be distanced beyond bridging from Mutabilitie. Even some three centuries later, Darwin hesitated for decades to publish his work on natural selection because he was aware that the potential audience he sought held fundamental preconceptions of reality, moral law, and social justice that were in violent disjunction with the underlying assumption of his theory that the natural order is without purpose or direction.[14] For Darwin, as for Mutabilitie, everything in nature is the product of random change. On the other side of the Darwinian watershed from Spenser's contemporary audience, we confront Mutabilitie's argument with a set of expectations Spenser could not anticipate. His problem rhetorically is not to reinforce the distance between his audience and Mutabilitie with irony: on the contrary, as with Despaire, he must gain her a hearing after giving her a voice. Thus the dyslogistic topoi of her prosopographia reinforce audience expectations, but pathetic topoi of fairy tale heroism and the ethos of her performance as advocate contradict those expectations. Similarly the indecorum between Spenser's dense, brilliant elocutio and Mutabilitie's inventio serves to cast an argument the audience might have expected in an entirely unexpected mode, its ingenious and delightful copia a source of eulogistic pathos inconsistent with its ethos. Such strategies have less to do with dramatic irony than with the induction of Socratic aporia to stimulate examination of the unexamined. Spenser subjects the conventional Boethian doctrine that Dame Nature rehearses to re-examination, and in so doing creates, or re-creates, like Boethius himself, a revitalized sense of the questions for which the concept of nature's providential order is the answer.

The tactics that court such re-examination give Mutabilitie seductive plausibility in performance despite an ethos of reputation strongly predisposing the audience against her; in this they attract an obvious comparison with Spenser's treatment of Despaire. Trevisan's warning and the patent dyslogia of appearance and setting make Despaire's threat both more obvious and more affectively personal than Mutabilitie's, but their similarities in rhetorical posture give them structural equivalence as loci of identical topoi and argue that the pleasing appearance of the latter merely makes her the more insidiously dangerous of the two. Unlike Darwin, Mutabilitie does not argue that since nature displays no purpose, hence no moral order, natural law is indecorous as the model for a just social order. On the contrary, like Despaire, she illegitimately appropriates the causal structure of providential will while denying its first premise. Nature remains Mutabilitie's model for all analogous orders of art, social justice, and history, but the model has no moral relevancy: in the chaotic dispositio of random chance the only decorum is paradoxically a radical non-decorum, an utter absence of fixed attractors or principles of organization. Despaire is a master rhetorician, hence a master of decorum: he tailors his argument to audience and occasion. He ostensibly evokes retributive justice as a fundamental topos of his inventio for Redcrosse because it is fundamental to the ethical topoi of the knight and consequently renders him vulnerable to suasion by pathos based on its implications. On another occasion, before another audience, while ostensibly appealing for justice, Despaire could readily argue by logos rather than pathos that there is no basis for justice of any kind, only amoral flux in nature and the local contingencies of power. The court on Arlo Hill provides that occasion and audience.

Mutabilitie invests Despaire in female guise: their allusive resonance creates a kind of parodic, dyslogistic resolution of the Hermaphroditic topoi resolved eulogistically in Dame Nature. Appropriately, as in Despaire's refutatio, the evidence here is no more in dispute than Spenser's humanist principles of causality at Despaire's cave. Redcrosse is guilty of the crimes Despaire catalogues, and Dame Nature concedes the proof in Mutabilitie's evidence from nature "that all things stedfastnes doe hate / And changed be." Dame Nature and Mutabilitie use the same exempla to support antithetical enthymemes. The envoy thus ends with Dame Nature demonstrating dramatically her structural identity with Spenser. She functions effectively less as Mutabilitie's judge than as her opponent in a debate and cites I Corinthians to win on grounds of scriptural ethos rather than logos: "But time shall come that all shall changed bee, / And from thenceforth, none no more change shall see. / So was the Titaness put down and whist" (vii.59.4–6).

5   PERORATIO

Spenser's two-stanza peroratio to *The Faerie Queene*, labelled by Lownes as an "vnperfite" canto viii, immediately follows this moment in the envoy. The "I" who speaks this peroration takes the stance which Spenser's narrator has assumed throughout the epic. "I" is not the creator of the speeches we have just heard but a fellow-member of the audience who first "thinke[s] on" the "speech whyleare / Of Mutability" and "then" on "that which Nature sayd" (viii.1.1, 2.1). Spenser represents this "thinking" as seriatim process, its direction tracking a path out of aporia charted by Plato and Boethius. He uses the first/then pattern to transpose an interpretive polarity into a sequence, debate into narrative. Temporal priority (when Fortune, then Providence) generates the logos of structural analogy to demonstrate both causal priority (because Providence, then Fortune) and logical priority (if Providence, then Fortune). The sovereignty of Mutabilitie over "all things," save "Heav'ns Rule" for which "she all vnworthy were," teaches the narrator to "loath this state of life so tickle, / And loue of things so vaine to cast away" (viii.1). He recognizes in her advocacy the general case of his enthymeme, drawn as an epiphonema from the specific case of Calidore's agony at the loss of Pastorella, that "worldly chaunces" afflicting the "ioyes of love" have a didactic purpose: "to let men weet, / That here on earth is no sure happiness" (VI.xi.1). Thus Mutabilitie completes the demonstration of despair as a state of frustrated courtship, complementing with social and erotic courtship the transcendent frustration invested in her cognate prosopopeia, Despaire. In sequence, thus in consequence, the narrator "then" turns to Nature, taking on her topoi in succession after those of Mutabilitie.

Boethian conventions thereby allow the narrator to resolve the dilemma of forced choice between antagonistic interpretations of Mutabilitie's undisputed evidence from nature. Fortune is didactically ordained by Providence: they are not static, competing answers to the same question but complementary components of a reciprocal dynamic in which one stimulates the question for which the other is the answer. Philosophically, dilemma generates dialectic; rhetorically, estrangement generates courtship. Spenser's narrator learns the lesson of Mutabilitie's speech by recognizing in her evidence his own state of estrangement from the same ultimate term that Mutabilitie courts by "seeking her Right." She courts the place decorous by right with her nature, her Artistotelian state of rest. Of course, her state of rest by natural right is change, and she is a summative exemplum of rational disorder, of courtship misperceived and misdirected by appetitive motives: "For thy decay thou seekst by thy desire" (vii.59.3). Her courtship of justice disguises social motives under transcendent topoi, and her very power to gain suasive identity with Spenser's audience through the pathos of shared estrangement undermines the ethos of her case for sovereignty. For if subjection to change evokes the sense of estrangement from our rightful place, then we can never justly, by right, be transcendent courtiers to change: "she all vnworthy were / Of the Heav'ns Rule."

Spenser's narrator, therefore, functions here to distinguish the pathetic and ethical persuasiveness of Mutabilitie's argument from its undisputed and powerful proof by logos that "all that moueth, doth in Change delight." In supplying the conventional Boethian answer to Mutabilitie's case for the "a-decorum" of nature, the narrator fulfills a rhetorical function equivalent to Una's during the confrontation of Redcrosse with Despaire, and once again attracts that episode into Spenser's strategy of circular closure. The "heauenly mercies" suppressed by Despaire in his propagandistic distortion of divine judgment become equivalent to the didactic purposes of providential will suppressed by Mutabilitie in her depiction of purposeless, directionless flux as the essence of natural order. Change is both the primal cause of estrangement from the "God of Sabbaoth" (vi.5–6) and, like all estrangements, the necessary condition of His transcendent courtship, but the burden of Mutabilitie's propaganda argues that all change is purposeless. She transmutates the doctrine of *felix culpa* into the primal enthymeme of despair, nothing to be done. This parallel not only confirms Mutabilitie's functional identity with Despaire but also locates Spenser's audience with Redcrosse as transcendent courtiers at a point of crisis, estranged in longing from the place of rest and "peace vniuersall" where contemplation delivers a true vision informing the ideal and universal polis of "the Host" governed in perfect justice by the "Lord of Hosts": Spenser's topos of the New Jerusalem defines the end (both object and conclusion) of all courtship where all estrangement is resolved: "For all that moueth doth in Change delight: / But thence-forth all shall rest eternally / With Him that the God of Sabbaoth hight" (viii.2.6–9).

Concomitantly, the didactic purpose attributed to Fortuna in the narrator's peroratio argues that those who so court are being courted in turn. The functional identity of providential will with "heauenly mercies" provides the ultimate exemplum of reciprocal courtship and the ideal of marriage as mystery, since the ordained didacticism of fortune proves the sacrificial caritas of supernal justice and provides the "lodestarre" whereby the creature's will to court lost identity finds immediate, equal, and reciprocal response in a providential will to court the creature. For Redcrosse, indeed for all Spenser's knights, the world in which they move is the world of Mutabilitie, and the flux of that fortune-charged place is educative: their learning and their courtship chart the same path. "All that moueth," the kinetics of their legends, define their courtship and provide the narrative dispositio to demonstrate the virtues they champion. Spenser's narrator in the final two-stanza peroratio replicates their courtship and summarily demonstrates the rhetorical implication of Fortuna's didactic purpose: he "moueth" both "from" and "because of" the lessons of Mutabilitie to an understanding of Dame Nature's judgment.

In so doing Spenser's narrator also moves finally into functional identity with his creator. The prayer in exclamatio concluding the peroratio and *The Faerie Queene*, "O that great Sabboath God, graunt me that Saboaths sight," is univocal: the longing it expresses to see from Arlo Hill the vision Redcrosse attained on the Mount of Contemplation and the estrangement that longing demonstrates leave no distance between the poet and his creature, or indeed between poet, bardic voice, and audience. Spenser as artist replicates the didactic function of providential will. We have come to Arlo Hill where the vision is possible because Spenser has led us here along a path out of (both arising from and away from) the aporia provoked by Mutabilitie's testimony, the sense of pathlessness between the exempla of Mutabilitie's world and the inventio of just, providential order that reason and desire would have that world prove. Often obtuse, occasionally trailing our understanding and sometime leading it, his naivety sometimes a source of ironic distance inviting amused collusion at his expense between Spenser and reader, the narrator was our surrogate, guide, and companion along this path, and his function, even at moments of ironic separation, was didactic. He taught while he learned or failed to learn, courting identity with his creator by striving to discern a decorous order underlying the seething flux of ever-changing copia by which Spenser imitated the world of Mutabilitie and reciprocally courted his audience.[15]

As a necessary condition of such reciprocal courtship, Spenser had travelled the road to Arlo Hill before us: whatever our apparent relation to narrator and poet, we have always participated after-the-fact in discovery – we have always been estranged from Spenser's understanding. At the summit of Arlo Hill his perspective merges with ours. With the prayer that ends Spenser's suasive courtship and our journey he demonstrates that this estrangement necessary to didactic mystery between poet and audience resolves ideally in the marriage of minds: we attain the end of the epic at the point of Spenser's acknowledgment that he has reached the end of his suasive purpose. He has no more to teach. Poet and audience become coincident in a single locus of common estrangement from the mystery they court.

6   ESTRANGEMENT: THE DIALECTIC IMPERATIVE

Rhetorically this prayer is an ambiguous instrument of closure. As an act of courtship, prayer implicitly assumes a will to reciprocal courtship of the suppliant by the transcendent courted. In its very form and conventions prayer thus confutes Mutabilitie's case for a sovereignty of purposeless change and so its generic topoi recapitulate in summary the burden of Spenser's entire dispositio. In particular its function reiterates Dame Nature's decision, evoking the lesson-response topoi of sacerdotal litany and affirming the ethos of her court on Arlo Hill as a temple incorporating both Mercilla's court and Isis's church.

Arlo Hill, however, is also a locus of decay from order to chaos described in topoi from Ovidian myth. Thus while its summit collocates with "Iustice … high adored," this union of ultimate terms occurs at the apex of Ovid's cone. Spenser's prayer looks to "that same time when no more Change shall be," locating him now within time and "Change," estranged from eternity as the events on Arlo Hill are estranged in the antique world when "all loued vertue" along the vector of moral disintegration leading to the now of Spenser and his audience. Diana's curse argues Mutabilitie's case.

The narrator's movement through the final two stanzas follows that vector, estranging us not just temporally but suasively from Dame Nature's decision. The prayer is no longer, or not now, simply a reiteration of her enthymeme: it is an act of pathos undertaken because the mutable fortune of Arlo Hill itself supports Mutabilitie and destabilizes the ethos supporting Dame Nature's decision. Natural cycles no longer function unambiguously as ironic refutations of Mutabilitie, since Ovid's cone turns cycles into spirals, exemplifying a transcendent will to chaos, not cosmos.

Spenser's peroratio mimics in affect this destabilized coda: it unites poet, narrator, and audience, but only to estrange them corporately and abruptly from the ultimate term of justice attained briefly at the end of the envoy. The peroration thereby addresses our corporate identity as courtiers within the flux of Ovidian history. No more than Redcrosse or Calidore can we remain in the paradisiac state of resolved courtship. As Berger observes, not even Spenser's corporate exemplar of courtship can ever resolve the transcendent estrangement that is the necessary condition of courtship. "Arthur as a minister of grace, an imitation of Christ, can redeem Britain from subjugation to the Earthly City, but Arthur is mortal and Britain will fall again."[16] Miller also doubts Spenser ever intended that Arthur should find Gloriana. He sees both as "synecdoches for the completion of Spenser's poem ... Arthur for its becoming complete and Gloriana for its being complete." Their union in marriage is "less an achievable telos than ... a kind of vanishing point."[17]

Rhetorically, as in the case of Amoret and Scudamour, the resolution of Arthur and Gloriana's erotic estrangement by marriage would prove the simultaneous resolution of transcendent estrangement. All courtship would cease. The moment of resolution on Arlo Hill is a point of structural closure only in the sense that it marks the point where a new cycle of courtship begins. Spenser's end returns us now to the beginning, still and again bereft of justice and its infolded virtues: compelled therefore, "pricking on the plaine," to seek them with only Spenser's vision and a prayer as borrowed armour to sustain us.

APPENDIX

Schematic of Classical Rhetoric and Glossary of Terms

DEFINITIONS

1 The art of persuasion
2 (Aristotle) To discover in each case the existing means of persuasion and to select the best means from those available and appropriate (Appropriateness=decorum: cf. Elocutio, B.iv below).

TYPES (Aristotle's categorization according to the purpose of a speaker and the role of his audience)

1 Judicial or Forensic (relating to law courts: the rhetoric of prosecution and defence)
Speaker: examine evidence and proof to dispose audience toward or against the client
Audience: reach a verdict about events in the past
2 Deliberative (originated in popular, political assemblies)
Speaker: persuade or dissuade about course of action or policy
Audience: "judge of things to come"
3 Demonstrative or Epideictic (public ceremonials or rituals)
Speaker: praise gods and heroes (e.g., eulogies, panagyrics), also came to include censure or denunciation of individuals and institutions
Audience: not called upon to reach a decision or act – only feelings and attitudes are affected.

OFFICES OR FACULTIES OF THE ORATOR

Inventio
a) Proof
  i) Inartificial (evidence in law court: e.g., sworn testimony, material proof)
  ii) Artificial (or "artistic")
  Ethos: proof based on authority of reputation or performance
  Pathos: proof based upon emotional response
  Logos: ("logical"): proof based upon enthymemes and exempla (sing. exemplum)
  includes
  Enthymeme: a proposition decorous with alogical, open systems; probable in contrast to the certainty of premises and syllogisms in logical systems
  Exempla: three types (in decreasing order of ethos): scriptural, historical, fabulous
b) Topoi (sing. *topos* from Gr. for "place," particularly a place where treasure is stored)
  Tested and approved ways of arguing a case, investigating a chosen subject, conducting an argument, treating a theme. Originally kept in lists by subject matter, especially topoi of praise (eulogistic) and blame (dyslogistic)
c) Commonplaces
  Collections of information, observations, maxims, proverbs, and ideas applicable to (therefore "common" to) more than one subject.

Dispositio   arrangement: disposition of arguments and structure of oration
  a) Exordium (introduction): aims to make the audience receptive, advertent, and pliable (benivolem, attentum, docilum)
  b) Narratio: a short statement of the facts of the case or general subject
  c) Propositio: states succinctly the specific concern of the oration; sets definite issue or problem before the audience.
  d) Partitio or divisio: divides topic under its main headings
  e) Confirmatio: develops all arguments on speaker's side of the case
  f) Refutatio or reprehensio: acknowledges contrary arguments in order to refute them
  g) Digressio: a departure from the main argument for the sake of pertinent and useful enrichment of the case. Peacham's *The Garden of Eloquence* gives as examples: "the declaration of deeds, the descriptions of persons, places and times, the reporting of apologies [fables] and similitudes" (Sonnino, *Handbook*, 74).

h) Peroratio (conclusion)
    summing up (enumeratio) of main points
    Amplificatio: impressive, emphatic statement of speakers position
    Commiseratio: appeal to the tender feelings of the audience

Memoria   the arts of commiting an oration to memory

Pronunciatio   the arts of effective oral delivery

Elocutio   (style and ornamentation)
  a) General styles
      i) Grand: impressive words ornately arranged (best for moving an
          audience); decorous with tragic, heroic, and sacred subjects
      ii) middle or tempered (best for pleasing): decorous with odes, lyrics,
          elegies
      iii) Low or plain: (best for teaching) decorous with pastoral, satire, and
          burlesque
          Any given rhetorical artifact, especially in English, will usually con-
          tain all three – they are not personal styles
  b) Qualities of style
      i) Purity and correctness
      ii) Clarity
      iii) Decorum: choice of genre, diction, imagery, sentence structure,
          rhythm, strategies of argument and proof, tropes, and schemes of
          ornament will depend upon such matters as subject, genre, occasion,
          audience, purpose of the oration.
      iv) Ornament: the "figures" of rhetoric (literally "attitudes" or different
          postures taken up by words on different occasions). The number of
          figures (tropes and schemes) defined by rhetorical theorists
          increased ten-fold between Aristotle's *Art of Rhetoric* and Peacham's
          The Garden of Eloquence, approaching 200 in the latter work, many
          involving distinctions without significant difference.

          I have attempted to keep the sample used analytically in this
      study as small and selective as possible, and to make the meaning
      of each figure clear from its context. Those used crucially or fre-
      quently are listed here together with a highly generalized descrip-
      tion of their functions.

          Allegoria: a species of narrative alluding to other sequences of
      events, inviting multiple interpretations, and a method of
      exegesis.

Antiphrasis: the use of a word to give it meaning antithetical to its normal connotations

Antithesis: a juxtaposition of contraries

Causa: a form of apologia accounting for present conditions through a narrative, historical or mythic, of their provenance

Epiphonema: a summary moral drawn as the conclusion of a narrative or argument

Epitheton: an adjective or other modifier attached to a substantive to praise, dispraise, amplify, or extenuate

Expolitio: occurs "when we dwell on the same topic and yet seem to say something ever new. It is accomplished in two ways: by merely repeating the same idea, or by descanting upon it. We shall not repeat the same thing precisely. Our changes will be of three kinds: in the words, the delivery, and the treatment" (Sonnino, *Handbook*, 93).

Hyperbole: transparent overstatement, revealing rather than concealing the truth

Icon: the description of a person by multiple comparison for purposes of praise or blame

Interrogatio: a question implicitly assuming the answer: effectively an assertion in the interrogative mode

Ironia: "a class of allegory in which the meaning is contrary to that suggested by the words" (Quintillian).

Metalepsis: a kind of metonymy or conceit in which a remote cause is signified by a series of metaphoric steps to a present effect; "the metaphor of a metaphor" (Sonnino, *Handbook*, 263).

Metaphora: differs from the modern "metaphor" in that it involves only one word used to suggest another word close to it in meaning

Metonymy: the substitution of the cause for the thing caused, e.g., the inventor for his invention, the container for the thing contained, the sign for the thing signified, and vice versa.

Oxymoron: the juxtapostion or collision of words signifying logical opposites in normal usage

Paroemion: alliteration of consonants

Paronomasia: a pun

Ploce: occurs "when one or more words are iterated for the purpose of amplifying our subject or drawing forth feeling of commiseration" (Sonnino, *Handbook*, 64).

Prosopographia: the description of persons by their form, stature, manners, studies, activities, affections

Prosopopoeia: to give a voice to non-human objects, inanimate or animate, or to personify abstractions

Pysma: series of questions asked without pause for answers; effectively an undefended series of assertions in the interrogative mode

Sententia: a maxim pertaining to "the maners, and common practises of men, which declareth by an apte breuity, what in this our lyfe ought to be done, or not done" (Rix, *Rhetoric*, 52).

Synecdoche: to represent the whole by a part, genus by species, and vice versa

Topothesia: the description of an imaginary place. Peacham notes it is a figure used by poets, not by orators (Sonnino, *Handbook*, 212).

Notes

1 In correspondence with me dated 12 June 1981 Hamilton quotes a letter to him from James Murphy received the previous week.

2 For a schematic outline of classical rhetoric and a glossary of rhetorical terms used in this study, see *Appendix*, 205–9.

3 For an excellent summary of the issues see W.J. Kennedy's introductory essay, "Rhetorical Criticism and Literary Theory," in his *Rhetorical Norms in Renaissance Literature*, 1–19. See also Henderson, "Rhetorical Criticism from E.K. to the Present."

4 On rhetorical instruction at Merchant Taylors' School when Spenser attended, see Cain, *Praise in the "Faerie Queene,"* 6. Cf. Barker, "Merchant Taylor's School." Sloane ("Schoolbooks and Rhetoric") argues persuasively that Erasmian pedagogic intentions for copia were primarily concerned with inventio rather than elocutional ornamentation. Ong provides an evocative sense of the insidious and pandemic influence of rhetorical theory and practice on every aspect of Tudor education in *Rhetoric, Romance and Technology*, especially in his essays on "Oral Residue in Tudor Prose Style" (23–47), "Tudor Writings on Rhetoric, Poetic, and Literary Theory" (48–103), and "Ramist Classroom Procedure and the Nature of Reality" (142–64). For a concise survey of Ciceronian textbooks and methods of instruction, see Freedman, "Cicero in Sixteenth-and Seventeenth-Century Rhetoric Instruction." Hardison ("Humanism") summarizes Erasmian influence on English education.

5 For a useful summary of allegoria and the other genre available to Spenser see Sonnino, *A Handbook to Sixteenth-Century Rhetoric*, 225–32. Murrin gives an incisive account of evolutionary variations in "allegory" as a rhetorical term, ranging in designation from simple trope to "extended tropological discourse" in *The Veil of Allegory*, 54 ff.

6 "Allegorical theory practically demands Platonism for its understanding, or rather Neoplatonism, since the Renaissance Platonists read their master by means of Plotinus and Proclus" (Murrin, ibid., 90). Bieman in *Plato Baptized* traces with admirable thoroughness and economy the complex evolution of Platonism into Neoplatonism and demonstrates its pervasive presence in Spenser's work. Cain (*Praise in the "Faerie Queene"*) attributes Spenser's making Una the "first encomiastic type of Elizabeth" in the poem to her embodying generally "the oneness behind multiplicity," and particularly "the unity that underlies the many facets of the queen's praise." See also Hankins, *Source and Meaning in Spenser's Allegory*, 234–77 and Nohrnberg, *The Analogy of "The Faerie Queene,"* 527–68.

7 Two modern studies provide exceptions. Rix, *Rhetoric in Spenser's Poetry* (1940), applies sixteenth-century sources of rhetorical theory to Spenser's work and selects illustrative examples from throughout the canon; in keeping with tradition he restricts himself to figures of elocutio, but does so systematically and thoroughly. Cain (*Praise in the "Faerie Queene"*) breaks with tradition to provide acute analysis of topoi and strategies of encomium in selected passages of description involving characters he considers iconically representative of Queen Elizabeth in *The Shepheardes Calender* and *The Faerie Queene*; Cain thus restricts his interpretation of the distributio of praise primarily to an allegoria on Elizabethan occasions.

8 In addition to the works by W. J. Kennedy, Murrin, Ong, and Sloan cited above, see G. A. Kennedy, *Classical Rhetoric and Its Christian and Secular Tradition*, Murphy, ed., *Renaissance Eloquence*; Vickers, *Classical Rhetoric in English Poetry* and *In Defence of Rhetoric*.

9 Montrose used the term "orientation" to characterize a tentative conceptualization of New Historicism, noting that "those identified with it, by themselves or by others, tend to be heterogeneous in their practices and reticent in their theorization of those practices. In brief their project is to resituate canonical literary texts among the multiple forms of writing, and in relation to the non-discursive practices and institutions, of the social formation in which those texts were initially produced – while, at the same time, recognizing that this project of historical resituation is necessarily the textual construction of critics who are themselves historical subjects." He summarizes the issues involved in this dichotomy between new historical and new critical

topoi with exceptional clarity in the opening section (303–7) of "The Elizabethan Subject and the Spenserian Text." The quotation is from p. 304.

10 Hamilton, "Our New Poet: Spenser, 'Well of English Undefyld,'" in Hamilton, *Essential Articles for the Study of Edmund Spenser*, 488.

11 Miller, *The Poem's Two Bodies*, 118–19.

12 Ryle, *Dilemmas*, 1.

13 See for instance Kane's postmodernist strategies in *Spenser's Moral Allegory*.

14 This incipient, if not actual, "dilemma" has sufficient force to occupy Clark Hulse, Richard Strier, and Andrew D. Weiner in a special issue of *Studies in Philology*. Significantly, it also engaged A. C. Hamilton and Louis Adrian Montrose in controversia as the topic inaugurating the Kathleen Williams Lectures on Spenser and His Age in 1987. See Benson, "Spenser at Kalamazoo," 51–3. See also Howard, "The New Historicism in Renaissance Studies."

15 Lodge, *After Bakhtin*, 14.

16 Goldberg, *Endlesse Worke*, 29n12. Anderson's essay is "Whatever Happened to Amoret?".

17 Pechter, "In Defence of Jargon," 171. I am grateful to my colleague Heather Jackson for referring me to Pechter's witty sanity.

18 Burke, *A Rhetoric of Motives*, 208. For an earlier attempt to apply Burke's notion of courtship as an approach to Spenser's poetry see Dixon, "Rhetorical Patterns and Methods of Advocacy in Spenser's *Shepheardes Calender*." Angus Fletcher anticipated, with evident lack of enthusiasm at the prospect, the possibility of an "attempt to press rhetoric into critical service in reading Spenser." As if to minimize the chances of encouraging such a specter, he gives his speculation maximum obscurity as an addendum to a lengthy footnote at the last extremity of an excellent book and suggests that "for such purposes Kenneth Burke's notion of the 'caricature of courtship' … would seem a useful starting point" (*The Prophetic Moment*, 302n38). Burke's section on the "caricature of courtship" deals with Kafka. I have found his "The Paradigm of Courtship: Castiglione" (221–33) to be a more decorous and fruitful point of departure, and I am generally indebted to the entire Part 3 ("Order") of Burke's study (183–333).

19 Goldberg, applying Barthes rather than Burke, arrives at a similar delineation of this invocation, noting that the common posture of poet to muse, Lady, and patron presents "relationships of power refigured in each stanza of the Proem." He finds in these figurations an assertion of reflexive empowerment for the poet through his medium of courtship (*Endleese Worke*, 21). Cain (*Praise in the "Faerie Queene,"* 9 ff.) suggests that Spenser's praise of Elizabeth through "cultic images" identifying

her with Venus, Diana, and Astraea and "deifying icons implying proximity to God himself" represents an adaptation of elocutional strategies of comparatio recommended by Scaliger and Quintilian.

20 Spenser, "*The Faerie Queene*," ed. Hamilton (New York: Longman, 1977; reprint with corrections 1980). All citations of *The Faerie Queene* and "A Letter of the Authors to Sir Walter Raleigh" are to this edition, which will be cited henceforth as Hamilton (1977).

21 On Neoplatonic triads generally see Wind, *Pagan Mysteries in the Renaissance*. Cain sees the triad as an instrument of encomium in the Proem to Book I where Elizabeth as goddess, mirror of grace, and great lady of the greatest isle mediates, in the "middle term . . . presented serially" between the heavenly and the earthly (*Praise in the "Faerie Queene,"* 53). Nohrnberg associates Neoplatonic triads primarily with Spenser's use of the Graces (*The Analogy of "The Faerie Queene,"* 74, 461–2) and with the Christian Trinity in the puzzle of Triamond and his brothers (617). See also Bieman, *Plato Baptised*, 49–50, and her ingenious "composite schema of Platonic, Biblical, and Neoplatonic language" (133).

22 Cf. Hamilton (1977, 3) who cites Sidney's identification of "the skill of the artificer" with "that Idea or fore-conceit of the work, and not the work itself." Hamilton argues that "the presence of this 'Idea' in *The Faerie Queene* justifies Williams' assertion that 'from the first book to the fragmentary seventh the reader becomes increasingly aware of a clear and comprehensive vision, and of a steady purpose which impels him, through a mass of significant detail, towards a final unity.'" Hamilton's quotation is from Williams, "'Eterne in mutabilitie,'" 115.

23 Hamilton (1977), 737.

24 On Elizabeth's own rhetoric of chastity, her "polliticke" use of its topoi to consolidate her authority and counter the "patriarchal" topoi of her parliament and privy council in their arguments for a dynastic marriage, see Montrose, "The Elizabethan Subject and the Spenserian Text," 309–18. See also Miller, *The Poem's Two Bodies*, 5–6.

25 For a contrary view see Kouwenhoven, *Apparent Narrative as Thematic Metaphor*. Kouwenhoven starts from the assumption that the letter to Raleigh is a definitive statement of Spenser's intention and the epic is the unemended fulfilment of those intentions, and argues that "magnificence" rather than justice is the virtue that "infolds" all others; it becomes "another word for each of these virtues when 'perfect'" (16–18).

26 In exploring this "analogy of private and public orders" Nohrnberg adduces exempla of analogous imagery drawn from common sources in the elocutio in Books II and V. (*The Analogy of "The Faerie Queene,"* 285–425). Nohrnberg's elocutional evidence demonstrates both his copious

learning and the presence of the Platonic analogy, but I obviously remain unpersuaded that it demonstrates the notion in his structural model that the work, in effect, folds back on itself at the juncture between Book III and IV, making the book of justice an analogous "sequel" (285) to the book of temperance rather than the focus of a "grammar" ordering dialectically the virtues demonstrated in all preceding books.

27 Miller, *The Poems Two Bodies*, 180n15.

CHAPTER ONE

1 Greenblatt, *Renaissance Self-Fashioning*, 174.

2 Miller, *The Poem's Two Bodies*, 154.

3 Cain, *Praise in the "Faerie-Queene,"* 178.

4 Montrose, "The Elizabethan Subject and the Spenserian Text," 319–20. See also Helgerson, "The New Poet Presents Himself."

5 Although he does not use rhetorical terminology, Dunseath seems to have these distinctions in mind when he argues that "Spenser is a better teacher than Aquinas precisely because he is not a teacher in the strict sense of the term. His technique works not by precept nor by description but by example. His is a poetry of awareness, not resolution" (Dunseath, *Spenser's Allegory of Justice*, 230).

6 Barthes, "Myth Today," 129.

7 Said, *Orientalism*, 203.

8 Ibid., 231.

9 Bal's *Narratology* provides a serviceable catalogue of the terms and issues involved in this lively controversia as well as an excellent bibliography.

10 Alpers, *The Poetry of the "Faerie Queene,"* 5. While Alpers deals sensitively with elocutio, he does not engage dispositio as a suasive element, perhaps because he doubts its relevance. His term "tact" (131) expresses a relationship of poet to audience that evidently precludes any comprehension of decorum between the elocutional texture of the individual stanza and the distributional structure in which it functions. The books, therefore, "have no structures," only immediate textures of pathos. Alpers argues this enthymeme by "appeal to the common reader's experience ... the intense absorption in details of the moment, the even progression from line to line and stanza to stanza, the difficulty in remembering details of earlier cantos and books" (112). Proof by ethos evoking experience of "the" common reader is, of course, irrefutable, even if the experience of another reader is contradictory; obviously I also find it unpersuasive. Cf. Dundas, "The Rhetorical Basis of Spenser's Imagery."

11 Carscallen, "The Goodly Frame of Temperance," Hamilton (1977), 348.
12 Goldberg is a perceptive representative of commentators who charac-
    terize our response to such narrative disruptions and dislocations with
    the terminology of pathos: "satisfaction," "frustration," "pleasure,"
    "desire," and "anxiety" (*Endlesse Worke*, 2–3 and passim). His study
    demonstrates that even discontinuous narrative is suasive; the disconti-
    nuities provide him with exempla for his proof by logos. Kouwen-
    hoven seems to treat continuity as the *sine qua non* of narrative; thus
    the "disconnected" nature of Spenser's "fiction *qua* story" represents
    merely "the illusion of narrative" (*Apparent Narrative*, 10).
13 "A Letter of the Authors," Hamilton (1977), 738. Cain (*Praise in the
    "Faerie Queene,"* 73) argues that the emphasis on the "celestial *genus*"
    of Una and Caelia, each an *icon* of Elizabeth, "intimates, in a non-
    iconic way, the eternal beyond the narrative flux and implies that the
    queen is a celestial Idea that sheds meaning upon the milieu of experi-
    ence and history." I would only stress that the "eternal beyond the nar-
    rative flux" is demonstrated by that flux.

CHAPTER TWO

1 These topoi have been collected and catalogued in two standard
    works: Krappe, *The Science of Folk-lore*, and Thompson, *Motif Index of
    Folk Literature*. On the general relationship between fairy tale and epic,
    I am indebted to Campbell, *The Hero with a Thousand Faces*, and
    Langer, *Philosophy in a New Key*, especially Langer's ch. 7, "Life
    Symbols: The Roots of Myth."
2 These strategies have been extensively and cogently addressed by
    other commentators. I find the following particularly useful for the
    investigation of rhetorical structure: Alpers, "Narration in *The Faerie
    Queene*"; Dees, "Narrator of *The Faerie Queene*"; and Hinton, "The Poet
    and His Narrator." Dees also provides an insightful epitomization of
    the commentary in his "Narrator of *The Faerie Queene*."
3 Metonymia (L. *transmutatio*) is a trope defined by Susenbrotus (*Epitome
    troporum ac schematum et grammaticorum et rhetorum* [Zurich, 1541], 7f)
    as the substitution of the cause of a thing for the thing itself: "we do
    this in several ways, substituting the inventor for his invention ... the
    container for the thing contained or vice versa ... an author for his
    work ... the sign for the thing signified" (tr. Sonnino, *Handbook*, 184–5).
4 For an extensive summary of the Dragon's cumulative functions in
    Book I, see Kaske, "The Dragon Spark and Sting in the Structure of
    Red Cross's Dragon-Fight."
5 See Skulsky's excellent summary and bibliography in "Despaire."

6 Beckett, *Waiting For Godot*, 15f. "Nothing to be done" is also the first line spoken in the play (7), and recurs twice before the occurrence quoted here.

7 Hume, *A Treatise of Human Nature* (1739–40), I.iii.

8 MacLure, "Nature and Art in *The Faerie Queene*," Hamilton (1972) 179.

9 I borrow this pun from Nyquist's witty and disturbing anatomy of a sustained critical and editorial reconstruction of Milton's text, "Textual Overlapping and Delilah's Harlot-Lap."

10 Roberts in his "Circe" (165–7) traces concisely the traditional topoi Spenser draws upon. He notes that Busirane and Mutabilitie, two of Spenser's strongest voices of refutatio subsequent to Acrasia, are also Circean (166).

11 Hamilton (1977), 281, summarizes allegorical interpretation of these topoi.

12 Alpers, in his "Bower of Bliss," gives an insightful, balanced, and economical summary of the vexed controversy generated by this passage and its significance as "a touchstone for larger issues of poetics" and of poetic response.

13 Hamilton (1977), 168.

14 Miller (*The Poem's Two Bodies*, 156) uses this line as an exemplum in proof of an interpretive formulation evidently derivative from that most effective of rhetorical analysts – Karl Marx, in his critique of German ideology. Miller argues that the substance of Guyon's exclamatio can be accounted for "only" through "a profound mystification of authority" such as that represented by "belief in a hierarchy of body and soul" which gives the soul "ontological privilege ... typically expressed as a form of the authority to govern." I would qualify Miller's exclusivity: the Marxian formulation is "only" one possible enthymeme decorous with such rhetorical fundamentals as identification of analogous patterns of priority and the mystery of the other.

CHAPTER THREE

1 Lewis, *The Allegory of Love*, 338.

2 Craig notes that both Renaissance Platonism and Ramist logic "acknowledged no fundamental distinction between dialectic and poetry ... In respect to words as well as ideas, the poet ideally is a dialectician ... For Ramists, "words are a form of argument because the 'notation' or etymology of a word bears some logical relation to the 'notion of the thing,'" and the etymology required is the "logical one which explains the cause why this name is imposed for this thing." Craig, "The Secret Wit of Spenser's Language," 316. Hankins (*Source*

and Meaning, 235) points out that Critias is the interlocutor most often named by Plato: he appears in five dialogues.

3 Hill traces the topoi of Platonic love for this defence in "Colin Clout's Courtesy," 223–5.

4 Berger, "The *Faerie Queene* III," 415.

5 Cf. Williams, "Eterne in mutabilitie," 211. For a thorough analysis of Belphoebe's prosopographia as an encomiastic icon of Elizabeth and Elizabethan imperialism see Cain, *Praise in the "Faerie Queene,"* 86ff. Cain finds a tempering of comic excess even in the sustained eulogistic mode of the description. Miller (*The Poem's Two Bodies*, 233) also interprets the equivocal praise of Belphoebe's virginity as political allegory, a dyslogistic view of Elizabeth's failure to ensure dynastic succession. Spenser's criticism of Elizabeth is "deeply implicit ... [and] tends to emerge, if at all, through equivocation" from "within what is ostensibly a language of praise." See also Anderson, "Belphoebe."

6 Cain (*Praise in the "Faerie Queene,"* 104) notes that "the spectacle of Amoret's 'trembling hart' drawn from her breast and 'Quite through transfixed with a deadly dart' ... perverts one of Spenser's favourite images for oratorical effect, the pierced heart." See also Hyde, "Busirane."

7 This oxymoronic juxtaposition, like most rhetorical figures, can equally function eulogistically. Cain (*Praise in the "Faerie Queene,"* 78 and *passim*) discusses what he terms the "Virgo-Venus paradox" as a topos of encomium to Elizabeth in Book I. Cf. Miller, *The Poem's Two Bodies*, 224–5.

8 Berger ("*The Faerie Queene* III," 418) gives this hierarchical structure a Jungian context, interpreting it as psychological allegory. "Together with Florimell, the twins are infolded into the more complete image of the feminine psyche [than that offered by the Venus/Diana model, a "one sided masculine caricature"] of which Britomart is the exemplar offered in *The Faerie Queene.*"

9 Cf. Bieman's assertion of "the absolutely central importance of the reciprocal erotic activity between Venus and Adonis" (*Plato Baptized*, 223). She stresses the specifically Neoplatonic analogue to the fundamental rhetorical structure I outline here and uses the term "participating" as a functional synonym for my "courting." See also Geller, "Venus and the Three Graces." On the controversy concerning a Platonic presence in the Garden, which Roche (*Kindly Flame*, 120) describes accurately as "pointless," see Hankins, *Source and Meaning*, 234–9. On the role of *Symposium* see Brooke, "C. S. Lewis and Spenser," Hamilton (1972), 15.

10 Miller (*The Poem's Two Bodies*, 261–2) summarizes the interpretive problematic represented by Spenser's topothesia of the Garden, and elaborates Roche's argument that the Garden is not visualizable (*Kindly*

Flame, 118–22) with a geometrical analogue: "We are asked to follow rapid shifts in perspective that move, so to speak, along two different axes – for the perspective shifts from that of matter and that of form as well as shifting from point to point in the cycle of natural life" (272). In my view, those axes are temporal and logical respectively, resolving implicitly into a causal cycle. Bieman, however (*Plato Baptized*, 221), issues a salutary warning that any reading of Spenser's radically "equivocal text" which "achieves apparent clarity ... is clearer than the poetry."

CHAPTER FOUR

1 Cf. Cain (*Praise in the "Faerie Queene,"* 106) who identifies the Hermaphroditus as not only an emblematic *typus matrimoniae* but also, as "child of Mercury and Venus," an emblem "fusing rhetoric and desire," respectively (in my terminology) the instrument and motive of courtship. Silberman ("Hermaphrodite") notes the relationship between this eulogistic Hermaphroditic exemplum at the end of III:1590 and the dyslogistic allusion to one of its sources, the Ovidian well of Salmacis (I.vii.5) where Redcrosse's appetitive motives bring "illicit coupling" with Duessa and subsequently, hence consequently, the tyrannous aegis of Orgoglio. See also Silberman's "Hermaphrodite and the Metamorphosis of Spenserian Allegory."
2 Goldberg, *Endlesse Worke*, 66–7 and *passim*.
3 Cf. Dunseath (*Spenser's Allegory of Justice*, 8–9) who cites exempla of continuities between Books III, IV, and V and takes issue with Roche's "tacitly claim[ing]" that "the whole love affair of Britomart and Artegall" is covered in Book III and IV. Dunseath argues that any explanation of their romance "which does not include Book Five, where the romance itself has its most crucial trials, is partially incomplete" (10n14). Bieman also takes Roche to task for "confin[ing] his examination of the image of Britomart to the Books of Chastity and Friendship and, not surprisingly in the light of that limitation, [finding] her an unreal character." "Britomart in Book V of *The Faerie Queene*," 156. See also Fletcher, *Prophetic Moment*, 205.
4 Hamilton (1977), 423; Murrin, *Veil of Allegory*, 95–6.
5 Goldberg, *Endlesse Worke*, 130.
6 Ibid., 5–6.
7 Roche, *Kindly Flame*, 16–17. See also Cheney's "Triamond" for an excellent summary of allegorical commentary on this episode.
8 "As 'great tort' he epitomizes all other tyrants in the poem who extort property." Hamilton (1977), 530, gloss to V.i.3.7–9.
9 Ibid., 424.

10 Ibid., 495.

11 Goldberg, *Endlesse Worke*, 134.

12 For an contrary, entirely dyslogistic reading of Venus and her Temple
    see Goldberg, *Endlesse Worke*, 89ff. He sees the temple as Lust's cave,
    the garden as "a garden of the dead," and Venus as simply a "figure
    of power," not one justly exercising power: "in her temple only she
    has power, and the only joy in the temple is her joy." Clearly, I do not
    find this episode to be as univocal as Goldberg does. His identifying
    Britomart and Arthur with Scudamour (130) also seems insufficiently
    discriminating; both motive and action demonstrate that for Britomart
    and Arthur Amoret is precisely not a "commodity," an object of
    exchange to be bartered. Admittedly, however, we are probably, in this
    instance, listening to different voices. Goldberg "hears" Ate and Venus
    as "various" but evidently synonymous "names" for the "general
    term, Desire" and argues (98) that "conventional readings" opposing
    Ate and Venus "leave the narration behind ... to find it voicing the
    commonplaces of Renaissance culture." It is fair to counter, however,
    that Goldberg here leaves the narration behind to find it voicing the
    commonplaces of postmodernist culture.

13 For a view of Scudamour's assuming the voice of narration quite con-
    trary to mine, one I can only characterize as nihilistic, see Goldberg,
    ibid., 62–3.

14 Cain (*Praise in the "Faerie Queene,"* 167–8) identifies the Thames-
    Medway wedding procession with an Orphic hymn in its emblemizing
    of concord derived from discord, and notes that the hymn stresses the
    indecorum of the "erotic parallel between Scudamour and Orpheus"
    immediately preceding.

15 Hamilton (1977), 425.

16 Goldberg, *Endlesse Worke*, 135ff.

17 Ibid., 144. Cf. Miller, *The Poem's Two Bodies*, 69n5.

CHAPTER FIVE

1 Aptekar (*Icons of Justice*, 109–10) notes that Dante relegates the violent
   and fraudulent to the lower circles of Hell. Dante's cone of disorder
   shapes the infernal regions as a spiral, and the hierarchical position of
   the violent and fraudulent in this cone as courtiers to Satan identifies
   their degree of moral chaos. The consequences of their sins are
   "polliticke" rather than, like those of incontinence, private. Thus
   Aptekar observes that Dante "following Aquinas, regards injurious
   malitia as the chief assailant of justice" (110).

2 Burke, *A Rhetoric of Motives*, 208.

3 The quotation is from Miller, *The Poem's Two Bodies*, 129. See also Aptekar, *Icons of Justice*, 111; Nelson, *Poetry of Spenser*, 302; and Cheney, *Spenser's Image of Nature*, 151. Fletcher (*Prophetic Moment*, 291) notes a similar double-vision in our experience of the Blatant Beast under submission to Calidore in the final canto of the legend of Courtesy.

4 Justice as a corporate synecdoche for other virtues has had some currency as a topos, and several commentators have alluded to it. Cain (*Praise in the "Faerie Queene,"* 5) cites Scaliger's *Poetices libri septem* 3.12 (1561) on the tradition of an encomiastic *Aeneid* in the Renaissance, noting that Scaliger describes Aeneas "as the ideal hero whose every venture exemplifies princely virtues, *collectively* understood as justice" (emphasis mine). Yates, in her *Astraea*, notes that the "attribution to Elizabeth of all the virtues was a commonplace which fits very easily into the Astraea theme, for Justice is an imperial virtue, and also the virtue which is theoretically supposed to include all the others" (65). When Astraea comes again she brings with her not only justice but all other banished virtues, as Ariosto says" (65–6). Cf. Cicero: "[*justitia*] *haec enim una virtus omnium est domina et regina virtutum*" (*De Officiis*, III.vi.28). Such considerations support Fletcher's characterization of Book V as "a planlike document ... an historicist myth, a blueprint for the historical dimension of the mythology elsewhere in the poem" (*Prophetic Moment*, 136).

5 Cain (*Praise in the "Faerie Queene,"* 125) notes that in Merlin's account of Britomart's progeny (III.iii.21–24), "Spenser departs from Ariosto to avoid, as he habitually does, the Virgilian encomiasitic motif of the Golden Age returned."

6 Cain (ibid., 3) notes the historical existence of a "special affinity" between epideictic and deliberative rhetoric, and quotes Aristotle (*Rhet.*I.9): "what you might suggest in counselling becomes encomium by a change in the phrase." Cain also cites Erasmus's defence against the charge that his *Panegyricus* (1504) flattered Philip of Burgundy: "no other way of correcting a prince is as efficacious as offering the pattern of a truly good prince under the guise of flattery to them, for thus do you present virtues and disparage faults in such a manner that you seem to argue them to the former while restraining them from the latter." Cf. Miller (*The Poem's Two Bodies*, 157) and his witty discussion of the strategic use of precedent in political rhetoric to bring into being the prior condition claimed as proof (107ff).

7 Cain, *Praise in the "Faerie Queene,"* 147.

8 Not all commentators take a dyslogistic view of the episodes. For a more eulogistic, and decorously contextualized, perspective than most on these historical allusions, see Fletcher, *Prophetic Moment*, 146–7; 152,

and his section "Beyond Culture: Idealized Imperialism" (204–14). "History," he concludes, "is Platonically the shadow of the ideas the poem intends to allegorize, and its historical allusions are *figurae* born of those ideas" (214). Cf. Aptekar, *Icons of Justice*, 8.

9 Miller (*The Poem's Two Bodies*, 127) sees Gloriana as a similar locus, functioning as an agent of temporal and transcendent linkage. He argues that the poem's "geneological foreconceit" elaborates "narrative and symbolism ... with respect to two distinct moments, the one in which Arthur acts and the one in which Spenser writes. As both the object of Arthur's quest and an honorific name for Elizabeth, 'Gloriana' links these two moments typologically."

10 Thompson provides a thorough exploration of this issue in her *Under Pretext of Praise*. See also Kennedy, *Rhetorical Norms*, 79–94.

11 Hamilton (1977), 525.

12 Cain (*Praise in the "Faerie Queene,"* 19) notes a similar strategy of careful qualification to create a sovereign worthy of praise in Colin's encomiastic ode to Eliza in the "Aprill" eclogue.

13 Phillips summarizes the formal, demonstrative procedures of Renaissance political theorists in treatises on justice which "consistently define and expound it in terms of three major topics or places: namely, Justice, Equity, and Mercy or Clemency." He argues that it is these topoi rather than "the requirements of narrative consistency [that] determined Spenser's selection and arrangement in Book V of narrative materials which he wrote at different times and with different purposes in mind." Phillips, "Renaissance Concepts of Justice," Hamilton (1972), 473.

14 Anderson, "'Nor Man It Is,'" Hamilton (1972), 447. Cf. Aptekar (*Icons of Justice*, 116–17), who cites Bradner, Gough, Davis, and Hamilton in arguing that "generations of readers have disliked the Legend of Justice, principally because they have disliked Artegall."

15 Cited by Hamilton (1977), 532. On etymologlical and mythic analogues to Talus see Fletcher's excellent summary (*Prophetic Moment*, 138ff; also 189). On the iconographic topoi of Talus's iron flail, see Aptekar, *Icons of Justice*, 42–52.

16 "Auxillary" is Cornford's translation of Plato's "Epixouros," a term which has resisted any more satisfactory rendering into English. See *The Republic of Plato*, 102n1.

17 Fletcher, *Prophetic Moment*, 167.

18 "In the native English conception, law is logically prior to equity, hence the maxim 'Equity follows law.'" Kermode, "*The Faerie Queene*, I and V," Hamilton (1972) 284. Cf. Fletcher, *Prophetic Moment*, 161–2; 171.

19 See Kristellar et al, ed., *The Renaissance Philosophy of Man*, 223–54.

20 On the "deep affinity between the original idea of nature, upon which is built the medieval legist's natural law, and the idea of justice," see Fletcher, *Prophetic Moment*, 284–7.

21 Fletcher, arguing that the Giant "betrays his followers even more fearfully than he upsets the state," treats him as an exemplum of fraud, a locus of disordered wit and hierarchical indecorum rather than usurped power (ibid., 243–4). Aptekar (*Icons of Justice*, 37), by contrast, treats him as an exemplum of illegitimate usurpation of sovereignty, of hierarchical indecorum in a strictly social sense. Dunseath, however, treats him as an exemplum of transcendent hierarchical indecorum. He briefly identifies the exordium, narratio, confirmatio, and refutatio of the Giant's speech, and catalogues the scriptural topoi undermining his ethos of reputation (*Spenser's Allegory of Justice*, 100ff). For Dunseath, the "arguments pro and con are not about social issues, but upon God's order, which is the cause–hence the thoroughly theological bent of the arguments" (97). I contend, of course, that within Spenser's rhetorical structure these diverse treatments are complementary, not contradictory: his hierarchical model will accommodate all without absurdity.

22 On Artegall's echo of Job, cf. Dunseath, ibid., 104. For a discussion of the principles underlying Spenser's conception of legal system as an analogue to cosmic order authorizing evolutionary as opposed to revolutionary change, see Fletcher, *Prophetic Moment*, 182–4.

23 Aptekar (*Icons of Justice*, 36–7) quotes Raleigh's *Maxims of State*: "The First way to suppress Sedition, is Eloquence and excellent Persuasion, which oftentimes worketh grat Effects among the Multitude ... If Persuasion cannot prevail, then Force must compel."

24 Hough, *A Preface to the "Faerie Queene,"* 195; Alpers, *The Poetry of "The Faerie Queene,"* 300. Both cited by Hamilton (1977), 525.

25 On the Giant as an exemplum of Fortuna, cf. Fletcher, *Prophetic Moment*, 246 and Aptekar, *Icons of Justice*, 38.

CHAPTER SIX

1 Structurally, of course, Radigund will also serve as a dyslogistic analogue of Elizabeth. Miller conjectures that "emasculating political subordinates who regarded themselves as her natural superiors was undoubtedly one of the small consolations afforded by Elizabeth's royal office" (*The Poem's Two Bodies*, 164).

2 Aptekar does not contextualize the Radigund incident as I do, within the courtship sequence from prior books which includes Britomart's submitting herself to Busirane's rhetoric, and so takes a dyslogistic

view contrary to mine of Artegall's ethos in his strategies of resistance to Radigund's rhetoric. Aptekar treats them as exemplary of fraud rather than tested chastity (*Icons of Justice*, 119ff).

3 Cf. Goldberg, *Endlesse Worke*, 106–8.

4 Aptekar (*Icons of Justice*, 136ff) discusses the iconography of "Fraude" common to both Dolon and Archimago.

5 On the scriptural allusion to Christ at Gethsemane in Britomart's wakeful watch see Elizabeth Bieman, "Britomart in Book V of *The Faerie Queene*," 164–5.

6 Fletcher (*Prophetic Moment*, 233) notes that in Roman law *dolus malus*, deliberate fraud, is opposed to "the spirit of *aequitas*." *Subtilitas*, a form of *dolus malus* representing "adherence to the strict letter of the law" accounts for Artegall's entrapment by Radigund's law and lore. Fletcher argues that in Dolon Britomart, "unlike Sir Artegall, ... can *experience* the error of *dolus malus* in an experimental fashion so that, unlike him, she will not fall into the trap of excessive legalism" (Fletcher's emphasis).

7 Cf. Fowler's argument that the two loci are antitypes in his *Triumphal Forms*, 51. Cited by Hamilton (1977) 573.

8 Thus Cheney, for instance, (*Spenser's Image of Nature*, 170), while acknowledging Britomart's "conspicuous tendency to be upset by the thought of her future husband," refers to "the vision of bearing a lion by one's crocodile suitor" as "only the most bizarre of a series of reports concerning Artegall." This "report," however, unlike those of Merlin, Redcrosse, Talus, and, implicitly, Busirane, is *sui generis*. Aptekar, while taking a dyslogistic view of Artegall's behaviour during and after thralldom to Radigund, nevertheless argues that "with all its strange aspects, the episode of the crocodile epitomizes Spenser's complex view of justice," and sees the crocodile as "Britomart's assailant and her saviour; he becomes, it would seem, her slave" (*Icons of Justice*, 88; 97). Bieman ("Britomart in Book V," 168–9) interprets the crocodile after submission to Isis's rod as the eulogistic Osiris, "higher alter-ego" of the dyslogistic, subdued Typhon. See also Dunseath, *Spenser's Allegory of Justice*, 172–77. Graziani accepts without amelioration the dyslogistic properties of the crocodile, but again attributes them to Spenser rather than Britomart, arguing that they accommodate a political allegory on the threat to Elizabeth Tudor from Mary's supporters. The subjugation of the beast thus asserts that their suppression is a restoration of hierarchical order and just sovereignty. See Graziani, "Elizabeth at Isis Church," 376–89.

9 Goldberg (*Endlesse Worke*, 104) argues that it is appropriate for Britomart in IV.ix "to demand that Scudamour tell his story, for it is her

story too." I would argue, however, that the events at Isis's Church prove her reading of Scudamour's story as her own to be a misreading.

10 Cf. Fletcher (*Prophetic Moment*, 280ff) who presents an allegorical motive for Spenser's intensive use of psychomachaic topoi in his dispositio of Britomart in Book V. The "pyschological change" in Britomart, he argues, is linked to "traditional thinking on natural equity" which related it to the "conscience of the law" and Chancery, the court of equity. Spenser "wants to determine the sacral-psychological source of any virtue, and for equity this source is the conscience of the hero." The "guiding idea" for the "spirit" of equity is cognate with the rhetorical principle of decorum; it "seems to be a willingness to modify rigid principles to suit varying historical circumstances" (283).

11 Pollente (ii.18) and Grantorto (xii.23), and presumably Duessa (x.4), share Radigund's fate, the first two dispatched by Artegall's sword Chrysaor and the last by Mercilla's executioner, while the Souldan not only loses his head to Arthur but goes all to pieces, as it were (viii.42). Cf. Bieman, "Britomart in Book V," 159; 173n12; 17.

CHAPTER SEVEN

1 To limit the rhetorical resonance of this moment by interpreting it allegorically as a simple appropriation of Britomart emblematically to advocate traditional topoi of domestic submission for women seems unduly reductive. For a contrary view to mine, see Miller, *The Poem's Two Bodies*, 217ff. See also Benson, "'Rule Virginia.'"

2 See chapter 5, section II.

3 Hamilton, *The Structure of Allegory in "The Faerie Queene,"* 170.

4 Fletcher, *Prophetic Moment*, 279.

5 Dunseath, to my knowledge, is the first commentator on Book V to give this scene of reconciliation serious allegorical analysis. Although he does not use the rhetorical term, Dunseath (*Spenser's Allegory of Justice*, 187) reads the swearing of mutual fealty as proof of Artegall's redeemed ethos.

6 Iconographic and etymological readings of this topos are equally dyslogistic. Using iconographic topoi as proof, Aptekar (*Icons of Justice*, 82–3) identifies the Armada of Philip II as the likely historical exemplum of this runaway, self-destructive technology. Cf. Fletcher, *Prophetic Moment*, 210.

7 Apteker, *Icons of Justice*, 123.

8 On the etymology of "Malengine," Aptekar (ibid., 115) cites Upton's rendering "*malum ingenium*" and Le Duchet: "Malengin: *dolus malus*: c'est l'action d'une personne ingénieuse à mal faire." Aptekar also

notes (129–30) that the topoi of Malengin's prosopographia have been taken as allusions to the Irish, and she draws parallels to the emblematic figure of Ripa's *Inganno*. Fletcher (*Prophetic Moment*, 234–5) treats the "metamorphic chain" of Malengin's protean change as an example of causal sequence projected in a narrative analogue, representing "the type of cosmogonic myth making so common in Spenser, whereby the origin of all evil is sought in a natural process exaggerated to the last degree."

9 Fletcher, ibid., 289.

10 Bieman, *Plato Baptized*, 185. Bieman suggests (182–5) that Spenser acknowledges in this ambiguity his own sense of vulnerability as a critic of the powerful and thereby makes "a covert gesture of self-justification against accusers past and future," accusers who would "colour" a "prudently equivocal prophet" with "cowardice." As the case I advocate above in chapter 5 against such accusers makes clear, I consider Bieman's extra-textual interpretation of this figure wholly decorous with Spenser's general strategies of praise in these final cantos of Book V. He evidently anticipates that he, like Mercilla, would become an exemplum of indecorum between performance and reputation.

11 Cf. Cain, *Praise in the "Faerie Queene,"* 137–45. Aptekar (*Icons of Justice*, 142–4) lends some support to the notion of a wider resonance for Duessa, finding iconographic relationships between Duessa and both Errour and Geryoneo's monster through the emblem of *Fraude*. She also notes a linkage between Duessa's beast from Revelation and the Blatant Beast (207–8). Fletcher, while stressing the trial as political allegory (*Prophetic Moment*, 236–42), notes that the ostensible charge against Duessa, treason, focuses a general principle: "absolute justice can only be reached after the experienced trial of a contrary absolute, which, we find, is not force but fraud. Force cannot betray; fraud can." For Fletcher too, therefore, the issues at stake in Duessa's trial go well beyond the specifics of Mary Stuart. "If injustice radically comes from or through betrayal, then injustice is subject not primarily to police correction but to a reformation of thought about the natural bonds of society. Such is the theory Spenser holds. The obvious emphasis on treason in Book V has often been called the bias of an Establishment poet. But it follows directly from a theory independently valid, both as political or human truth and as poetic truth" (235).

12 "Since the law comes into being when judges like Mercilla and Artegall decide on actual cases, law is the progeny of trial" (Fletcher, ibid., 169–70). Dunseath (*Spenser's Allegory of Justice*, 215) distinguishes the phases of "normal legal procedure" at Duessa's trial: arraignment, presenting of charges, prosecution, and defence.

13 On the descriptive topoi giving Mercilla's court, like those of Venus and Isis, the resonance of a temple, see Cain, *Praise in the "Faerie Queene,"* 137ff. Cain notes that, unlike other icons of Elizabeth in the epic, Mercilla's contains no physical description. "Instead, Mercilla is like a deity, apprehended indirectly through ritual objects." In this aspect Mercilla anticipates Dame Nature's appearance (VII.vii.5–13) for her juridical role on Arlo Hill.

14 Aptekar (*Icons of Justice,* 62–9) discusses the "complex psychological and political" iconography of Mercilla's chained lion, arguing that it exemplifies both political power under restraint and self-restraint.

15 On the major allusive exempla relating "peace" to "justice," see Dunseath, *Spenser's Allegory of Justice,* 63–5. On the appearance of "Iust Dice, wise Eunomie, myld Eirene" in Mercilla's iconographic prosopographia (ix.32.6) see Aptekar, *Icons of Justice,* 18. Dunseath (211) cites Bodin's *Republique* on the hierarchical relationship among Dice, Eunomie, and Eirene, with "Eirene" as "peace" or "harmonial justice" subsuming both prior elements in the series. On Truth as the "daughter of Time," and the reconciliation of Truth with the other three "daughters of God – Justice, Mercy, and Peace" and their "sacred marriage," see Fletcher, *Prophetic Moment,* 143–5; 279.

16 Fletcher (ibid., 288) seems to reverse the order of narrative, hence causal sequence, here. "The mere fact that Artegall has not done his full work, (Grey had not succeeded in Ireland) enables Envy's cloud to dim the lustre of his fame." Surely envy is cause not effect of Artegall's aborted mission. Cf. Cain, *Praise in the "Faerie Queene,"* 149, and Apteker, *Icons of Justice,* 204–5; 211–14.

17 Fletcher, *Prophetic Moment,* 136.

18 Neuse, "Book VI as Conclusion to the *Faerie Queene,"* Hamilton (1972), 367, 369. Miller (*The Poem's Two Bodies,* 33) notes economic factors that marginalized humanist courtiers during the 1590s and may have given a specific topical urgency to the debate among humanists over issues of reciprocal obligations and benefits between princes and their courtiers. For a persuasive analysis of Erasmian topoi and More's use of them in *Utopia* to provoke controversia among humanists, see Logan, *The Meaning of More's "Utopia."* For an excellent summary of the courtesy books and their occurrence in Spenser's canon see Whigham, "Courtesy as a social code," and Javitch, "Courtesy books." See also Whigham's *Ambition and Privilege.*

19 Cf. Burke, *A Rhetoric of Motives,* 227–31.

20 Cheney, *Spenser's Image of Nature,* 182. See also Borris, "Courtesy."

21 The *narratio* in classical rhetoric ususally follows the *exordium.* It provides a short statement of the facts of a case or the general subject and purpose of the oration. Most theorists recommend it be followed by

the *propositio* that states succinctly the specific concern of the oration, setting a definite issue or problem before the audience. Spenser's letter to Raleigh blends functions of both elements. Cf. Appendix.

22 Miller (*The Poem's Two Bodies*, 214) argues that Spenser so represents himself in the Briton Moniments and Elfin Chronicles. He takes the "role" of "inspired magician, culture bearer, or lawgiver," situated as Elizabeth's "humanist counselor-poet, who embodies the trope of Fairy instruction for Elizabethan England."

CHAPTER EIGHT

1 Cf. Cain, *Praise in the "Faerie Queene,"* 155ff.

2 Cf. Tonkin, *Spenser's Courteous Pastoral*, 24. Tonkin argues that "the equivocal formulation of the poet's question [in Pr.6] leaves doubt whether the court of the 'soueraine Lady Queene' is in antiquity or in modern times."

3 Neuse, too, worries about the "disturbing connotations of "purchase," "vse," and "apply" in this stanza, and notes the cognate indicators of ethos in Calidore's "hyperbolical near perjury" in protecting Priscilla's reputation ("Book VI as Conclusion," 378). Cain (*Praise in the "Faerie Queene,"* 174) notes that one etymological reading of Calidore's name is "cunning with gold (L. *callidus*)... from the beginning, financial imagery hints that Calidore can use courtesy for profit," and "like the mercenary Brigants, Calidore is putting a price on the pastoral." See also Miller, "Calidore," and Cheney, *Spenser's Image of Nature*, 185–6.

4 Tonkin, *Spenser's Courteous Pastoral*, 172–7. Cited by Hamilton (1977), 623. Cf. Cheney, ibid., 177.

5 According to Osgood's *Concordance*, the exact counts are Book I, 38; Book II, 37; Book III, 38; Book IV, 43; Book V, 38; Book VI, 79. Cf. Dixon, "Fairy Tale, Fortune and Boethian Wonder," 141–65.

6 Lewis, *Variorum*, 346. Cf. Williams, *Flowers on a Lowly Stalk*, 56–8, 135.

7 Gloss to VI.x.28.6, Hamilton (1977), 693.

8 Hamilton (ibid., 692–3), provides an informative reading, both detailed and economical, in his gloss to VI.x.24.

9 *Astrophil and Stella*, sonnet 71.

10 Cain (*Praise in the "Faerie Queene,"* 178) identifies Calidore with the poet as an Orpheus figure, and sees his deceptive friendship with Coridon, which functions in the narrative sequence causally to free Pastorella, as "duplicity ... effectively altruistic." For Cain, therefore, this "intimation of poetry's social irrelevance implicitly opposes *dulce* and *utile* and undoes the self-justifying idealism of the encomiast and the humanist promotion of Orpheus as civilizer." My analysis of the dynamics in this scene suggests that Calidore functions here not as the poet but as the poet's courtly audience; poetry is not irrelevant,

although its audience, at considerable social cost, may misdeem it to be so. Cf. chapter 9, section II.

11 Cheney (*Spenser's Image of Nature*, 216–17) argues that the "very substitution of pastoral for epic anticipates the limited and anticlimactic nature of the victory possible in the area of courtesy." Cf. Cain, *Praise in the "Faerie Queene,"* 32.

12 Cheney (ibid., 230–1) treats Colin as Spenser and his appearance as one of "the contemporary allusions" that, like those in the final cantos of Book V, effect "an immediate relevance to the fictional situations." See also Fletcher, *Prophetic Moment*, 291–2 and Cain, *Praise in the "Faerie Queene,"* 175–9.

13 Cf. Fletcher's argument (*Prophetic Moment*, 218) that "the language of the trial is so precisely legal that we are entitled to discern in it a legislation of the whole order of nature and destiny." Fletcher sees the "frontal" issue of the Cantos as "the political allegory of rebellion ... Assuming that the cosmos is the largest possible image of political order, we can move inward from Mutabilitie's insurrection, applying its lessons of cosmic error to the field of human politics, which is the subject of Book V."

14 Goldberg (*Endlesse Worke*, 148–9) attributes "the profound ambivalence surrounding social representation" to this problem of justice, the conflicting motives of the one and the many. He uses "naming," a complex signifier in his analysis, as exemplary of alienated essence, representing "social acts of identification [that] alienate the self, making misidentification, misrecognition, and misrepresentation the norm of society."

CHAPTER NINE

1 Cited by Hamilton (1977), 711.

2 Hamilton, ibid.

3 Blissett, "Spenser's Mutabilitie," 26. Blissett argues that cantos vi and vii are that "rare phenomenon in Renaissance literature, a poem without analogies" (27). He suggests the term "retractation" rather than "envoy" for the Chaucerian analogue, but applies it only to the two stanzas comprising VII.viii which I refer to as a "peroratio" below, and prefers *epyllion* ("little epic") for the two Mutabilitie Cantos (35). Miller (*The Poem's Two Bodies*, 43) notes that Spenser "echoes recognizably" the *Troilus* envoy in his envoy to *The Shepheardes Calender*. See also Zitner's incisive summary of the issues of continuity and closure raised by the Mutabilitie Cantos in his *"The Faerie Queene, Book VII."*

4 *Iteratio* is a scheme used for repetition, recapitulation, and summation, occurring "commonly," reports Puttenham, "in the end of every long tale and oration" (Sonnino, *Handbook*, 124).

5 For an analysis of Spenser's "historical vision" as both "retrospective" and "evolutionary," and the dynamic generated by this combination, see Berger, *"The Mutabilitie Cantos,"* 147.

6 Hamilton (1977), gloss to VII. title, 714.

7 For Fletcher this dynamic of dilation links the Giant with scales and his followers by anticipation to Mutabilitie. "Their hope is not equalization and amelioration ... but rather a flattening out of historical time which corresponds to their flattening out of space. They would destroy the process of dilation which Nature had prescribed for Mutabilitie" (*Prophetic Moment*, 245). In my terminology, they demonstrate a radical failure to "get their priorities straight."

8 Cf. Bennett, "Spenser's Venus and the Goddess Nature of the *Mutabilitie Cantos*," 172ff. Bennett cites sources linking Nature to the revelation of God and Christ as the "Word made Flesh." Cited Hamilton (1977), 725.

9 Hamilton (1977), gloss to VII.vi.37.1.

10 MacLure ("Nature and Art," 10) argues that "the legitimate offspring of the marriage of nature and art is the state; their pre-marital affair produces a love-child, the pastoral pleasuance." For extended analysis of relationships between pastoral discourse and the courtship of power, see Montrose, "Eliza, Queene of Shepheardes and the Pastoral of Power" and "'The Perfecte Paterne of the Poete.'"

11 *Ominatio* is a figure, according to Peacham, in which "the orator fortelleth the likeliest effect to follow of some evil cause" (Sonnino, *Handbook*, 136).

12 Cain (*Praise in the "Faerie Queene,"* 12ff) traces in Boccaccio and Comes the attributes of Orpheus, "the humanists' favorite archetype for the successful poet," which include "teaching them to build cities, to keep civil laws, and to accept the institution of marriage." He argues elsewhere (156) that "as encomium of the queen becomes less and less evident in the books added in 1596, Spenser brings the role of poet increasingly into focus; in one sense, the poet becomes the hero of Book VI." Miller discusses at length the role of *The Shepheardes Calender* as an instrument of Spenser's social courtship, arguing that his address in the envoy "implicitly characterizes the text as an ambitious 'new man' seeking to overcome the disadvantage of low birth through patronage and conspicuous ability" (*The Poem's Two Bodies*, 39). Referring to the dedicatory sonnets for *The Faerie Queene*, he notes "the poet's lack of a prescribed 'place' in this pageant" with its heraldic order of hierarchical sequence, and contends that Spenser "had to define a role for the poet in the Elizabethan court and justify it, in part, on the vatic power to foretell and so forestall disaster" (58).

13 Hawkins, "Mutabilitie and the Cycle of the Months," 87.

14 See Gould, "Darwin's Delay" in his *Ever Since Darwin*, 21–8.

15 For a contrary view see Cain (*Praise in the "Faerie Queene,"* 183), who distinguishes the voice of the peroratio from that of the narrator, finding it "akin to that speaking in the proems, separate from the narrator and close to the actual poet." "*Poeta* and *vates*," he argues, "fall into subordination before the ordinary visionary who is simply Christian man at prayer." Goldberg (*Endlesse Worke*, 42), referring specifically to IV.i.1, observes that "since the text is treated as having already been written, and by another, the narrator positions himself not as its author but as its reader – that other – and he defines his relationship to the text in his feeling with the text."

16 Berger, *Allegorical Temper*, 102.

17 Miller, *The Poem's Two Bodies*, 138.

Bibliography

The following abbreviations are used for citations of periodicals:

BJRL   *Bulletin of the John Rylands Library*
ELH   *English Literary History*
ELR   *English Literary Renaissance*
JEGP   *Journal of English and Germanic Philology*
MLR   *Modern Language Review*
MP   *Modern Philology*
NLH   *New Literary History*
PMLA   *Publications of the Modern Language Society of America*
SEL   *Studies in English Literature*
SP   *Studies in Philology*
SpN   *Spenser Newsletter*
SpStud   *Spenser Studies*
TSLL   *Texas Studies in Literature and Language*
UTQ   *University of Toronto Quarterly*

Alpers, Paul J. *The Poetry of the "Faerie Queene."* Princeton: Princeton University Press, 1967
– ed. *Elizabethan Poetry: Modern Essays in Criticism.* Oxford: Oxford University Press, 1967
– "Narration in *The Faerie Queene.*" ELH 44 (1977): 19–39
– "Bower of Bliss." Hamilton, *Spenser Encyclopedia*, 104–7
Anderson, Judith H. "Whatever Happened to Amoret? The Poet's Role in Book IV of *The Faerie Queene.*" *Criticism* 13 (1971): 180–200

– "'Nor Man It Is': The Knight of Justice in Book V of Spenser's *The Faerie Queene.*" PMLA 85 (1970) 65–77; rept. Hamilton (1972), 447–70
– "Belphoebe." Hamilton, *Spenser Encyclopedia*, 85–7
Aptekar, Jane. *Icons of Justice: Iconography and Thematic Imagery in the "Faerie Queene" V.* New York: Columbia University Press, 1969
Aristotle. *The "Art" of Rhetoric,* ed. and tr. John Henry Freese. Loeb Classical Library. Cambridge: Harvard University Press, 1926
Bal, Mieke. *Narratology: Introduction to the Theory of Narrative,* tr. and rev. Christine Van Boheemen. Toronto: University of Toronto Press, 1985
Barker, William W. "Merchant Taylor's School." Hamilton, *Spenser Encyclopedia,* 468
Barthes, Roland. "Myth Today" in Susan Sontag, ed. *A Barthes Reader,* 93–149. New York: Noonday Press, 1982
Beckett, Samuel. *Waiting For Godot: A Tragicomedy in Two Acts.* New York: Grove Press, 1954
Benjamin, Walter. "The Storyteller: Reflections on the Works of Nikolai Leskov" in his *Illuminations.* ed. Hannah Arendt, tr. Harry Zohn. New York: Schocken, 1968
Bennett, Josephine W. "Spenser's Venus and the Goddess Nature of the *Mutabilitie Cantos.*" SP 30 (1933): 160–99
Benson, Pamela J. "'Rule Virginia': Protestant Theories of Female Regiment in *The Faerie Queene.*" ELR 15 (1985): 277–92
– "Spenser at Kalamazoo." SpN 18 (1987) 51–3
Berger, Harry, Jr. "*The Faerie Queene* III: A General Description" in Hamilton (1972), 395–424
– *The Allegorical Temper: Vision and Reality in Book II of Spenser's "Faerie Queene."* New Haven: Yale University Press, 1957
– "The Mutabilitie Cantos: Archaism and Evolution in Retrospect" in Harry Berger Jr., ed. *Spenser: A Collection of Critical Essays,* 146–76. Englewood Cliffs, NJ: Prentice-Hall, 1968
Bieman, Elizabeth. "Britomart in Book V of *The Faerie Queene.*" UTQ 37 (1968): 156–74
– *Plato Baptized: Towards the Interpretation of Spenser's Mimetic Fictions.* Toronto: University of Toronto Press, 1988
Blissett, William. "Spenser's Mutabilitie" in Millar MacLure and F.W. Watt, eds. *Essays in English Literature presented to A.S.P. Woodhouse,* 26–42. Toronto: University of Toronto Press, 1964
Bond, Ronald B. "Blatant Beast." Hamilton, *Spenser Encyclopedia,* 96–8
Borris, Kenneth. "Courtesy." Hamilton, *Spenser Encyclopedia,* 194–5
Brooke, N.S. "C.S. Lewis and Spenser: Nature, Art, and the Bower of Bliss." *Cambridge Journal* 2 (1949) 420–43; rept. Hamilton (1972), 13–28
Burke, Kenneth. *A Rhetoric of Motives.* Berkeley and Los Angeles: University of California Press, 1969

Cain, Thomas H. *Praise in the "Faerie Queene."* Lincoln NB: University of Nebraska Press, 1978

Campbell, Joseph. *The Hero with a Thousand Faces.* Bollingen Series xvii, 2nd ed. Princeton: Princeton University Press, 1968

Carscallen, James. "The Goodly Frame of Temperance: The Metaphor of Cosmos in *The Faerie Queene,* Book II." *UTQ* 37 (1968) 136–55; rept. Hamilton (1972), 347–65

Castiglione, Baldesar. *The Book of the Courtier.* tr. Charles S. Singleton. Garden City, NY: Anchor Books, 1959

Cheney, Donald. *Spenser's Image of Nature: Wild Man and Shepherd in "The Faerie Queene."* New Haven: Yale University Press, 1966

Cheney, Patrick. "Triamond." Hamilton, *Spenser Encyclopedia,* 698–9

Cicero. *De oratore.* ed. and tr. E.W. Sutton and H. Rackham. Loeb Classical Library. 2 vol. Cambridge: Harvard University Press, 1942

Craig, Martha. "The Secret Wit of Spenser's Language" in Paul Alpers, ed., *Elizabethan Poetry: Modern Essays in Criticism,* 447–72. Oxford: Oxford University Press, 1967; rept. Hamilton (1972), 313–33

Cullen, Patrick. *Infernal Triad: The Flesh, the World and the Devil in Spenser and Milton.* Princeton: Princeton University Press, 1974

Dees, Jerome S. "The Narrator of *The Faerie Queene*: Patterns of Response." *TSLL* 12 (1971): 536–68

– "Narrator of *The Faerie Queene.*" Hamilton, *Spenser Encyclopedia,* 498–500

Dixon, Michael F. "Rhetorical Patterns and Methods of Advocacy in Spenser's *Shepheardes Calender.*" *ELR* 7, no. 2 (1977): 131–54

– "Fairy Tale, Fortune and Boethian Wonder: Rhetorical Structure in Book VI of *The Faerie Queene,*" *UTQ* 44 (1975): 141–65

Dundas, Judith. "The Rhetorical Basis of Spenser's Imagery." *PMLA* 8 (1968): 59–75

Dunseath, T.K. *Spenser's Allegory of Justice in the "Faerie Queene."* Princeton: Princeton University Press, 1968

Fletcher, Angus. *The Prophetic Moment: An Essay on Spenser.* Chicago: University of Chicago Press, 1971

Fowler, Alastair D.S. *Spenser and the Numbers of Time.* London: Routledge & Kegan Paul, 1964

– *Triumphal Forms: Structural Patterns in Elizabethan Poetry.* Cambridge: Cambridge University Press, 1970

Freedman, Joseph S. "Cicero in Sixteenth- and Seventeenth-Century Rhetoric Instruction." *Rhetorica* 4, no. 3 (1986): 227–53

Geller, Lila. "Venus and the Three Graces: A Neoplatonic Paradigm for Book III of *The Faerie Queene.*" *JEGP* 75 (1976): 56–74

Goldberg, Jonathan. *Endlesse Worke: Spenser and the Structures of Discourse.* Baltimore: Johns Hopkins University Press, 1981

Gould, Stephen Jay. *Ever Since Darwin: Reflections in Natural History*. New York: Norton, 1977

Graziani, Rene. "Elizabeth at Isis Church." PMLA 79 (1964) 376–89

Greenblatt, Stephen. *Renaissance Self-Fashioning: From More to Shakespeare*. Chicago: University of Chicago Press, 1980

Hamilton, A.C. *The Structure of Allegory in "The Faerie Queene."* Oxford: The Clarendon Press, 1961

– ed., *Essential Articles for the Study of Edmund Spenser*. Hamdon, CT; Archon, 1972. Cited as Hamilton (1972)

– ed., *The Faerie Queene*. London: Longman, 1977; reprint with corrections 1980. Cited as Hamilton (1977)

– gen. ed., *The Spenser Encyclopedia*. Toronto and London: University of Toronto Press and Routledge, 1990

Hankins, John Erskine. *Source and Meaning in Spenser's Allegory: A Study of "The Faerie Queene."* Oxford: The Clarendon Press, 1971

Hardison, O.B. Jr, "Humanism." Hamilton, *Spenser Encyclopedia*, 379–81

Hawkins, Sherman. "Mutabilitie and the Cycle of the Months." *English Institute Essays* (1961): 76–102

Helgerson, Richard. "The New Poet Presents Himself: Spenser and the Idea of a Literary Career." PMLA 93 (1978): 893–911

Henderson, Judith Rice. "Rhetorical Criticism from E.K. to the Present." Hamilton, *Spenser Encyclopedia*, 602–4

Hill, R.F. "Colin Clout's Courtesy." MLR 57 (1962) 492–503; rept. Hamilton (1972), 220–37

Hinton, Stan. "The Poet and His Narrator: Spenser's Epic Voice." ELH 41 (1974): 165–81

Hough, Graham. *A Preface to the "Faerie Queene."* London: J. Duckworth, 1962

Howard, Jean E. "The New Historicism in Renaissance Studies." ELR 16 (1986): 13–43

Hulse, Clark, Strier, Richard, Weiner, Andrew D. "Spenser: Myth, Politics, Poetry." SP 85, no. 3 (1988)

Hume, David. *A Treatise of Human Nature*. 1739–40

Hyde, Thomas. "Busirane." Hamilton, *Spenser Encyclopedia*, 123–5

Javitch, Daniel. "Courtesy books." Hamilton, *Spenser Encyclopedia*, 197–9

Kane, Sean. *Spenser's Moral Allegory*. Toronto: University of Toronto Press, 1989

Kaske, Carol V. "The Dragon Spark and Sting in the Structure of Red Cross's Dragon-Fight: *The Faerie Queene* I.xi-xii." SP 66 (1969) 609–38

Kennedy, George A. *Classical Rhetoric and Its Christian and Secular Tradition from Ancient to Modern Times*. Chapel Hill: University of North Carolina Press, 1980

Kennedy, William J. *Rhetorical Norms in Renaissance Literature*. New Haven and London: Yale University Press, 1978

Kermode, Frank. "*The Faerie Queene*, I and V." BJRL 47 (1964) 123–50; rept. Hamilton (1972), 267–88

Kinney, Arthur F. "Humanist Poetics." Hamilton, *Spenser Encyclopedia*, 553–4

Kouwenhoven, Jan Karel. *Apparent Narrative as Thematic Metaphor: The Organization of "The Faerie Queene."* Oxford: The Clarendon Press, 1983

Krappe, A.H. *The Science of Folk-lore*. London: Methuen, 1930

Kristeller, Paul Oskar. *Renaissance Thought and Its Sources*. ed. Michael Mooney. New York: Columbia University Press, 1979

– et al., eds. *The Renaissance Philosophy of Man*. Chicago: University of Chicago Press, 1948

Langer, Susanne K. *Philosophy In A New Key: A Study in the Symbolism of Reason, Rite, and Art*. 3rd ed. Cambridge: Harvard University Press, 1957

Lewis, C.S. *The Allegory of Love*. Oxford: Oxford University Press, 1958

– *The Works of Edmund Spenser: A Variorum Edition*, ed. E. Greenlaw, C.E. Osgood, et al. 6 vols. Baltimore: Johns Hopkins University Press, 1932–49.

Lodge, David. *After Bakhtin: Essays on Fiction and Criticism*. London: Routledge, 1990

Logan, George M. *The Meaning of More's "Utopia."* Princeton: Princeton University Press, 1988

Machiavelli, Niccolo. *The Prince*, ed. and tr. Robert M. Adams. New York: Norton, 1977

MacLure, Millar. "Nature and Art in *The Faerie Queene*." ELH 28 (1961): 1–20; rept. Hamilton (1972), 171–88

Miller, David Lee. *The Poem's Two Bodies: The Poetics of the 1590 "Faerie Queene."* Princeton: Princeton University Press, 1988

– "Calidore." Hamilton, *Spenser Encyclopedia*, 127–8

Montrose, Louis Adrian. "'The Perfecte Paterne of the Poete': The Poetics of Courtship in *The Shepheardes Calender*." TSLL 21 (1979) 34–67

– "Eliza, Queene of Shepheardes and the Pastoral of Power." ELR 10 (1980): 153–82

– "The Elizabethan Subject and the Spenserian Text" in Patricia Parker and David Quint, eds., *Literary Theory/Renaissance Text*, 303–40. Baltimore and London: Johns Hopkins University Press, 1986

More, Thomas. *Utopia*, ed. and tr. Robert M. Adams. New York: Norton, 1975

Murphy, James J., ed., *Renaissance Eloquence: Studies in the Theory and Practice of Renaissance Rhetoric*. Berkeley and Los Angeles: University of California Press, 1983.

Murrin, Michael. *The Veil of Allegory: Allegorical Rhetoric in the English Renaissance*. Chicago: University of Chicago Press, 1969

– "The Rhetoric of Fairyland" in Thomas O. Sloan and Raymond B. Waddington, eds., *The Rhetoric of Renaissance Poetry from Wyatt to Milton*. Berkeley: University of California Press, 1974

Nellist, B. "The Allegory of Guyon's Voyage: an Interpretation." ELH 30 (1963): 89–106

Nelson, William. *The Poetry of Spenser: A Study*. New York: Columbia University Press, 1963

Neuse, Richard. "Book VI as Conclusion to the *Faerie Queene*." ELH 35 (1968) 329–53; rept. Hamilton (1972) 366–88

Nohrnberg, James. *The Analogy of "The Faerie Queene."* Princeton: Princeton University Press, 1976

Nyquist, Mary. "Textual Overlapping and Delilah's Harlot-Lap" in Patricia Parker and David Quint, eds. *Literary Theory/Renaissance Texts*, 341–72. Baltimore and London: Johns Hopkins University Press, 1986

Ong, Walter J. *Rhetoric, Romance and Technology: Studies in the Interaction of Expression and Culture*. Ithaca NY: Cornell University Press, 1971

Osgoode, C.G. *A Concordance to the Poems of Edmund Spenser*. Gloucester, MA: Peter Smith, 1963

Parker, Patricia. *Inescapable Romance: Studies in the Poetics of a Mode*. Princeton: Princeton University Press, 1979

Peacham, Henry, the Elder. *The Garden of Eloquence*, 1577 ed. London: Scolar Press, 1971

Pechter, Edward. "In Defence of Jargon: Criticism as a Social Practice." *Textual Practice* 5, no. 2 (1991): 171–82

Phillips, James E. "Renaissance Concepts of Justice and the Structure of *The Faerie Queene, Book V*." *Huntington Library Quarterly* 33 (1970): 103–20; rept. Hamilton (1972), 471–87

Pico della Mirandola. "Oration on the Dignity of Man" in Paul O. Kristeller et al, eds. *The Renaissance Philosophy of Man*. Chicago: University of Chicago Press, 1948

Plato. *The Republic of Plato*, tr. Francis M. Cornford. New York and London: Oxford University Press, 1945

Rix, H.D. *Rhetoric in Spenser's Poetry*. State College, PA: Pennsylvania State College, 1940

Roberts, Gareth. "Circe." Hamilton, ed., *Spenser Encyclopedia*, 165–7

Roche, Thomas P., Jr. *The Kindly Flame*. Princeton: Princeton University Press, 1964

Ryle, Gilbert. *Dilemmas: The Tarner Lectures 1953*. Cambridge: Cambridge University Press, 1954

Said, Edward W. *Orientalism*. New York: Vintage Books, 1979

de Saussure, Ferdinand. *Course In General Linguistics*, ed. Charles Bally, Albert Sechehaye, and Albert Riedlinger, tr. Wade Baskin. New York: McGraw-Hill, 1966

Silberman, Lauren. "Hermaphrodite and the Metamorphosis of Spenserian Allegory." ELR 17 (1987): 207–23

– "Hermaphrodite." Hamilton, *Spenser Encyclopedia*, 357–8

Sirluck, Ernest. "A Note on the Rhetoric of Spenser's 'Despaire.'" *MP* 47 (1950): 8–11

Skulsky, Harold. "Despaire." Hamilton, *Spenser Encyclopedia*, 213–14

Sloane, Thomas O. "Schoolbooks and Rhetoric: Erasmus *Copia*." *Rhetorica* 9, no. 2 (1991): 113–29

Sonnino, Lee A. *A Handbook to Sixteenth-Century Rhetoric*. London: Routledge & Kegan Paul, 1968

Spenser, Edmund. *The Faerie Queene*, ed. A.C. Hamilton, rept. with corrections 1980. New York: Longman, 1977

Stillman, Carol. "Poetics, Precedence, and the Order of the Dedicatory Sonnets to *The Faerie Queene*." *SpStud* 5 (1985): 143–8

Thistleton-Dyer, T.F. *The Folk-Lore of Shakespeare*. London: 1883

Thompson, Geraldine. *Under Pretext of Praise: Satiric Mode in Erasmus' Fiction*. Toronto: University of Toronto Press, 1973

Thompson, Stith. *Motif Index of Folk Literature*. 6 vol. Bloomington: Indiana University Press, 1955–58

Tonkin, Humphrey. *Spenser's Courteous Pastoral: the "Faerie Queene" VI*. Oxford: Oxford University Press, 1972

Vickers, Brian. "Epideictic and Epic in the Renaissance." *NLH* 14 (1983): 497–537

– *Classical Rhetoric in English Poetry*. London: Macmillan, 1970

– *In Defence of Rhetoric*. Oxford: Oxford University Press, 1986

Whigham, Frank. *Ambition and Privilege: The Social Tropes of Elizabethan Courtesy Theory*. Berkeley and Los Angeles: University of California Press, 1984

– "Courtesy as a Social Code." Hamilton, *Spenser Encyclopedia*, 195–6

Whitaker, Virgil K. "The Theological Structure of *The Faerie Queene*, Book I." *ELH* 19 (1952): 151–64

Williams, Kathleen. "'Eterne in Mutabilitie': The Unified World of the *Faerie Queene*." *ELH* 19 (1952): 115–30

– "Venus and Diana: Some Uses of Myth in *The Faerie Queene*." *ELH* 28 (1961): 101–20

Wind, Edgar. *Pagan Mysteries in the Renaissance*. London: Faber and Faber, 1967

Wittreich, Joseph. "Apocalypse." Hamilton, *Spenser Encyclopedia*, 46–8

Yates, Frances A. *Astraea: The Imperial Theme in the Sixteenth-Century*. London: Routledge and Kegan Paul, 1975

Zitner, Sheldon P. "*The Faerie Queene*, Book VII." Hamilton, *Spenser Encyclopedia*, 287–9

Index

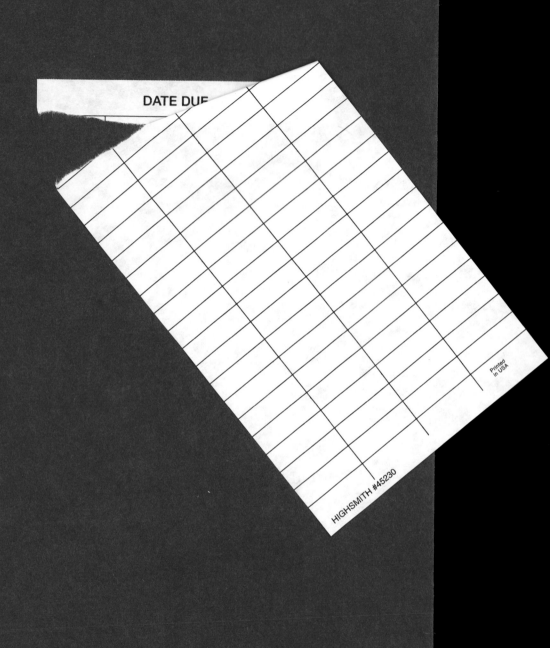

DATE DUE

HIGHSMITH #45230

Printed
In USA